Women and Nature

WOMEN IN THE WEST

Series Editors

Susan Armitage
Washington State University

Sarah J. Deutsch
Clark University

Vicki L. Ruiz
Arizona State University

Elliott West
University of Arkansas

Glenda Riley

Women and Nature

SAVING THE "WILD" WEST

University of Nebraska
Press   Lincoln & London

LIBRARY OF CONGRESS CATALOGING-IN-PUBLICATION DATA

Riley, Glenda, 1938–
   Women and nature : saving the "Wild" West / Glenda Riley.
      p.   cm. — (Women in the West)
   Includes bibliographical references and index.
   ISBN 0-8032-3932-7 (cloth : alk. paper). — ISBN 0-8032-8975-8
(pbk. : alk. paper)
   1. Women environmentalists—United States. 2. Women conservationists—United States. 3. Environmentalism—United States.
4. West (U.S.)—Environmental conditions. I. Title. II. Series.
GE55.R55   1999
333.7'2'0820973—dc21   98-35168
                                                              CIP

Dedicated to

C. Warren Vander Hill

consummate provost and

congenial colleague

who thought "green"

long before it was

fashionable

CONTENTS

ILLUSTRATIONS

Following page 96

INTRODUCTION

During the mid 1980s, Utah's Great Salt Lake swelled and crested at over four thousand feet, ravaging the wetlands of northern Utah. At the same time, naturalist Terry Tempest Williams's mother fell victim to incurable cancer. In *Refuge: An Unnatural History of Family and Place* (1991), Williams described the link she gradually discovered between natural and personal disaster, as well as the critical bond between nature and humankind.

Williams further revealed that she sought solace and encouragement in the environment. The land taught her many useful lessons: "to be quiet and unobtrusive" and "to find grace among spiders with a poisonous bite."[1] In turning to nature to heal the sting of her mother's death, Williams searched for the meaning of the cosmos and her place in it.

This alone was unremarkable, for generations of women have revered nature and explored their relationships with it. What is extraordinary—and lamentable—is that Americans so often overlook Williams's long string of predecessors in the telling of the saga of the West.

Williams wrote during the closing decade of the twentieth century, thousands of years after early migrant tribespeople began to inhabit western lands, hundreds of years after Spanish people traveled northward to what they called *El Norte*, nearly four hundred years after the first European settlers landed at Jamestown with their eyes already turned westward. During that entire time, women were *of* the western land: they cultivated it, cherished it, preserved it, prayed over it, spoke or wrote about it, and turned to it for comfort.

Yet western history, environmental history, and even women's history have had relatively little to say about women's interactions with nature. This omission is gradually being remedied, with particular success during the past two decades. Scholars are especially beginning to study women nature writers. In addition, the achievements of women mountain climbers, park rangers, founders of national parks, and activists in the Progressive conservation campaign have recently received attention.

Despite such writings about women, however, many scholars and laypeople still hold a narrow, uninformed view of environmentalism and its leaders. For instance, a 1997 advertisement in a leading American magazine claimed that "in the 1880s" John Muir "became the country's first environmentalist." Although the U.S. Congress had already established Yellowstone in 1872 as the country's earliest national park, the advertisement maintained that Muir "helped establish the world's first national park."[2] Obviously, misinformation rules—even about leading male environmentalists.

In the meantime, the question remains largely unasked—and unanswered—whether women played anything more than a marginal or perhaps "cooperative" role in the attempt to safeguard the American West. This study maintains that untold numbers of women—who were largely of European descent and from the middle and upper classes—merit belated recognition for their immense exertions and crucial contributions to the American environmental movement in the trans-Mississippi West, including Alaska and Hawaii. The sheer number of environmentally active women is overwhelming and proves the point that, historically, the conservation movement has included a significant female component.

But there is more to be found in the following pages. How, for example, did women engage nature on so many fronts when they were allegedly wary of the outdoors? In large part, the idea of female fear of nature is a myth. A significant proportion of American women loved nature. They drew upon a longstanding tradition of outdoor activity established by generations of European, especially English, women predecessors. In addition, American women made the physical world more attractive and hospitable to themselves by gradually feminizing the "wild" West. On one level, women revised perceptions of western landscapes. Their written and visual images offered a new view of nature, one that welcomed women. Frequently, women's interpretations of western landscapes even appeared soft and sensual rather than harsh and threatening. At the same time, women feminized the outdoors by imposing a female presence on the West—in the form of "ladies" campgrounds, or by developing clothing that accommodated outdoor activities but still fell into the realm of what was considered "proper." Women even posed for photographs while sitting on mountain peaks with tea cups and saucers in their hands.

This study also indicates that women approached nature with different perceptions and assumptions than men. The disparity derived, at least in part, from white European societal values that urged men to exploit western lands in the name of progress but encouraged women to save and protect their families, cultures, and surroundings. Female environmentalists seldom had to persuade other women of the wisdom of preserving western lands. The message already had a special female resonance.

In addition, women environmentalists often held a wider definition of environmentalism than did men. As "social conservators," women typically believed they should safeguard not only landscapes but also native peoples and historic structures. Thus, women's interpretation of environmental conservation included far more than land and its resources.

The conservation movement gained much from women's widespread presence. Environmentalism would have been far less effective had it not been for the thousands of women who supported it. A groundswell of sentiment that came from the people, both men and women, gave a tremendous impetus to the conservation movement, as well as contributing an incredible breadth of programs and projects. Also, in recasting the public perception of "wilderness," women made both the outdoors and concern about its future palatable to a wider audience. In addition, women stimulated economic endeavors related to environmental concerns, including nature writing and photography, health spas and resorts, and outdoor clothing and equipment. Women even associated the environmental ethic with such enduring American values as Mom, family, and flag waving.

In turn, women received much from their participation in environmentalism. Almost all learned the importance of networking, organizing, lobbying, and using the political structure to gain their objectives. Many learned to speak in public, pursue advanced degrees, and revise customary notions of acceptable female clothing. Some even came to see the outdoors as a feminist paradise where they could climb mountains, revel freely in nature's beauty, and experience the independence of the open road. In other words, whether consciously or not, women environmentalists widened their own sphere of activity and action.

To relate this complicated story, the opening chapter of this book supplies historical background and establishes the interest of numerous American women—in the East, South, and West—in nature and the environment well before the conservation ethic began to flourish in the United States after the Civil War. Additionally, it points out that women forerunners of the environmental impulse existed in all parts of the early United States. It also examines a number of central questions: why men generally receive credit for the development of environmentalism; how gender issues positively and negatively influenced the work and reputations of environmentally minded women; and how and why Anglo-European traditions and biases became embedded in the movement.

Chapter 2 explores the European—especially the English—background of American women's environmental thought and activities. From botanists and nature writers to mountain climbers and the Victorian "lady travelers," women on the other side of the Atlantic set high standards and offered exemplary models for their counterparts in America. White, well-to-do American women may have had the education and leisure time to become environmentalists, but they also had a strong cultural heritage of interacting with nature.

The main body of the study—chapters 3 through 8—concentrates on the years between the early 1870s and the early 1940s, which was the developmental period of environmental conservation and the era in which women's efforts receive the least attention. Each of these chapters showcases an individual woman and describes several others—usually westerners themselves—who worked as avid and effective environmentalists.

Each of these chapters also considers a distinct category of women. In part, women have been grouped for ease of handling large numbers of case studies. In addition, each kind of woman advocated slightly disparate environmental values and programs. Most importantly, however, women environmentalists are arranged by type so that their similarities and differences are readily apparent.

These chapters begin with women scientists (chapter 3) who had a clear-cut and predictable interest in nature and environmental programs. Nature writers and visual image-makers, who also had a long tradition of considering and supporting nature, follow (chapters 4 and 5). Next are women who are less readily identified as environmentalists and thus are usually ignored. These include club women (chapter 6), climbers and other athletes (chapter 7), and tourists (chapter 8).

The final two chapters extend the story. Chapter 9, "Beyond the Land," examines the expansion of women's environmentalism into another kind of preservation, that of native cultures and historic sites. Chapter 10, "Since 1940," brings the story to the present, including Rachel Carson and ecofeminism.

The conclusion encourages a broadening of historical scholarship to integrate women's environmental endeavors and achievements. It maintains that not only have women environmentalists spoken wisely and well, but a long and rich historical heritage inspires, bolsters, and strengthens their ideas. Further, it argues that the inclusion of women in environmental history—and of the recent scholarship regarding such women—recasts our understanding of the conservation movement.

Because some nomenclature has become specialized during recent years, a note is in order about the terminology used throughout these chapters. Generally, the following pages employ generic and historical meanings. More specifically, rather than indicating the scientific management of natural resources to sustain their yield, the term "conservation" carries the dictionary definition of preserving, guarding, protecting, and preserving from loss, decay, injury, or violation. The phrase "conservation movement" denotes the formal activities of people interested in preserving nature. "Environmentalism" is utilized throughout as an umbrella term to indicate the beliefs and practices of those pursuing conservation and preservation. When "preservation" is used specifically to apply to the built environment, the expression "historic preservation" is employed.

The terms used in this book for racial or ethnic groups are fairly standard. *African American* and *black* are used interchangeably. Indians are referred to as *Native Americans* and *American Indians*. The term *Hispanic* is used for those of Spanish backgrounds.

Some explanation is also in order concerning the focus on the trans-Mississippi West. Certainly, women worked to conserve and preserve landscapes all over the United States. But a study of their efforts would provide material for an encyclopedia rather than a book-length study.

More significantly, the "wild" West attracted an enormous share of environmentalists' attention. The West's vast lands, rich resources, and astonishing vistas begged for deliberation and planning before they disappeared forever. Furthermore, the West stood as the last bastion of American character, culture, and natural wealth. Could a nation that so closely identified itself with the West subject the region to misuse and outright abuse? Obviously not.

For women, the West had all these attractions and more. The region offered them relative freedom and an abundance of "good" causes, most of which sat on their own doorsteps. Women received societal approval for their efforts on behalf of the West, whereas feminist activity often elicited a hostile response. Women could be activists, and thus subtle feminists, within the conservation movement without raising too many hackles or being labeled "strong-minded women."

Naturally, in the process of research and writing I have incurred many debts. I especially wish to thank Anne M. Butler, C. Warren Vander Hill, and W. Clark Whitehorn for reading the manuscript and offering invaluable suggestions. Had it not been for the steady, efficient effort of graduate assistants Mary Margaret Weber and Deborah L. Rogers, the research would never have been completed nor have remained organized. Also, the Department of History and Ball State University assisted the project through released time, financial aid, and the more intangible catalyst of reassurance and encouragement.

In the course of the project I also relied upon the skills and kindness of many dedicated and hard-working archivists and librarians. These include Rose Byrne, Riva Dean, Susan Peters, Deborah Shelton, and Kim Frontz at the Arizona Historical Society in Tucson; Emily Bergman, Kimberly Balcom, Sharon Johnson, and Kevin Mulroy at the Autry Museum of Western Heritage in Los Angeles; Kim G. Walters at the Southwest Museum in Los Angeles; Peter Blodgett at the Huntington Library in San Marino, California; Susan Bock, Susan Dean, and Kim McCusker in the Special Collections Department of the University of Colorado at Boulder Libraries; Marty Covey and Bruce Montgomery of the Western Historical Collection at University Libraries of the University of Colorado at Boulder; Lisa Backman and Eleanor Gerhes in the Western History/Genealogy Department of the Denver Public Library; Kathy War in the Women's Archives at the University of Nevada–Las Vegas; Lee Mortensen at the Nevada Historical Society in Reno; Kathryn M. Totton in the Special Collections Department and Susan E. Searcy, Manuscripts Curator, both at the University of Nevada–Reno; Jim Bradshaw at the Nita Stewart Haley Memorial Library in Midland, Texas; Alan Barnett, Alan Overstreet, and Linda Thatcher at the Utah State Historical Society in Salt Lake City; and Gary A. Lundell and Carol Wynne in Manuscripts and University Archives at the University of Washington Libraries in Seattle.

In addition, helpful but unidentified staff members furthered the research at the Iowa Historical Society in Des Moines and Iowa

City; University of New Mexico Libraries, especially in the Southwest Collection; the Barker Texas History Center at the University of Texas at Austin; the Kansas State Historical Library in Topeka; the Minnesota Historical Library in St. Paul; the Montana State Historical Society in Helena; the Montana State University Library Special Collections Department in Bozeman; the Nebraska Historical Society in Lincoln; the South Dakota State Historical Resource Center in Pierre; the State Historical Society of North Dakota in Bismarck; the University of Oklahoma Western History Collection in Norman; the Wyoming American Heritage Center at the University of Wyoming in Laramie; and the Wyoming State Archives in Cheyenne.

Also, numerous, nameless librarians assisted me at the Bodleian Library, the University Museum, and the Ashmolean Museum in Oxford, England. I was drawn to Oxford by the abundance of documents and artifacts available regarding European and English women's relationships with nature, as well as the Bodleian Library's rich exhibit on women and natural history. In none of these was I disappointed.

In the United States, Jean Ford, director of the Nevada Women's History Project, was kind enough to give me research materials, while Virginia Grattan shared her photographs of Mary Colter with me and gave me permission to reprint them. Toni Dewey and Vic Danilov of the projected Women of the West Museum in Boulder, Colorado, explored my ideas at the same time they fed and housed me.

For all this assistance I am grateful. I hope I have woven the strands into a useful finished product.

Women and Nature

I

"Wimmin Is Everywhere"

During the early 1890s, political humorist Josh Billings looked around the United States—at reform campaigns, the Farmers Alliance, and politics—and declared: "Wimmin is everywhere."[1] If anyone had bothered to delve a little deeper, they would have seen that Billings's statement applied to the emerging American conservation movement as well.

The vast numbers of environmentally minded women in the late nineteenth- and early twentieth-century United States are almost unbelievable. With a little digging, their stories trickle forth from any research or archival collection. With a bit more effort, the trickle soon turns into a flood. From birders, botanizers, and other naturalists to travelers and tourists, women were present in force. Almost always, women's interest in nature turned into concern for the environment's future. Thousands of women, usually westerners themselves, seemed especially anxious to save the American West for the use and enjoyment of coming generations.

•

Women's environmentalism is not as surprising as it may seem. Looking back into history prior to the development of the conservation ethos reveals that American women long possessed a meaningful relationship with the physical environment. Well before the use and misuse of the American West became an issue, American women lived close to the land and involved themselves in the outdoor world. A solid tradition of women's intimate alliance to nature occurred in every cultural group.

Even though late twentieth-century Americans have probably over-idealized Native Americans' environmental commitment, Indians commonly lived and worked in relative harmony with their surroundings. They generally perceived nature as a total cosmos, an interdependent system composed of the earth and its peoples, as well as an organizing theme of history.[2]

Among many Indian groups, women agriculturalists in particular had a finger on the earth's pulse. Such peoples believed that because women reproduced the species, they had a genius for other reproductive activities, including growing crops. Thus, because of their closeness to the earth, Indian women could judge the vigor or soreness of the land and try to remedy disorder.

Native women regulated the environment in other ways as well. They frequently served as resource managers, deciding the best time to hunt, fish, and gather. They had to determine when resources were plentiful or nearing depletion. As herbalists, medicine women, and apothecaries, they also knew what the produce of the earth could cure. Even landless, rootless native women scavenged whatever the land would yield. Meanwhile, Indian women who were explorers themselves, or assisted early European explorers, opened new areas to use.[3]

Even after white settlers arrived, bringing with them distinctive philosophies regarding the use of nature and its resources, many Indian women clung to traditional beliefs. Buffalo Bird Woman, a Hidatsa born around 1839, learned farming methods from the women of her family on land in what is today North Dakota. Although U.S. government policy eventually forced her to adapt to new methods and crops, Buffalo Bird Woman never understood the market economy. "My mother and my two grandmothers worked at clearing our family's garden," she said. Toiling with iron hoes and an old-fashioned digging stick, they produced corn and other commodities that Buffalo Bird Woman judged superior to the "new" crops. In 1911, she finally proved her point by winning a prize for the best corn at an agricultural fair, corn she had cultivated "exactly as in old times."[4]

Tension soon developed between Indian and white interpretations of nature. During the early 1900s, one American Indian woman repeated the longstanding charge that if land offered even a hint of profit, thoughtless and greedy whites had no concern for either natural beauty or human history. "White people," she claimed, "plow up the ground, pull up the trees, kill everything. . . . the spirit of the land hates them." According to her, Indians refrained from hurting the earth, while whites' penchant for destruction hastened the end of the world.[5]

Like Native Americans, people of Spanish heritage developed their own beliefs regarding the environment. Although some sought riches and depleted resources, many others developed an environmental philosophy.[6] Also like Indian women, Hispanic women frequently lived in communication with the land, as farmers, ranchers, shepherds, and *curanderas* who could use nature's products to cure human ailments. When early Hispanic women writers characterized the land as blessed, filled with a long tradition of families tied to and nourished by it, they depicted typical attitudes. Rather than regarding wilderness as empty and primal, these women invested the landscape with generations of people whose lives were integrated with nature.[7]

Similar attitudes appeared in the work of female artists of Spanish heritage. Drawing on Indian women's traditions and their own propinquity to nature, Hispanic women artists incorporated nature into everything from rugs to houses. According to one *enjarradora* (a woman who embellished architecture), nature was ever-present in Hispanic adobe buildings, for mud was "the flesh of the earth."[8]

Again like Indians, Hispanics soon saw many of their beliefs regarding landscape fall victim to white ideas.[9] After their arrival in North America during the late 1500s and early 1600s, European colonists often ignored Hispanic values, even overriding native land management policies, which were well suited to the culture and physical environment of indigenous peoples.[10]

•

Among their cultural baggage, European immigrants brought well-formed attitudes toward physical resources. Generally, these were male in orientation. For one, Euro-Americans generally feared wilderness, which they perceived as unoccupied, primitive, and threatening. For another, male settlers believed they had to conquer nature before it conquered them. They also defined nature—in this case, the enemy—as female. Everything from sermons, laws, and essays proclaimed an intention to subdue the *virgin* environment, to master *Mother* Nature.[11]

At the same time, however, American male colonists came from countries—especially England—already beset by overpopulation and inadequate resources. Thus, they brought with them notions of forest preservation, marsh reclamation, and fish and game conservation, all of which they enacted into colonial statutes. In 1701, Pennsylvania's charter required that, for every five acres cleared, one acre be left forested. From American Indians, white settlers borrowed the use of fire to modify forest growth.[12]

After the American Revolution ended in 1783, the thirteen Anglo-European dominated states also moved toward economic autonomy and an industrial revolution. The male colonists' opinions regarding nature and its appropriate use multiplied. During the 1820s and 1830s, romanticism vied with capitalism concerning interpretations of nature. While capitalists generally argued for the taming of nature, romantics idealized it and reveled in its "wildness."[13]

During the Civil War era of the 1860s and 1870s, nature and questions regarding its future continued to engage the minds of numerous Americans. Although the Civil War and Reconstruction diverted interest to slavery, war, and survival, nature held its own. Awareness of the value of plants, animals, landscape, and wilderness grew during these years. Meanwhile, the rapid population growth on the Great Plains provoked interest in a region thought by some to be a vast desert and by others a lush garden. With the rise of the westward movement came an infusion of additional values, beliefs, and attitudes toward the land, some exploitative, others environmental in tone.[14]

By the time the conservation movement emerged in the 1870s, 1880s, and 1890s, interest in nature and support for its preservation existed in the East, South, and West; from the Gulf of Mexico to the Great Lakes; from the seashores to the plains. In addition,

Native American environmental beliefs exerted a growing influence on white thinking. During the late 1800s, American Indian and Hispanic values informed the philosophies of such early environmentalists as George Bird Grinnell, Ernest Thompson Seton, and George Perkins Marsh.[15]

•

As these developments took place, American women pursued a host of nature-related activities and frequently demonstrated attitudes that diverged from what male leaders espoused. For example, colonial women often showed a keen awareness of nature and an interest in studying and classifying aspects of it. Jane Colden of New York City developed into an avid botanist who by 1757 had compiled a catalogue of more than three hundred local plants.[16]

Other women ascribed spirituality to nature. Phillis Wheatly was an eighteen-year-old African slave who wrote poetry. Drawing on classical literature, Wheatly lauded nature's beauty and divine creation in this excerpt from a poem written in 1773:

> See in the east the illustrious king of day!
> His rising radiance drives the shades away.[17]

After the American Revolution, women—primarily middle- and upper-class whites—continued to study nature. Because they could work from their parlors without fear of criticism for deserting their homes and families, such women primarily collected and classified botanical specimens. As early as 1824, botanist Amos Eaton reported that "More than half the botanists in New England and New York are ladies."[18]

At the same time, women regularly prepared landscape and fossil drawings for state geological survey reports. Since these women also worked largely at home, society considered their labor "genteel." One of the earliest, Orra White Hitchcock, illustrated her husband's publications during the 1830s and 1840s while he held tenure as the first state geologist of Massachuetts.[19]

Between the 1830s and the late 1850s, many other middle- and upper-class white women delved into nature in socially acceptable ways, including attending lyceum lectures on scientific topics, collecting and identifying plants, and painting nature. In 1831, Maria Martin, a Charleston, South Carolina, nature painter, first met ornithologist John James Audubon, who soon employed her to provide delicate watercolor backgrounds for the birds he painted for *Birds of America.* In 1833, Audubon, who admired Martin's penchant for fine detail, wrote that "the insects she has drawn are, perhaps, the best I've seen."[20]

During the antebellum era, white women developed a particular outlook on nature. Like Phillis Wheatly before the American Revolution, antebellum white women seemed especially interested in connections between nature and morality. According to transcendentalist Margaret Fuller, nature provided the path to spiritual and all other revelation, a conviction with which many woman agreed.[21]

After the Civil War, nature-oriented women continued to live and work all over the United States. Kate Furbish built a reputation as an innovative botanist. After her father died in 1873 and left Furbish a guaranteed income so that she did not have to marry, she spent thirty-five years collecting, classifying, and capturing in watercolors the flora of Maine, especially in swamps, which she found a "delightful retreat." Furbish published articles in the *American Naturalist,* lectured, helped found the Josselyn Botanical Society of Maine, and discovered two plant varieties, which were later named for her.[22]

Throughout the United States, countless other women engaged nature in some way. For instance, amateur fossil and mineral collectors brought in valuable research specimens. It was during the 1870s and 1880s that Erminnie Adelle Platt Smith established a reputation as an ethnologist.[23]

By the time conservation evolved into an ideology, Euro-American women in all parts of the country embraced it with enthusiasm. Once such leaders as John Muir declared the wilderness "fun," meaning an opportunity for recreation and travel, more and more women began to partake of nature's wonders.[24] Soon, countless women committed their time and energy to the conservation ethic.

•

Despite women's dedication, however, the customary view holds that early environmentalism originated with such well-known policy shapers as John Muir, Gifford Pinchot, and Theodore Roosevelt. A similar persuasion claims that legislators and their laws rescued the western environment from overuse.

In part, such misconceptions derive from the perennial mistake of equating visibility with significance. From Gifford Pinchot to lesser-known legislators, these men made the headlines, not to mention the history books. Even recent histories claiming to include individuals who "have influenced the environmental movement in the United States" read like directories of white male environmentalists.[25]

But visibility is not the only test of importance, power, and contributions. Nor do politics constitute the whole of history. Women, unable to vote until 1920 and seldom allowed to hold high political office, appeared to be little more than bit players on the national political scene. At local and state levels, however, as well as in communities and families, women often wielded far more influence than did nationally known politicians.

The propensity of male conservation leaders to take credit for themselves further compounded the historical problem. During the early 1940s, when career forester Gifford Pinchot looked back on the origins of the conservation movement, he wrote that the "conservation" idea flashed into his mind as he rode his horse Jim through Rock Creek Park in Washington DC. On that afternoon in 1907, Pinchot explained, a new policy for the "use of the earth for the good of man" hit him. He carried what he termed his "brain child" to President Theodore Roosevelt. The president, in turn, made what Pinchot called "an as-yet-unnamed program" into "the most significant achievement" of his administration.[26]

Despite a tendency for politicians to make great claims for themselves, it seems unconscionable for Pinchot to grab such praise for himself and Roosevelt. A number of scholars maintain that Pinchot contributed little new to conservation thought and that he actually drew heavily on the ideas of George Perkins Marsh. Others go so far as to attribute environmentalism to the romantic tradition or to nature writers, seeing Pinchot's and Roosevelt's actions and achievements as simply a logical "culmination" of events.[27]

Even if one grants Pinchot and Roosevelt a pivotal role in promoting environmental programs, the work of millions of average nineteenth- and early twentieth-century Americans laid the groundwork for their efforts. Grass-roots Americans, including a sizeable number of women, played a crucial part in developing awareness, idealizing nature, and exploring environments.

•

If numerous white American women supported environmentalism during the late nineteenth and early twentieth centuries, why are they not included in history books and other accounts? Why are the names and contributions of women who interacted with and worked for nature overlooked, ignored, even suppressed, while the assumption that conservation was largely a male movement remains vital?

A partial answer lies in English conservation history. The tendency to overlook American women's connections to their environment stems, in part, from early European women scientists and naturalists, who typically harbored a continental disdain for American science and intellectual endeavor in general. Such women often disregarded American women's efforts and mistakenly concluded that few American women interacted with the physical world. As a result, European women's attitudes suggested that American women had little concern for nature.

American women compounded the matter by giving the impression that, at best, they could only imitate their English sisters. Some observers condemned American women's enthusiasm for English books as puerile imitation rather than a sign of genuine interest. Moreover, even when American women wrote their own essays and books, they continued the English tradition of incorporating established domestic metaphors and a romanticized, female language into their work.[28]

For their devotion to the accomplishments of their English sisters, American women suffered in the United States. The male scientific establishment failed to understand the terms of female writings and dismissed them as fanciful ravings. Indeed, male scientists found it difficult to comprehend such works as educator and botanist Almira Hart Lincoln Phelps's 1829 work, *Familiar Lectures on Botany: Practical, Elementary, and Physiological.* Phelps offered an image of Eve hovering over her garden, a mother nourishing her plants. This Eve also knew science; she could classify the flora before her. By combining motherhood and science, as well as urging women to pursue the "mysteries" in the "temple of science," Phelps appealed to nineteenth-century women. But it is also likely that in the eyes of male scientists, Phelps's women looked like dabblers rather than serious students of nature.[29]

During the nineteenth century, women environmentalists continued to be overlooked because most were nonprofessionals. In a culture dominated by male professionals, the female amateur lacked standing. Especially during the 1870s, 1880s, and 1890s, the very decades when American science professionalized, most women amateurs found themselves demeaned or ignored.

Even women who were professionals had a difficult time gaining recognition in the scientific and conservation establishments. A telling example was that of chemistry instructor Ellen Swallow Richards, who held a Ph.D. from the Michigan Institute of Technology. Beginning in 1873, Richards worked to bring domestic science and emerging ideas regarding ecology together to form environmental science. Yet in November 1892, after Richards announced the new science in Boston, her declaration received less than a page in the *Boston Globe.* In the style of the era, the *Globe* described Richards as "Mrs. Robert Richards" and filled most of the page with illustrations of the previous evening's gathering and descriptions of the fashions worn. The term "environment" failed to appear in the account. Only today is Richards belatedly recognized as the founder of ecology.[30]

In addition, throughout the nineteenth century and even into the twentieth, many Americans, including historians and other scholars, believed that women feared nature. These observers fell victim to a widespread myth—perhaps aimed at keeping "uppity" women at home—that females dreaded the outdoors. Of course, some women did perceive the outdoors as a terrifying place, as did some men, but for the most part the stereotype of women cowering in their homes was unfounded.

How, then, did such an inaccurate idea originate? It began partly with nineteenth-century commentators and scholars who customarily divided the world by gender: autonomous men farmed, hunted, or earned wages, while maternal women cooked, cleaned, and produced goods at home. This model cast women as conservative and timorous, men as intellectual and progressive. It made men the center and women constellations. Given such a prototype, it is unsurprising that a concomitant belief developed: aggressive men sallied forth into the world of nature; passive women stayed indoors.[31]

Novelists further contributed to the myth of female fear of nature, especially among women who relocated in the nineteenth-century American West. Male novelists often used landscape as a symbol of a woman's entrapment—of her inability to stand up to forces larger than herself. Although the best-known example of such female terror is found in Ole Rolvaag's *Giants in the Earth* (1929), an earlier work, Hamlin Garland's *The Moccasin Ranch: A Story of Dakota* (1909), recounts an equally revealing example.

Garland's Blanche Burke was driven to distraction by isolation, a bleak landscape, and the Dakota wind. "Now the wind had dominion over the lonely women," Garland wrote, "wearing out their souls with its melancholy moaning and its vast and wordless sighs." When Blanche had to return home from town, "She was like a prisoner whose parole had ended."[32]

Surely women like Blanche Burke existed throughout the West in the nineteenth and twentieth centuries. But the rich scholarship of the last two decades indicates that the majority of women coped, eventually prevailing over their physical environments. Sheer numbers of women who lived, worked, and played in nature disprove the notion of female fear—and the supposition that women were not involved in nature and its preservation. Even before John Muir and others suggested that wilderness could mean play and sport, so many women who loved the outdoors existed in the annals of American history that it gives lie to the old shibboleth.

Women could, and often did, go where they chose in the outdoor world. After all, the "domestic sphere" was easily enlarged if one felt so inclined. Wherever men and children went was women's sphere, including the outdoors. In addition, nature was filled with such "domestic" phenomena as pregnancy, birth, families, nurturance, and death. Understandably, women frequently used female metaphors in describing nature; women themselves saw nature as their appropriate realm.

Nor did these women creep into nature reluctantly, hiding behind the backs of men. They frequently led the way, ready to meet and embrace nature. Women—perhaps pluckier, healthier, or more optimistic than Blanche Burke—exulted in the physical splendor of the West, rhapsodizing over "flowers up to your neck" and calling the region a "paradise in the Wilderness."[33] In fact, in the American West so many women ventured into every aspect of the environment that they deserve some discussion here.

Numerous women worked directly on the land. U.S. census data indicate that the number of women who farmed on their own increased during the closing decades of the nineteenth century.[34] Such figures exclude additional women on the land: Indian women who farmed, women who hired out as farm laborers, former wives who continued to run family farms and ranches after divorce or the death of a spouse, and Mormon women who managed family farms while their husbands lived with other families or went on missions.[35]

Another important group of female farmers who tackled the environment on their own were "girl homesteaders." Largely white but sometimes women of color, these unmarried women took up land between the 1870s and 1920s and demonstrated a better rate of "proving up," or finalizing their claims, than did male homesteaders.[36]

Such women feared neither hard work nor nature. Single, divorced, or widowed, these women killed snakes, hunted wild game, built their own claim shacks, plowed their own fields, and harvested their own crops. From Oklahoma Territory to Dakota Territory, women homesteaders learned how to drive wagons and plows and to care for a variety of stock.

Moreover, using guns to protect themselves while in the physical environment seemed natural to many women homesteaders and other farm women. As early as 1869, Kansan Eliza J. Wyckoff carried a revolver in one hand whenever she went to the well for water; other times she hid it in a drawer. As late as 1916, after Utah's Myrtle Rigby built a tiny homestead cabin in Chalk Creek Basin east of Coalville, Rigby took her rifle wherever she and her horse Toby went, including hunting and trapping.[37]

Other women grew up punching cows and, as adults, ran ranches on their own.[38] As early as 1862 and continuing both during her marriage and after separating from her husband, María de Jesús Domínquez of Los Angeles owned a highly successful stock business.[39] During the 1870s, the "Cattle Queen of New Mexico," Susan McSween [later Susan McSween Barber], operated a thriving ranch at Three Rivers, New Mexico. It was said that she could "shoot a gun, brand a cow, make a souffle or play Beethoven."[40]

Later, during the 1880s, Wyoming settler Minnie (Ma) Frederick built a ranch on the Texas Trail near Fort Laramie that eventually covered more than sixty thousand acres. One icy night, she slipped and fell while checking her cattle, thus sustaining a disabling injury. For the last fifty years of her life, Minnie ran her ranch from a chair in the middle of the kitchen, wielding what one of her employees called an "iron hand."[41]

Western women proved themselves free of fear of the environment on virtually every other front. Certainly, mid-nineteenth-century women went wherever men dared to go—and other places as well. As early as 1846, thirty-two women marched across the Great Plains toward California with the Mormon Battalion.[42] In 1855, Mountain Charley (Mrs. E. J. Guerin) dressed in men's clothes and led a wagon train to California, thus entering an occupation she followed for thirteen years. Ten years after Mountain Charley's debut, Lucy Rice, a "Teamstress" in Gold Hill, Nevada, drove freight wagons over the Sierra Nevada to Virginia City.[43]

Women continued such outdoor exploits throughout the century. In 1899, a party traveling from Texas to Arizona even ran into two female tramps who hopped railroad cars along the Pecos River in Texas.[44]

Women also participated in mining rushes, which took them into the supposedly feared wilderness. In 1877, Nellie Cashman set out as a lone woman with a party of Alaskan miners and eventually built a reputation as "the West's only girl mining expert." Other women, on their own or with families, took part in the Alaskan and Klondike gold rushes. In 1898, a young woman who had spent days packing goods through treacherous White Horse Pass was moved to write, "It was a lovely sight; So grand and lovely one could look, From early morn till night."[45]

Early twentieth-century women continued to show interest in mineral resources and the environment. In 1914, Josephine C. Scott of Nevada and her husband, George, prospected through southern Nevada, Death Valley, along the Walker River, and through Bridgeport over Sonora Pass. Using horses and burros, the Scotts traveled one thousand miles in six months, during which Josephine drove the team and acted as bookkeeper, miner, cook, and doctor.[46]

In addition to the above activities, western women traveled and camped. During the late 1890s and early 1900s, Luella Moyer of Wyoming claimed that "the average ranch woman of any means at all did more traveling than the same class of women in the East."[47] In 1919, when three ranchwomen camped in Utah's Horseshoe Canyon for "leisure and exploration," they ignored the rain, instead reveling in "the exquisite, sensuous joy" of the experience.[48]

Perhaps some women feared nature, but the women described above and many others relished it. During the early 1900s, Florence Hughes of Wyoming, who regularly entertained herself by fishing, hunting, and trapping, admitted, "I was kind of a tomboy and I loved that kind of life, I loved it."[49] Thus, it is unsurprising that numerous nineteenth- and twentieth-century women had an intense interest in the environment and its preservation.

•

Yet female environmentalists have been generally overlooked. In addition to the factors discussed above, several gender issues shrouded, and even led to the trivialization of, women's participation in the early American conservation movement.

Frequently, the male establishment disdained women because they thought and acted differently than the vocal, ruling group of men. More specifically, although it is difficult to document, nineteenth- (as well as twentieth-) century white women seemed to hold a different interpretation of nature than most men.[50]

The few scholars who have analyzed women's perspectives suggest that women defined nature and wilderness in a distinctive way. These researchers concluded that men (with the possible exclusion of Muir's followers) perceived environmental resources as usable assets, whereas women more typically looked to the land for counsel. Rather than aiming to control and harness the environment, women sought guidance. As recently as 1978, one female traveler following the route of the Esclante expedition in the Southwest explained, "For me the landscape was not something to conquer or to survive—it was something to admire and enjoy."[51]

Moreover, women must have presented a subtle threat to the male establishment. During the late nineteenth and early twentieth centuries, women became the conservators and social reformers of society. They served as culture-preservers of families, religions, and cultural and racial groups. It was only a matter of time before women would claim conservation of the natural environment as their own. Men could not, however, bar women from environmentalism; men needed women's numbers, as well as their organizational and lobbying skills.

•

Yet another reason that women's efforts go unrecognized is that some women remained in the background. They accepted Victorian teachings that women should stand behind men, offering examples, encouraging, pushing, even prodding. As a result, men received kudos, while women's efforts went unremarked.

For example, John Muir's mentor was a woman. Sometime during the late 1860s, Jeanne Smith Carr, writer and wife of a professor of chemistry and natural history at the University of Wisconsin in Madison, first met student John Muir at an annual fair of the state agricultural society. Because Muir's wood carvings and machinery models had not made the prize categories, Carr requested that officials create a "special" prize recognizing Muir's unusual "creativity."[52]

From those days forward, Muir carried on regular correspondence with Jeanne Carr, as well as frequently visiting her and husband, Ezra Slocum Carr. Carr said she received "hundreds of letters, scraps of journals—from the Canada woods . . . to the swamps of Florida," even a letter with a drawing of a grasshopper at the top and a pattern of tracks around its edges. Carr might have added that she encouraged Muir to take up nature writing as a profession, introduced him to New York editors, critiqued his manuscripts, told him when it was time to wed, and, during the late 1870s, picked out "Louie," an active outdoorswoman in her own right, who married Muir in 1880.[53]

In addition to Carr, John Muir turned to numerous other women for guidance and models. During the 1900s to 1920s, Muir wrote numerous letters to botany enthusiast Katharine Putnam Hooker. Although he did not know naturalist Florence Merriam Bailey as well as Hooker, Muir also wrote to Bailey, including a note in 1907 to thank her for her "grand photographs of the Enchanted Mesa," a sight he had not yet seen for himself.[54]

Lesser-known men also depended on women. Although Nebraska legislator Julius Sterling Morton introduced the bill establishing Arbor Day in 1872, his wife, Caroline Joy French, provided the inspiration. French had designed the Morton home, Arbor Lodge, and had laid out the trees, many of them with her own hands. She also managed the lodge and farm. Was Arbor Day Morton's or French's idea? Even though documents do not reveal the answer, one of the Morton sons went on record as saying, "Had it not been for her [his mother], none of us—including father—would have amounted to much."[55]

•

Lastly, contemporary scholarship is at fault for women's near invisibility in the American conservation movement. Historians of women and other researchers have spent far too much time on the nineteenth-century concept of domesticity and not enough on the opposition to that philosophy. Misled by nineteenth- and early twentieth-century prescriptive literature, analysts accepted the idea that women typically remained within their "proper realm"—the home and family. But if women stayed in their sphere, why did domestic proponents devote so many words to cajoling women into doing so?

It is probably true that a significant number of nineteenth- and early twentieth-century women followed advice and remained within prescribed bounds. After all, the women's sphere provided safety and security. Also, adherence to domestic values may have been a regional phenomenon. Someday, comparative regional studies may demonstrate that more eastern and southern women followed the tenets of domesticity than western women. Certainly, although women carried such ideas westward with them, domesticity gradually lost its grip. Nor did domesticity have much appeal to women of color, poor women, and wage-earning women.

Numerous other women chose a variety of ways to thwart domestic principles. Some, like editor, novelist, and nature writer Sarah Josepha Hale, employed cunning. At the same time that she subverted customary beliefs, Hale publicly maintained she hewed the traditional line. Others chose to follow domesticity's competing ideal, which emerged during the mid 1800s. Long overlooked and undervalued, this model promoted a healthy, outdoor, "all-American girl."[56]

Still other women rejected societal expectations out of hand. For instance, a significant number of women escaped domestic ideology by living alone and supporting themselves. Graceanna Lewis—a Quaker naturalist from Chester County, Pennsylvania, who never married—lectured on birds, identified a new bird species, and in 1868 published her *Natural History of Birds*. Similarly, in 1869 Mary Treat began to develop her interest in insects and birds. Because her husband had drifted away to New York City, Treat had to support herself, which she did by writing about natural history, including her most popular book, *Home Studies in Nature* (1880).[57]

Certainly, the women's sphere expanded slowly, bit by bit, here and there, in marriage and without it, at home and in wage work, so that it has taken scholars a long time to notice, much less to understand, the magnitude of the changes. But an incipient revolution indeed existed.

•

With women restored to their rightful place in the early environmentalism, it becomes apparent that the movement developed from the bottom up. Examples of grass-roots action are everywhere. In 1902, a little-known New York botanist, Elizabeth Gertrude Knight Britton, helped establish the Wild Flower Preservation Society of America, serving as its secretary, treasurer, and driving force. By the mid 1920s, Britton had devised conservation activities for schools and garden clubs and had served as chair of the conservation committee of New York State's Federated Garden Clubs. During the 1920s, ornithologist Margaret Morse Nice wrote books, articles, and research reports on Oklahoma birds and spoke out on environmental issues, including the uncontrolled use of pesticides and abuses in wildlife refuges.[58]

Clearly, those at the top of the environmental movement acted on widespread, popular sentiment.[59] If Muir, Pinchot, and others had not had extensive public awareness and support—much of it created by and among women—they would have achieved little or nothing. Clearly, John Muir understood this fact in 1909 when he recruited masses of women in his opposition to San Francisco officials who lobbied to utilize Yosemite National Park's Hetch Hetchy Valley as a reservoir for their city.[60]

In another way, however, early environmentalism *was* top-dominated: it attracted primarily white people of the middle and upper classes. Among women, this race and class stratification occurred for several reasons. For one, by the late nineteenth century, nature study had become a staple ingredient in the lives and education of well-to-do white American women. Consequently, these women were quick to understand the environment's vulnerability and the need to work on its behalf.

Other factors favored white women's participation in environmentalism. These women had the time and interest to save forests and fields. Also, while such avenues as lobbying and speechmaking remained closed to poor women and those of color, they stood open to white women. In addition, because white women organized clubs, traveled, picnicked, camped, and birdwatched together, they tended to invite women similar in race and class to join them.[61]

Meanwhile, by the late nineteenth century, Native Americans had lost their standing as the original American environmentalists. Further embittered by their loss of southwestern lands to whites, they had little reason to help conserve these lands, especially white-dominated parks, campgrounds, and wilderness areas. Among Native American women, probably few cared about their exclusion from the developing conservation movement. Indian women faced their own problems, including reservation living, lack of education, alcoholism, and urban migration.[62]

It is likely that similar dynamics operated among women of Spanish heritage, a growing number of whom lived in urban barrios where they had limited time or energy for political or community activities.[63] Hispanic women often had to fight for survival: to keep their families together, put food on the table, and gain education for their children. Bedeviled by low wages, poor health conditions, and a growing rate of absentee or single parenthood, such women worried more about keeping their babies alive than about saving forests.[64] Hispanic women also waged a difficult battle to preserve their own culture. The Pro Raza Society and other groups dedicated to perpetuating Spanish heritage and background meant more to these women than environmental organizations.[65]

Only those Hispanic women who lived on the land and who were of the upper classes had the freedom to develop an interest in nature and its preservation. Beginning in 1824, Eulalia Elias spent sixteen years managing one of her family's thirty ranches and land grants, the Babocomari, in what became southeastern Arizona. Although she grazed some forty thousand head of cattle, Elias bought additional land and rotated her herds so that the grass on her ranch remained luxuriant and its stream clear.[66]

Later, during the 1920s and 1930s, Ynes Mexia of Mexico City and San Francisco brought botanical specimens from Mexico, Brazil, Peru, Ecuador, Chile, and Argentina that garnered praise from

renowned botanists. She also developed an environment awareness, in particular recognizing the collector's role in denuding the
environment. When she ordered a tree felled, Mexia felt what she
called a "pang" for the tree.[67]

For another group, African-American women, the legacy of
slavery may have stood between them and environmental action.
Some writers suggest that African-American slaves learned to hate
the land on which they were forced to labor, but others claim that
African Americans regarded the land they cultivated as spiritual,
only disliking the "wilderness" beyond their homes as terrifying
"bush" country.[68]

After slavery's end, the majority of African-American women in
the South, North, and West used their energy to battle lynching,
fight health threats, and establish much needed schools and playgrounds for their children. Even black women homesteaders who
fell in love with western landscapes discovered that poverty and
prejudice hindered their ability to invest themselves in the land.[69]

Besides, black women were told they had little stake in nature.
As early as 1837, Englishwoman Harriett Martineau claimed that
"black women ploughing in the field" had little relation to the
"scarlet and blue birds" flitting overhead or the "persimmon
sprouting in the woods."[70]

Later, a prejudiced social system discouraged African Americans from picnicking, camping, and traveling. Although the National Park Service never established an explicit segregation policy, local practice effectively barred black Americans from parks
and other facilities. Consequently, black western women often expressed the concern that although they paid taxes, they lacked access to such public facilities as parks.[71]

In addition, because most African-American women operated
in different circumstances than white women, they developed
their own perceptions of nature, ecology, and environmental crisis.
As black Americans became urban dwellers—23 percent of the
black population by 1900—the safety of swimming beaches, preservation of sequoia trees, and the future of the American eagle
meant less and less to them. One black woman explained that
her people's history had even taught her to avoid unsettled areas,

for the urban ghetto meant security. For black people, what she called the "great out-of-doors" was a place of attack, lynching, and murder.[72]

Much like other western women of color, American women of Asian heritage also believed that local causes had a higher priority than environmental issues. In Hawaii during the 1930s, Florence Wai Kyiu Young Doo tried to overcome widespread prejudice by becoming a spokesperson for the Chinese community and serving as the first president of the American Chinese Club's Women's Auxiliary. During the same era, Auko Furukawa Fukitani and Sei Tanizawa Soga, both of Honolulu, acted as interpreters and go-betweens for the Japanese community.[73]

Besides confronting immediate issues, women of color contributed to environmentalism in quieter, less structured ways accessible to them. They attacked nearby environmental threats by organizing cleanup projects to remove garbage or programs to transform public health. Or they expressed themselves in a subtle form, perhaps by withholding their cooperation from the building of such endangering forces as railroad yards and garbage dumps.[74]

•

Even white women faced barriers to their admission to the early conservation movement. Whereas it is true that white female environmentalists did not have to fight for the right to speak—as in the abolitionist movement—or campaign for the right to vote—as did American suffragists—they did have to negotiate acceptable gender roles in environmental organizations and programs. Just donning the freeing trousers that men took for granted became a disputed matter.

Despite such problems, women continued to engage in environmental activities. To their credit, they refused to be excluded. Also, women did not limit themselves to one line of attack on the male establishment. Instead, they used every tactic from separatism to integration. Women formed their own organizations, joined such existing ones as the Sierra Club, and entered the conservation movement through fathers, brothers, sons, and husbands.[75]

During the late nineteenth and early twentieth centuries, then, women widened their sphere to include nature and its preservation for the future. Although most women were indeed domestically oriented, they defined the physical world as domestic.

From parlor to politics, conservation-minded women urged and lived environmentalism. Consequently, "wimmin," especially white women, were everywhere in the early movement to save the "wild" West.

2

The European Legacy

American women who immersed themselves in nature were far from being "firsts." A longstanding European tradition, and especially a rich English heritage, underwrote their efforts and achievements. European women bequeathed to their white, well-to-do American peers and successors a dedication to nature and the outdoors. This cultural legacy was unparalleled in other cultures.[1]

Besides establishing models for white American women, European women's writings about nature contributed to American women's thinking. By 1845, one observer claimed that American women "eagerly bought, and read" European books.[2] As early as 1819, French writer Charlotte de La Tour's *Le Langage des Fleurs* offered female perspectives to botanists, while in 1830 Jane Haldiman Marcet's *Conversations on Vegetable Physiology* encouraged women to carry their ideas into their gardens and fields. In such works, European women were the first to feminize the physical world by using female images, domestic metaphors, and a romanticized female language.

In addition, by sometimes criticizing things American and at other times ignoring them, European women challenged American women to develop their own brand of natural science. American women especially reacted to the work of English women because of their common language and similar cultures. In 1832, American novelist and editor Sarah Josepha Hale published a collection of idyllic poetry about flowers, *Flora's Interpreter; or, The American Book of Flowers and Sentiments*, expressly to refute European criticism of American plants.

Moreover, English women urged—even ordered—their American counterparts to examine nature firsthand. As early as 1853, traveler and writer Fredrika Bremer preached that appreciation of nature would enhance the ability of such American women to function as civilizers of their nation.[3]

Even though such cross-fertilization is usually overlooked, it played a strong part in making certain American women more aware of, and eventually more concerned about, their physical surroundings. American women entered the conservation movement, at least in part, because of a strong European tradition of women engaging nature on many levels. Consequently, a more detailed examination of the European legacy follows.

•

Science and natural history long attracted European women, but because such endeavors were considered "unladylike," women had to insinuate themselves into scientific activities in subtle ways. French women, for example, often assumed a secondary role, including assisting husbands, offering patronage to protégées, and establishing salons.[4]

In England, women showed a similar interest in scientific matters. The first Duchess of Portland financially underwrote the engraving of plates for Robert Morison's *Plantarum historiae universalis Oxoniensis pars 3* (1699). Half a century later, English women constituted at least one-fourth of the subscribers, or financial supporters, of entomologist Benjamin Wilkes's *English Moths and Butterflies* (compiled from 1747 to around 1750).[5]

Some English women, however, were not content to stay in the background. The second Duchess of Portland, Lady Margaret Cavendish Bentinck Harley, became a collector herself, amassing huge natural history collections, particularly plants and insects. The depth and passion of her preoccupation created work for others, including field collectors, botanists, and catalogers. When Lady Hartley died in 1785, the sale of her collections, the largest in Britain, took thirty-eight days.[6]

Partly due to Lady Harley's example, early nineteenth-century English women took up the study of botany. Fortunately, botanical activities could easily be pursued in the breakfast room and parlor. Because botany was seldom a formal career for men or women at the time, it consisted of such tasks as collecting, categorizing, and illustrating, all of which fit women's lifestyles. Additionally, such activities had the support of fathers, uncles, husbands, and sons.

After marrying explorer Thomas Edward Bowdich 1813, Sarah Bowdich coauthored with her husband a series of widely read books about plants, birds, geography, and other similar topics. She illustrated these volumes with her own drawings and became the first English woman to collect botanical specimens in tropical Africa. After Edward died of fever in the Gambia in 1824, Sarah finished their work there, wrote an account of five new genera of plants among Gambian flora, and raised their three children. To some extent, the Bowdiches' popular manual, *Taxidermy*, which went through multiple editions, eased her financial burden.[7]

Gradually, then, botany became a socially acceptable endeavor for women. As early as 1842, botanist Lydia Becker, who later developed a natural system of plant classification, advocated science education for women in *Botany for Ladies*. In 1869, one woman even recommended that the achromatic microscope, "the companion of every intelligent family," should be a fixture in parlors.[8]

English women were not only botanists, however. They engaged in virtually every aspect of natural history from ornithology to geology. Such women as Mary Anning and the three Philpot sisters, all of Lyme Regis in Dorset, energized the "Golden Age" of British geology during the first half of the nineteenth century. In 1821, Anning found a nearly complete ichthyosaur, an extinct reptile. In 1828, she unearthed the first British example of a fossilized flying reptile. Only a year later, Anning discovered the fish *Squaloraja*, thought to be a transition between sharks and rays.[9]

The Philpot sisters—Mary, Margaret, and Elizabeth—also built a remarkable collection of fossils. Paleontologist Louis Agassiz named one species of fish *Eugnathus philpotiae* after the sisters. As with Anning's finds, leading scientists often used the sisters' discoveries to develop theories, yet the women received no recognition.[10]

Gradually, expanding attitudes created a climate of opinion in which English women could extend their scientific interests and even specialize, at least on an unpaid basis. During the 1880s, entomologist Eleanor Anne Ormerod associated herself with the Royal Agricultural Society of England, which gave her efforts a cachet of professional acceptance. Unlike male consultants to the society, however, Ormerod received no financial compensation. After the society appointed her as honorary consulting entomologist in 1883, she spent ten years preparing posters and reports, assisting members with queries, and lecturing to teachers. Ormerod's most well known book, *Guide to the Methods of Insect Life* (1884), later became *A Text-Book of Agricultural Entomology* (1892).[11]

Twentieth-century English women continued to pursue scientific interests. During the early to mid 1900s, Miriam Rothschild devoted her research to the parasites, notably fleas, that live in or on birds. Called the "Queen of the Fleas," Rothschild carried on work begun by her father.[12]

For all their scientific curiosity and expertise, however, English women naturalists had difficulty discussing such topics as plant sexuality and bird mating. During the mid 1850s, it was much more typical for women naturalists to search for moral lessons from what Margaret Gatty called "God's Creation, Nature." In 1857, Gatty presented her parables from nature, in which she described "the patient moon" which never tires "of her task of shedding rays of hope and promise to the world." Gatty concluded that humankind must learn to look to the environment for God's guidance.[13]

Eventually, British feminism helped relieve such constraints on women. As a result of the crusade for women suffrage, which began in the early 1800s and peaked during the years of parliamentary reform in 1909–11, English women gradually enjoyed a new openness and more equal footing with men. For women naturalists that meant more access to the scientific establishment, its language, and its concerns. In 1904, the Linnean Society admitted its first women members, many of whom distinguished themselves in their work.[14]

Clearly, English women naturalists established a precedent of scientific participation for other English-speaking women of the upper classes. They lent "female" terminology and images to women's scientific observations. Moreover, their work, which insisted on the application of British standards to American plants and animals, spurred women's interest in developing an American science. American naturalist Almira Phelps's *Familiar Lectures on Botany* (1829) not only argued for American women's participation in natural history but also urged women to help classify and name plants and animals of the New World. Soon, American women vied to outdo English women in the race to collect, classify, and name American flora and fauna.[15]

•

European women nature writers were also numerous and influential. Because society considered nature within women's sphere, female authors wrote prolifically about all aspects of the physical environment. Although they did not usually espouse environmental ideas, they did take a protective approach to landscapes, plants, insects, and animals.

By midcentury, English women nature writers appeared on every front. They especially appealed to children, who they believed had unformed attitudes about nature. As early as the 1790s, nature writer Priscilla Wakefield emphasized for her young readers both nature's spiritual component and women's values regarding nature. Writing in epistolary format, a popular style of the day, Wakefield urged young people to study nature as a way of understanding "the Divine Being" and the physical universe. In 1814, Wakefield turned her attention to animals, in which she saw the "Power of God." She asserted that men treated animals with more cruelty than did women, and she implored her youthful audience to learn from women to seek the "wisdom and goodness of the Deity" in everything from the "minutest fly" to frogs and spiders.[16]

Other nature writers also hoped to impress children with a benign outlook on nature and its creatures. In 1872, Christina Rossetti's *Sing-Song: A Nursery Rhyme Book* implored children to avoid cruelty to insects, emphasizing that whether insects experienced pain was not the issue. Because Rossetti and others saw childhood as the formative period for attitudes toward animals, they believed a child's treatment of insects would determine his or her later humanitarian inclinations.[17]

•

Besides writing about nature, European (especially English) women created visual images of nature. In so doing, they contributed specific, often "female," ways of perceiving the physical environment.

An important case was Maria Sibylla Merian, who as early as the late 1600s and early 1700s raised silkworms and caterpillars in her garden in Frankfurt, Germany, and sketched the way she perceived insects who lived on host plants. In 1683, Merian published her first collection of engravings with commentary. Other volumes followed, as did a 1699 trip to Dutch Surinam to study insects. During the latter 1700s, Linnaeus honored Merian by citing her work over one hundred times.[18]

Were Merian's insects totally objective and true to their actual state? No. Merian, heavily influenced by Dutch still-life painters, had her own vision. She often portrayed insects on food plants as dwarfed by their hosts and sometimes further overshadowed by animals in the background. In addition, some of Merian's editions appeared in such fine color that it is believed that Merian, or perhaps her daughters, did the tint work personally. Reviewers and readers judged the insects in the colored edition far more attractive than those in black and white.[19]

Later, Englishwoman Marianne North presented flowers as profuse and luxuriant. A sense of nature as fertile and bounteous informed her work. The walls of the Marianne North Galley at England's Royal Botanic Gardens at Kew, which contained 832 of North's botanical paintings when it opened in 1882 and today houses 848, are filled, floor to ceiling, with dots of color, trumpet-like flowers, and tangled leaves and vines. North's colorful, dramatic, stylized portrayal of nature and her full-lipped blooms strike the viewer as a forerunner of Georgia O'Keeffe's "sexual" rendering of southwestern plants and flowers.[20]

Marianne North's landscapes of the American West, painted in 1875 and later donated to the Royal Botanic Gardens at Kew, also characterized nature as feminine and approachable. North's paintings of giant redwood trees showed colorful bark and leaves that would feel like velvet if one could touch them. In her travel diaries, North put into words what her artist's eye saw. California's "Big Trees" of the Mariposa Grove had "rich red plush bark" set off by "the light green eclipse of feathery foliage above."[21]

North became one of the few English women to decry the exploitation of landscapes. During her trip to California in the mid 1870s, North recorded in her travel diaries her growing sadness at the wanton destruction of redwood trees. Californians were "gradually sawing them up for firewood," she wrote, "and the tree would soon be extinct." North added that "it broke one's heart to think of man, the civiliser, wasting treasures." During an 1882 trip to the United States, when she saw that the center had been hacked from a redwood tree so that a coach and team could drive through it, North pronounced the action "barbaric."[22]

Besides such nature illustrators as Merian and North, female photographers influenced the way people understood landscapes. After photographer Anna Atkins's illustrated books on algae and ferns helped open science and photography to women during the 1840s, other English women thronged to photography and established their own traditions. By the 1890s, women photographers even became involved with documentary and reportage.[23]

During the early 1900s, the number of women nature photographers multiplied. Working in gardens and fields, these women captured everything from flowers and trees to landscapes and seascapes. Not only did they mediate aesthetic standards of natural beauty, but they also modified environments to suit their artistic desires. They used light and shadows to get the effects they wanted, or clipped grasses and flowers to fit their conceptions of nature. Until the outbreak of World War II, these women photographers presented an ordered environment that most people found attractive and appealing.[24]

Another type of visual image-maker, women gardeners, also shaped nature to suit themselves and their clients. Certainly, through most of the nineteenth century, women had little to do with England's truly magnificent gardens, which were planned and managed by employed gardeners who resented intrusions by amateurs. English women, especially those in the lower classes, might have herb, vegetable, or flower gardens, but it was not until the latter part of the 1800s that women asserted themselves in the formal garden.[25]

Gardener Jane Loudon challenged the restrictions on women as well as customary methods of gardening. In 1830, she married a gardening journalist who trained her in gardening and aesthetics. Although gardening was becoming more scientific, Loudon simply wanted to help people, especially women, enjoy and identify plants. Consequently, she choose to represent plants for what she termed their "design qualities" rather than for botanical interest.[26]

Beginning in 1840, Loudon prepared text and watercolor illustrations for over twenty books, all of which she hoped would draw women to gardening. Throughout her career, she also attempted to bring together untamed nature and art. Although she admired the "grace and elegance of wild flowers," Loudon believed a garden's benefit was "the trimness and neatness of art." Using soft-hued watercolors, she presented romanticized wildflowers. For formal arrangements, she grouped gorgeous blossoms according to various color schemes. The alluring and stunning results revealed nature as seen through Jane Loudon's eyes.[27]

By the end of the century, in part due to Loudon's influence, numerous women took up gardening and began to write about it as well. In 1898, Pomeranian author Elizabeth von Arnim published *Elizabeth and Her German Garden*, followed the next year by *The Solitary Summer*. Because von Arnim had a passion for natural landscapes, as well as an appreciation of solitude in her garden, her themes reinforced developing environmental philosophies of the time.[28]

Scores of other gardening authors followed, the most significant of whom was Gertrude Jekyll. Described as the first horticultural Impressionist, she brought to her gardening a background in art, decorative embroidery, and interior decoration. To Jekyll, a landscape designer was first an artist, second a gardener, and never a scientist. Beginning at age fifty-six and wearing commodious rubber boots that became her trademark, she designed and planted some of the most exquisite gardens of the late nineteenth and early twentieth centuries, wrote ten books in nine years, shot and developed her own garden photographs, and designed her own garden vases.[29]

Despite her occasional eccentricities, Gertrude Jekyll clearly believed herself an arbitrator of landscape aesthetics. To her, an appealing landscape was a three-dimensional setting that looked "right" from all viewpoints and in all lights. To achieve these goals, a gardener must be a creative genius. According to Jekyll, "For planting ground is painting a landscape with living things and I hold that good gardening takes rank within the bounds of the fine arts, so I hold that to plant well needs an artist of no mean capacity."[30]

Among her many other achievements, Jekyll established principles that would have appealed to environmentalists: wild rather than regimented gardens, plants and trees in their natural forms, and landscapes that suited their surroundings. In addition, Jekyll had an environmentalist's love of nature that she imparted to adults and children alike. "It is good to live," she wrote in 1900, "and all the more good to live in a garden."[31]

Gertrude Jekyll wielded widespread influence in her own day, both at home and abroad. During the early 1900s, her words were already repeated in American books on gardening.[32] Today, Jekyll's writings are widely available in Europe and the United States, with the gift shop at the Royal Botanic Gardens in Kew featuring her books, photographs, and memorabilia.

·

European women also had a long history of activism toward nature, both through organizations and as individuals. Although the women's club movement that developed in the United States in the late nineteenth and early twentieth centuries was uniquely American, European women joined forces on such immediate problems as unemployment.[33]

Moreover, English women had a long tradition of joining existing organizations, many of which were environmental in tone. The Royal Society for the Protection of Birds, which originated as the Fur, Fin, and Feather Folk in 1889, vowed "to refrain from wearing the feathers of any birds not killed for the purpose of food, the Ostrich only excepted."[34]

When animal welfare became an issue during the 1880s, English women formed a number of all-female, single-issue organizations, which supported the 1881 proposal in Parliament that experiments on animals be prohibited by law. Women's writings about the issue reveal a belief in strong ties between women, animals, and nature. "Nature," one pamphlet stated, "is no mere mechanism, inanimate, and insensible to defiance and outrage." Rather, nature was like women, "whose real law is sympathy." Women termed vivisection a "horror" that tortured animals and allowed them no recourse. Frequently, women placed the blame on male shoulders: "men of science are murderers and torturers."[35]

Besides action taken by women in organizations, individual women activists campaigned for a variety of causes. Female patrons of male naturalists were the first environmental activists. In an era when little government or corporate funding existed, Mary Somerset, Duchess of Beaufort during the 1600s and early 1700s, supported the work of such natural scientists as entomologist Moses Harris, naturalist Martin Lister, and botanist Jacob Bobart. In France during the late 1700s, Josephine Bonaparte financed botanical illustrator Pierre Joseph Redouté.[36]

Later, particular women took a variety of approaches to the issue of preserving nature. Entomologist Eleanor Anne Ormerod argued for the use of insecticides against pests that devastated crops and other plants. Although her position would be unpopular today, she took pride in her crusade to bring an arsenic compound called Paris green to Great Britain. In 1892 she declared, "Surely it should be recorded of me, 'SHE INTRODUCED PARIS-GREEN INTO ENGLAND.'"[37]

Yet other individual English women wrote and lectured on behalf of environmental matters. Women's rights advocate Frances Power Cobbe helped found both the Victoria Street Society for the Protection of Animals (1875) and the British Union for the Abolition of Vivisection (1898) and also spoke out strongly on behalf of animal rights. In 1897, Cobbe contributed to the first issue of a monthly magazine called the *Animals' Friend*, which stressed the relationship of women and anti-vivisectionism.[38]

Certain European women scholars and intellectuals also expressed an interest in environmental concerns. Women founders of the social sciences explored the ethics of stewardship. Such figures as Mary Wollstonecraft, Florence Nightingale, and Beatrice Webb developed an environmental ethic and, in particular, opposed degradation of the land and its resources.[39]

Despite this heritage, during the early twentieth century neither women's clubs nor environmental causes appeared to grip European women as firmly as they did American women. Perhaps when European environmental history is revised to include women, the latter perception will prove unfounded. Presently, however, the history of European women's environmentalism has yet to be written. Because women are generally absent from European environmental histories, the full extent of their activities remains unknown.[40]

•

If we turn to mountain climbing and other sports, the European background to American women's athletics is both apparent and clearly significant. American women who scaled mountains and pioneered other outdoor activities drew on a colorful history, especially involving English women.

Because historical data regarding European women is sketchy, historians of mountaineers disagree on the matter of which woman first scaled a mountain. They discount native women who may have climbed many mountains, but for whom records are lacking. By default, then, the honor goes to a white European woman, a Madame Harsberg of Hamberg, Germany, who ascended the Montanvert in 1789.[41]

Chroniclers mention other ascents by women in subsequent years, yet details are wanting. All agree, however, that in 1808 an eighteen-year-old French peasant named Marie Paradis, perhaps with considerable male assistance, made her way up Mont Blanc,

Europe's highest mountain. Paradis operated a tea room at the base of Mont Blanc and was anxious for the publicity her stunt would bring. She did not hide her motives: "Thanks to the curiosity of the public, I have made a very nice profit out of it; and that was what I reckoned on when I made the ascent."[42]

Other women followed, but their climbs were poorly documented. It is known that, in 1810, sixty-five guides escorted the Empress Josephine to the top of the Montanvert. In 1822, a Mrs. and Miss Campbell crossed the Col du Géant on Mont Blanc, which inspired a male climber to remark, "These ladies have shown how female intrepidity may finally surmount danger, where even the experience of guides may fail."[43]

Sixteen years passed before Frenchwoman Henriette d'Angeville tackled Mont Blanc. In 1838, at age forty-four, she attempted to scale the summit. Because critics labeled d'Angeville's plans foolish and unfeminine, she made out a will. She departed wearing a self-designed climbing outfit of nailed boots, knickerbocker trousers, a short blouse, a fur-lined bonnet and cloak, and a veil. The second day of the ascent d'Angeville suffered from what she called "two enemies of equal violence—suffocating palpitations of the heart when I walked, and a lethargic drowsiness" whenever she stopped. Despite these attacks, d'Angeville persisted on sheer will power and achieved her ambition to be the first woman mountaineer to reach the top of Mont Blanc under her own power. After the Mont Blanc success, d'Angeville continued climbing mountains into her sixty-ninth year.[44]

By midcentury, numerous other women longed to visit Europe's great mountains, if not actually reach the summits. In 1850, 1856, and 1858, an English woman known only as Mrs. Cole visited Italian mountains, passes, and valleys, particularly Monte Rosa. In *A Lady's Tour round Monte Rosa* (1859), Cole regaled readers with the delights of mountain travel. "I desire to give," she stated, "the benefits of my experience to others, in the hope of inducing them, and especially members of my own sex, to follow my example."[45]

Still, mountain climbing in Europe remained primarily a male sport. When the British Alpine Club organized in 1857, it barred women from membership. The following year, the first truly dedicated woman climber, Lucy Walker, began a remarkable twenty-one-year career, which revised some people's attitudes toward women climbers. Walker, who always wore a print dress on her trips, urged other women to try climbing. In 1871, she became the first woman to ascend the notorious Matterhorn. After the Ladies Alpine Club formed in 1907, Walker served as its president from 1913 to 1915.[46]

Despite their daring and growing proficiency, English women climbers continued to receive stinging disapproval from both men and women. Critics disparaged everything from women climbers' clothing to their "unwomanly" defiance of injury and death. As a result, women were seldom named in books and articles on climbing, were listed only briefly, or were mentioned by their initials rather than their first names. This is unfortunate, for their numbers were legion. During the late nineteenth century, such women as Anna and Ellen Pigeon, Isabella Straton, and Emmeline Lewis-Lloyd all proved remarkable climbers. During the early twentieth century, Emily 'Pat' Kelly pioneered solo climbing, while in 1921 Eleanor Winthrop Young helped found the Pinnacle Club, a British women's climbing organization.[47]

In addition to mountain climbing, European women took up other sports, notably riding and hunting. Early noblewomen in particular proved their prowess as riders and hunters. In France, Charlemagne and Hildegarde hunted, as did their six daughters. Marie Antoinette rode horses astride and dressed in breeches, while Louis XI's daughter Anne loved hunting. In England, Queen Anne was a hunting enthusiast, and Lady Mary Wortly Montagu specialized in stag hunting.[48]

After Queen Anne of Bohemia introduced the sidesaddle to accommodate women's full skirts during the early 1800s, riding became more difficult and thus more ornamental. Because it was hard to gallop and take jumps on a sidesaddle, women often worked behind the scenes raising hounds and training horses for the hunt. Still, some women persisted in hunting and jumping with sidesaddles. As early as the 1830s, a third pommel—or "leaping head"—was added to sidesaddles to give women more leverage.

By midcentury, balance straps followed. With more women riding and hunting, the safety-skirt, which tore off in emergencies, appeared and gained popularity during the 1870s.[49]

As the end of the nineteenth century neared, women continued to undertake a growing variety of sports. In 1894, Lady Violet Greville published a group of essays titled *Ladies in the Field.* In its preface, she claimed, "Women who prefer exercise and liberty. . . can remain essentially feminine in their thoughts and manners." Lady Greville also suggested that women "may even by their presence refine the coarser ways of men, and contribute to the gradual disuse of bad language in the hunting-field, and the adoption of a habit of courtesy and kindness."[50]

In the volume's first treatise, concerning riding in Ireland and India, Lady Greville stated that "of all the exercises indulged in by men and women, riding is perhaps the most productive of harmless pleasure" and creates "moral and physical well-being and satisfaction." She expressed her delight that women of the 1890s "rushed in where their mothers feared to tread" by trying all types of sports. In subsequent pieces, other authors explored activities ranging from hunting and tandem driving of horses to shooting, deerstalking, cycling, and punting, or boating.[51]

Two themes dominated the essays. Predictably, one was clothing. In "Tigers I Have Shot," Kate Martelli recommended a green cotton dress and a hat covered with the same material for hunting tigers and riding elephants in India. For punting in England, however, Sybil Salaman favored a serge skirt, "not too long," a loose blouse with sleeves that unbuttoned and rolled up, and "shoes with low heels, india-rubber soled preferred."[52]

The second issue concerned justifying the killing of wildlife. Kate Martelli explained that tiger hunting was not intended "to give the tiger a sporting chance." She added that hunters slaughtered tigers to protect "the natives and their cattle." Kangaroo-hunter Beatrice Jenkins shifted the matter to men's shoulders. "It has been said," Jenkins wrote, "an Englishman is never happy unless he is killing something, and nowadays, at any rate, his happiness seems increased if members of the weaker sex share this propensity with him." Much like Martelli, Jenkins argued that the Australian "pasttime" of hunting and killing kangaroos actually protected people and other animals.[53]

A strong anti-vivisectionist sentiment among English women encouraged many to spurn such arguments. In addition, numerous English women rejected killing as the goal of sports. More typically, English women showed concern with animal welfare and, of course, with their own appearance and health. When the *Sportswoman* began publication in London in 1908, it offered three reasons why women engaged in sports: "unborn desire for excitement," a love of fresh air, and an acceptable, fashionable means of amusement. *Sportwoman's* articles concerned the care of a variety of animals, female fashions and hair styles, the value of split skirts and riding astride, and the advantages of golf and archery for women.[54]

By the early 1900s, thousands of European women flocked to sports. Despite continuing criticism and other difficulties, they pursued their love of the outdoors. They especially enjoyed riding and hunting. A significant number of English women even attained the status of master of harriers. At the same time, more and more women discarded their sidesaddles in favor of cross-saddles. By the time World War II began, the majority of women used cross-saddles.[55]

Certainly, the English feminist movement encouraged sportswomen to assert themselves. In particular, middle- and upper-class European women, who could afford to engage in sport, sought freedom of action, opportunity to make decisions, and situations that challenged their abilities. On the one hand, they worked to maintain the image of dignified ladies seeking health, collecting information, and carrying their civilization to others. On the other, they exercised their independence along with their bodies.[56] Because of their devotion to climbing and other sports, late nineteenth- and early twentieth-century European women set a new pace for women in general, which helped open the way for American women.

•

A strong tradition of English women's travel writing also motivated American women. Although American women may have been exploring a new region—the American West—the custom of women traveling and relating their experiences in essays and books had a long background, especially among English women.

As early as the late seventeenth and early eighteenth centuries, the word pictures relayed by travelers began to reshape traditional thinking about nature. Such travelers added a new dimension to agriculturalists' usual perception of their immediate landscape as a garden combining charm and practicality. Landscape became an object to be observed from a distance. As was seen in seventeenth-century Dutch landscape paintings, the environment remained separate from humans. Landscape emerged as a social construction—something to be studied, appreciated, and esteemed.[57]

Of course, at that time men did most of the traveling and travel writing. European society considered women too domestic and weak to endure extensive journeys and judged their observations less than authoritative. The few eighteenth-century women who traveled and wrote about it—such as English novelist Ann Radcliffe, whose *Journey Made in the Summer of 1794* appeared in 1795—distanced themselves accordingly from their narratives by composing in the passive voice, avoiding self-references, and hedging their opinions in vagueness.[58]

As additional women ventured abroad, especially after 1870, they gradually attained more self-assurance. During the latter part of Queen Victoria's reign, women disdained male travelers' pursuit of camaraderie, danger, discovery, and science. Instead, women toured for general education and the cultural improvement of themselves and their readers. An unnamed Clevedon woman who left England to cross the Himalayan Mountains in India during the mid 1870s proclaimed that her writing about the expedition made "no pretension to a scientific character." Instead, she explained the journey "simply to explore an almost unknown country, and to enjoy the incidents of travel." Anticipating reproach that a mere woman dared to write such a work, she further dissembled; she added that she wrote only "at the earnest solicitation of her friends." She would be satisfied if others were able to follow "on paper my footsteps over untrodden paths."[59]

Meanwhile, other late nineteenth- and early twentieth-century English women sightseers probed the history, geography, customs, and physical environment of the nations they visited. In their writings, they conveyed their accumulated knowledge to women unable to travel themselves. Thus, women's travel writings not only helped objectify cultures and environments but also advanced women's emancipation through an enlarged view of nature and world civilizations.[60]

Women travelers often turned into botanical collectors as well, bringing back specimens of insects and plants to share with their homebound sisters. Margaret Fountaine first left England during the late 1870s, using her personal inheritance to fund her travels. In Geneva, Switzerland, in 1891, Fountaine began assembling what eventually became a formidable collection of butterflies. In Syria in 1901, she formed a personal alliance with diplomat Khalil Neimy, who shared her travels for the next twenty-six years. Fountaine died in Trinidad in 1940, bequeathing sixty years of travel diaries and a collection of twenty thousand butterflies to the Castle Museum in Norwich, England. According to Fountaine's instructions, Castle Museum officials waited to unseal her extensive—and, for her era, scandalous—travel journals until April 1978, a century after their writing.[61]

English naturalist Mary Kingsley, who toured West Africa in the mid 1890s, also gathered specimens. Her specialty was fish, which she collected for her patron institution, the British Museum. Wearing a proper Victorian skirt and shirtwaist, Kingsley employed her equally proper umbrella to prod a hippopotamus or take a marine sounding. In addition, she cleverly used her relatively acceptable activities to mask her pioneering anthropological studies of African tribes. Although what Kingsley described as a "distinguished and valued scientific friend" instructed her to take all human measurements "from the adult male," she resisted. Lest Kingsley be thought more of a rebel than she was, however, she refused to measure African men, not because she realized the importance of women and children, but because "men would not like it."[62]

English women tourists introduced other innovations in their work. Throughout the eighteenth century, their narratives helped define scenic tourism, which created concepts of landscape through viewing, sketching, and describing it. Accepting some "male" conventions and defying others, women travelers also participated in the development of a nature aesthetic. Generally, they provided more detail, emotion, and personal observations than male travel writers. More specifically, women sought the picturesque and the sublime in the environment. As English writer and feminist Mary Wollstonecraft put it, "the heart" should be allowed to "beat true to nature," rather than people subduing and shaping the environment to suit their own needs.[63]

Moreover, English women travelers encouraged landscape appreciation, notably through decorative English gardening, which applied the new aesthetic of natural scenery to domestic surroundings. Either inadvertently or perhaps purposefully, women's interpretations of nature provided an analysis of what men judged beautiful in nature, as well as a criticism of the ways men had traditionally arranged and managed the environment. Women usually characterized nature as female—a goddess, bountiful, wild—yet controllable.[64] The direct implication was that the environment could be managed in a more beneficial way than in the past, an important assumption for environmental reform.

English women sightseers helped develop another important tenet of environmentalism, a sense of possession of natural environments. When visiting the Rocky Mountains, Isabella Bird wrote, "Estes Park is mine."[65] Ownership of environments had important and far-reaching implications. In most women travelers' views, if one "owned" a piece of nature, one was also responsible for its future.

Women travelers interested in conserving and reshaping the environments and peoples they visited also cast themselves as philanthropists. As wives, mothers, seekers of improved health, and travelers, they grew committed to "saving" nature and natives wherever they went. These women thus threw a cloak of female respectability and benevolence around environmental values and activities.

Moreover, women tourists carried with them great curiosity, as well as a feeling of obligation, toward native peoples. During the early 1870s, English traveler Maria Theresa Longworth explained that she toured the United States "with the one object of seeing the country and understanding the people."[66]

At the same time, these women displayed prejudice by describing indigenous populations as exotic and aberrant to the norms they knew back home. Although English women travelers were usually less imperialistic and colonialist than male travelers, the women still revealed discriminatory attitudes, especially as they inadvertently established a hierarchy of cultures. In 1853, a Viennese visitor characterized California coastal Indians as having "a very low grade of civilization," while in 1880 Lady Duffus Hardy disparaged the Mormon practice of multiple wives and judged San Francisco's Chinese prostitutes as "female slaves of the most degraded class."[67]

One of the greatest contributions to the American West by Victorian "lady" travelers was publicizing the natural beauty of the region to European—and American—women and encouraging them to journey westward. As early as the 1870s, Isabella Bird began her career as the most well known English woman to visit and write about the United States. From Hawaii to the Rocky Mountain West, she toured unchaperoned in pursuit of improved health. In 1873, Bird tramped and rode horseback through Colorado's Rocky Mountains with only a male guide named Jim.[68]

Bird, who described the Rockies as "no region for tourists and women," not only camped out and rode through the Rockies but also attempted to climb Longs Peak. In her letters, later published in the English weekly *Leisure Hour,* she explained that Jim "dragged" her up Longs Peak, much "like a bale of goods." She also wrote that she found the Rocky Mountain area "glorious," the air "intoxicating," and the wildflowers "gorgeous." When Bird's letters appeared in 1879 as a book titled *A Lady's Life in the Rocky Mountains,* they piqued other women's interest in riding, camping, and traveling.[69]

Numerous other English women visited and wrote about the American West as well. In 1888, Rose Pender published *A Lady's*

Experiences in the Wild West in 1883, which described a four-month tour through such states as Texas, California, Utah, Wyoming, and Colorado, where Pender climbed Pikes Peak. Although Pender initially resisted the suggestion to attempt Pikes Peak because the mountain looked "so cold and so terribly high up," she eventually gave in to her companions' urging and climbed to the summit.[70]

Attired in a chintz skirt, a Norfolk jacket over a flannel shirt, old patent leather boots, and a hat with a full-face veil, Pender rode a mule up the slope to the snow line at 11,500 feet. When most of the party decided not to go any farther, Rose Pender, her husband, and one other man continued on foot. Even though Rose struggled through waist-deep snow and pushed on despite a "terrible pain" in her chest, the male climbers reached the summit before she did. After riding to the mountain's base camp, Rose bathed and joined her friends at dinner. She was surprised to learn that while she suffered no damage from the outing, the men complained of a variety of maladies, including grave sunburn.[71]

Pender's book, which received critical acclaim, eloquently depicted such sites as Yellowstone National Park and Yosemite's Inspiration Point. Still, Pender encouraged others to see them firsthand: "description is impossible. . . . see it for yourself." Like a true tourist, Pender was photographed in her "prairie attire" and also had photos taken of "horses and traps" to show her friends. Thus, on both a public and a personal level, Pender encouraged interest in western landscapes.[72]

California fared equally well at the hands of one of the nineteenth century's most imposing travel writers, Constance Gordon Cumming of Scotland, who visited Yosemite in 1878. Cumming told of the valley's "unique glory" filled with "granite crags and stupendous waterfalls." When she had only bread to eat and clear stream water to drink, she found herself fully "satisfied with bread here in the wilderness."[73]

Clearly, Victorian "lady" travelers contributed much to the construction of nature and to opinions about its conservation. They also set the pace and opened the way for American women sightseers. Although their numbers were few and they came from

middle- and upper-class backgrounds, Victorian travelers established a tradition of women touring and writing, of women ventur-
ing into botany and anthropology, of women creating landscapes
and espousing the preservation of nature wherever they went.[74]
From Isabella Bird to Mary Kingsley, they instituted an important
tradition for American travel-minded women.

.

In many ways, then, European women established approaches and
styles for white American women. From supplying a cultural heritage to specific work, interpretations, and even advice, European
women helped push their American sisters toward nature and the
physical world. From there, it was a short step to active environmentalism.

3

Botanizers, Birders, and
Other Naturalists

As in Europe, throughout the late nineteenth and early twentieth centuries, the American environment, especially the West, attracted millions of women—as botanizers, birders, collectors, geologists, and more. Like well-known environmentalist John Muir, these women combined a fascination with the outdoors and a growing concern for its welfare. Throughout their lives and careers runs the thread of environmental values.

Indeed, a vignette of one outstanding woman sounds like Muir himself. During the late 1800s, she tramped through the wilderness collecting specimens, wrote about the marvels of nature, dedicated a lifetime to its study and preservation, and urged Americans to cherish and protect the physical world surrounding them. This person was Alice Eastwood, one of America's leading botanists and a conservation advocate between the early 1890s and the late 1940s.

Born in Canada, Eastwood at the age of fourteen moved with her family to Denver. After graduating as valedictorian from East Denver High School in 1879, she taught there for the next ten years. During that era, the Rocky Mountains provided Eastwood's inspiration, joy, and source of energy. By railroad, horseback, buggy, and on foot, she probed crevices and hillsides, bringing back specimens of plants that well-known English naturalist Alfred Russel Wallace said "were altogether new" to him.[1]

In 1890, Eastwood left the classroom behind. Living from the income generated by modest real estate investments, she traveled to California, met with other botanists, and wrote *A Popular Flora of Denver, Colorado* (1893). In 1892, before her book even saw the light of publication, Eastwood moved to San Francisco to join herbarium curator Mary Katharine (Kate) Brandegee at the California Academy of Sciences. The employment of the two women was due to the exceptional foresight of academy founder Albert Kellogg, who ensured that the academy's minutes of 1 August 1853 read, "we highly approve the aid of females in every department of natural history, and . . . we earnestly invite their cooperation."[2]

Eastwood, who chose not to marry, achieved remarkable things in San Francisco. She pursued extensive fieldwork, finding a shrubby daisy subsequently named *Eastwoodia*. In 1905, she published *A Handbook of the Trees of California*, which included her own line drawings. The following year, as an earthquake and fire destroyed a majority of the academy building and its collections, Eastwood rescued 1,211 irreplaceable specimens that she had tucked away in case of such an emergency. She then decided to replace some of the other botany department specimens in forays to the coastal ranges and the Sierra Nevada. By her retirement in 1949 at age ninety, Eastwood had written over three hundred leaflets, articles, and books, including essays on gardens that gained her a reputation as the "gardener's botanist."[3]

During her years in California, Eastwood also discovered John Muir and the Sierra Club, which she joined in 1903. With other avid outdoors people, she climbed Mount Whitney. Eastwood learned not to overlook even the lowliest of plants in the environment. On her way to the academy each morning she collected specimens of flowers that she found between cobblestones. She admired these hardy "foreigners" but feared for their future. "This spontaneous vegetation," Eastwood commented, "indicates by its cosmopolitan character the final result of civilization. The tendency is to reduce mankind as well as plants to one dead level."[4]

•

Eastwood was part of a developing botanical tradition for American women. By the latter decades of the nineteenth century, some knowledge of botany had become a must for educated American women. Many women specialized in some aspect of botany. Despite one recent researcher's inclusion of only three women botanists in a collection titled *One Hundred and One Botanists*, numerous female botanists existed.[5] Another more enterprising investigator identified 1,185 active female botanists working during the nineteenth century. Such sources as botanical journals and club membership lists revealed that during the latter half of the century, 23 percent of these women prepared specimen collections, over half taught school, and a large number wrote books and articles.[6]

During the early twentieth century, women's commitment to botany—and to environmental values—grew. In the Southwest, when Edith Bellamy married botanist Forrest Shreve in 1909, she switched her interests from physics to plant physiology. During her early years in Tucson, Arizona, Edith shared her husband's fieldwork for the desert laboratory. He, in turn, supported her activities, cooked (because she had never learned how), and encouraged her maturation as an independent scientist. Although Edith Shreve published a classic study on transpiration in 1914, nepotism rules forced her to serve as a "voluntary investigator" for the desert laboratory. That did not stop her from writing and lecturing to others interested in nature, both past and future.[7]

In the Northwest, shortly after Lilla Irvin of Eugene, Oregon, graduated from the University of Oregon in 1908, she established a botany department at Eugene High School. In 1913, Lilla married John R. Leach, thus forming a team that regularly ventured into the field throughout Oregon on collecting jaunts. Because John Leach operated the Phoenix Pharmacy in Portland, Lilla organized their endeavors. John explained that "Lilla always travels in the lead and looks for flowers," while "my duty is to know maps, find trails, and keep an eye on the pack animals."[8]

Lilla Leach's work encompassed a wide range. Between 1915 and 1945, she discovered more than a dozen species and two new genera, *Kalmiopsis leachiana* and *Bensonia oregona*. Even though she received many awards and honors, she remained humble about her achievements. In describing one of her greatest finds, *Kalmiopsis leachiana*, she simply said: "I was in the lead where I usually walk in order to get the first chance over the burros to anything of interest that might be growing when suddenly I beheld a small patch of beautiful low growing, deep rose colored plants and because of its beauty I started running toward it and dropped to my knees. . . . I believed it was new."[9]

Following Alice Eastwood's lead, Lilla Leach also became an environmentalist. In 1931 in southwest Portland, she and her husband established a botanical garden, Sleepy Hollow, which they later deeded to the city. In addition, Lilla devoted time to such organizations as the Oregon Roadside Council and, after its founding in 1932, the Western Federation of Outdoor Clubs. From 1945 to 1948, she directed Save the Myrtle Wood, Inc.[10]

•

Besides botanists, women birders dedicated themselves to nature and its preservation. According to one observer, female birders "followed the birds into the woods and wrote about them and other aspects of nature with understanding and enthusiasm."[11]

Among such women, Florence Merriam Bailey stands out as the archetypal female ornithologist of the late nineteenth and early twentieth centuries. Although she lived in Washington DC, Bailey worked in the West, notably New Mexico. She first went west in 1891 and returned to the West many times, sometimes alone, other times with her biologist husband, Vernon Bailey, whom she married in 1899. While Vernon studied mammals, birds, reptiles, and plants, Florence concentrated on birds, which were her passion, her joy, and her conservation goal.[12]

As early as her Smith College days during 1882–86, Bailey had tried to protect birds from slaughter by companies that supplied feathers and whole birds for decorations on women's hats. When the Audubon Society was just beginning, she and another student organized a Smith College Audubon Society for the Protection of Birds. "The birds must be protected," the pair decided. "We must persuade the girls not to wear feathers on their hats." With her confederate, Bailey took her friends into the outdoors to observe birds. The conspirators said nothing about hat feathers; they simply left it to the birders "to hear the message nature holds for each human heart."[13]

Protection of birds proved a constant crusade in Florence Bailey's life. She wrote bird articles for the *Audubon Magazine* and protested what she called "bird murder" in such newspapers as the *Washington DC Evening Star* and *Watertown (New York) Times.* In 1913, when Congress considered a plumage law that would essentially stop milliners from using feathers and birds as decorations, Bailey disdained the "barbaric tastes" of those who wore feathers on their hats, supporting instead what she called "total abstainers." As a member of the Audubon Society and a teacher of bird classes, Bailey opposed the needless killing of birds to satisfy fashion's dictates.[14]

For her work, Bailey became, in 1929, the first woman ever elected a fellow of the American Ornithologists' Union, received an honorary LL.D. from the University of New Mexico in 1923, and has been called the "greatest woman ornithologist in the United States."[15]

During the early twentieth century, a growing awareness of the need for bird conservation developed among Americans in general, inspired by the efforts of such women as Florence Merriam Bailey. For instance, magazines such as *Bird-Lore*, which began publication in 1889 and became *Audubon Magazine* in 1941, proved instrumental in supplying information and supporting bird conservation.[16]

In addition, concerned people established bird clubs. In 1919, the Bird Lovers' Club of the Southwest Museum formed in Los Angeles. The group held bird walks once a week and study meetings once a month. On an early outing in 1921, the birders "walked through the hills to Eagle Rock Park," where they saw twenty-eight species of birds, including a ruby-crowned kinglet. The organization's membership was largely female, and the first two presidents, who presided for fourteen and sixteen years respectively, were women.[17]

Like most other naturalists, the Bird Lovers were also environmentalists who engaged in letter writing, lobbying, and speechmaking. In 1923, members protested the governor's cut in the budget of the state forestry department. Two years later the group fought the California Fish and Game Commission's decision to abandon protection of cormorants and pelicans. Meanwhile, the Bird Lovers tried to keep the designation of Eagle Rock Park as a protected haven for birds. In 1933, the group blocked the "commercialization" of Frazier Mountain Park.[18]

Farther west, in Hawaii, Mary Dorothea Rice Isenberg, born on Kauai, campaigned to bring the bird population back to the islands. She also served as a leader of the Hui Manu, organized in 1930 to reestablish the Hawaiian bird population.[19]

•

Women's dedication to scientific inquiry and environmental preservation appeared in many other areas of natural science as well. These women demonstrated scientific curiosity and a sense of adventure, often seeking exotic destinations and untried areas in which to collect.

Annie Montague Alexander of Hawaii fit this mold. She was not only a naturalist but an explorer as well. Everything interested Alexander, including plants, animals, insects, and rocks, especially fossils. After her family moved to Oakland, California, in 1882, Annie had hoped to become a nurse, but weak eyes interfered with her plans. Instead, she spent time traveling with her father on some occasions and with her friend, Martha Beckwith, a teacher at Mount Holyoke College, on others. Just as Mary Anning had encouraged the Philpot sisters in England in the early nineteenth century, Beckwith showed Alexander new paths. On a 1901 trip into California's Sierra Nevada, Beckwith taught Alexander how to collect specimens, observe birds, and study rocks.[20]

Following Beckwith's lead, Alexander soon expanded her horizons. She attended classes at the University of California in Berkeley, explored Shasta County, and, in 1903, began collecting the skulls of wild animals. By 1906, Annie was off to Alaska in search of wild bears. Two years later, fearing the disappearance of animals in the wild and hoping to stimulate interest in the natural history of the West, Alexander established the Museum of Vertebrate Zoology at the University of California, Berkeley. During the next decade, Alexander joined forces with Oakland teacher Louise Kellogg. The pair's answer to the rapid disappearance of indigenous animals in the West was to collect and preserve specimens of everything from shrews to gophers so that others would have knowledge of such species.[21]

During their time together, which extended into the 1930s and 1940s, Alexander and Kellogg collected assiduously. From Arizona to Alexander's native Hawaii, they gathered 6,744 mammals, birds, reptiles, and amphibians for the Museum of Vertebrate Zoology alone. Alexander could not resist the opportunity to collect. Once, while fishing, she wielded her rod to bring down a bat, thus adding it to her specimens.[22]

Alexander is also remembered as a philanthropist. Like European women who established salons, funded collections, and acted as patrons, she preserved facets of nature. Not only did she establish Berkeley's Museum of Vertebrate Zoology, but she helped endow its Museum of Paleontology as well. As a result of her successful speculation in the stock market, Alexander contributed nearly a million and a half dollars toward the two museums.[23]

As atypical as Alexander may seem for women in the late nineteenth and early twentieth centuries, she had a great deal of company. In Iowa as early as the 1870s, the Davenport Academy of Science's 206 members included 59 women. In 1879, the academy elected a woman president, probably a first in the United States. By the early 1880s, seven Iowa women, whose specialties ranged from geology to paleontology, were listed in *Cassino's Directory of American Naturalists*. One-tenth of the Iowa weather service's meteorological observers were women, while a Muscatine woman served as the entomology editor for the *Iowa State Register*.[24]

In some areas, women even made discoveries that still bear their names. Laura Linton, who studied at the University of Minnesota during the late 1870s, did the field work that identified a mineral closely related to thomsonite, yet with its own distinct characteristics. In 1879, the gemstone received the name lintonite in Linton's honor.[25]

By the the early 1900s, entomology in particular attracted a

49

growing number of women. Similar to English women, American women studied insects and reptiles, species to which women were thought to have an inherent aversion. Miriam A. Palmer, associate in entomology at Colorado State College, specialized in aphids, while in St. Louis Nellie Harris Rau developed a proficiency in wasps. When entomologist Edith Patch wrote a short history of women entomologists in 1939, she set the beginnings in the early 1880s. In her own day, Patch indicated that fifty women held membership in the Entomological Society of America and the American Association of Economic Entomologists.[26]

•

From botanists to entomologists, then, women naturalists emphasized the intertwined topics of physical science and environmental conservation. Some, like Florence Merriam Bailey, chose to protect live birds in their natural habitats, while others, like Annie Montague Alexander, believed that preservation could best be achieved through the establishment of museums. Whatever their environmental persuasion, however, such women faced similar problems in pursuing their goals.

Especially during the late nineteenth century, the so-called wilderness was not believed to be accommodating to women. Women were perceived as delicate and timid, while nature was full of such hazards as rough terrain and wild animals. How could women in the field, many people asked, maintain appropriate clothing and behavior, as well as protect themselves from harm?

There was no question that field conditions proved arduous for women. Everything from inclement weather to mosquitoes, spiders, and other insects besieged collectors in the field. Florence Bailey wrote of difficult trips by wagon and pack animal (horse, donkey, mule, or burro) across western prairies, mountains, and deserts, as well as twelve- to fifteen-hour days in the field. Annie Alexander recorded wind, sleet storms, thundershowers, rain, cold, and frozen specimens. With Louise Kellogg, she camped in tents, crawled under barbed-wire fences, set traps in the dark and rain, hiked and climbed miles carrying steel traps, and walked over lava beds. When botanist Sara Allen Plummer Lemmon and her husband made what she called "A Botanical Wedding Trip" in 1880 into California's Santa Catalina Mountains, she reported that they slept in a cave on a bed of dried grass, where they fought off pack rats and other small animals.[27]

In spite of such obstacles, female naturalists pushed ahead, conquering the West in their own way. They impressed their female personalities on the region, creating decorum and safety where none had existed before. They also faced issues that did not exist for their male counterparts.

One of the most troublesome of these was clothing. During the last three decades of the nineteenth century, most American women still aspired to be what social commentators called "ladies." Consequently, early female naturalists wanted to wear acceptable clothing that was also appropriate to their endeavors.

In 1880, botanist Sara Lemmon attempted to combine fashion and functionality by donning "a short suit of strong material, the best of firm calfskin shoes. . . . substantial leather leggings. . . . a broad-brimmed hat with a buckskin mask, and heavy gloves." She carried with her a botanical portfolio and a wooden staff. Despite her unusual appearance, which became one of her hallmarks, she went on to become an excellent botanist, speaker, and flower painter. Together the Lemmons discovered 3 percent of California's vascular plants. One colleague even ventured that Sara Lemmon "may have been responsible for much of the work that made her husband famous."[28]

Meanwhile, other women naturalists learned that they had to adjust their clothing to fit their activities. Like women living on farms and ranches, women naturalists discovered that heavy brush and branches tore "proper" riding and other outdoor outfits beyond repair.[29]

During the 1890s, Alice Eastwood tried to solve the dilemma by adopting a skirt that reached to her shoe tops rather than the prevailing standard—a trailing skirt trimmed with braid. Yet, such skirts still hindered her in the field. In 1893, yards of corduroy heavy with wet snow dismayed Eastwood as she climbed California's Mount Shasta with a party of more sensibly clad men. After that, she switched to clothes she designed and made herself. With a nod to the fashionable and feminine, Eastwood created a blue denim outfit using a cotton nightgown as a bustle. It incorporated a skirt open in front and back, which she fastened for walking by buttons concealed inside a flap. When she rode a horse, Eastwood fastened the buttons on the front to the corresponding buttonholes on the back to make an effective riding skirt.[30]

By the 1900s, clothing styles had relaxed somewhat for women, especially those engaged in sports or the outdoor life. In 1914, as Texas botanist Dr. Mary Sophie Young urged her team of burros through the trans-Pecos district of West Texas, she wore high-laced leather boots, an ankle-length skirt topped by a long-sleeved blouse, and a broad-brimmed straw hat. Similarly, in her later years, Alice Eastwood often wore high boots, a calf-length dress with long sleeves, and a crushed-denim hat with flowers for decoration.[31]

Other women simply gave up the struggle to remain fashionable. Such women as Ellen Schulz Quillin and Annie Alexander wore leggings and breeches, or trousers. By the late 1930s, when Nevada botanist Edith Van Allen Murphey began government fieldwork on Indian reservations, she favored knee-high boots, breeches, a long-sleeved shirt, and a floppy brimmed hat and carried a long-handled, double-bladed hoe.[32]

Still, some twentieth-century female naturalists clung to a modicum of modesty and femininity in dress, carrying female standards with them to mountaintops or seashores. In 1923, California birders at Playa del Rey sported high-topped shoes, ankle-length suits, white blouses and ties, and wide-brimmed felt hats decorated, oddly enough, with bird feathers. In these outfits, the birders did not let the outdoors deter them or dampen their spirits. They did what they pleased, including squatting in the sand to eat the lunches they had brought along in voluminous handbags or lounging at the ocean's edge, skirts pulled over their legs and booted feet pointed toward the waves.[33]

In the realm of clothing and fashion, women could not seem to win. On the one hand, if women argued over birds on hats, or the right to wear trousers in the field, they spent precious time and energy that their male peers expended on other activities. Also, women's issues often appeared silly to male associates and the larger public. On the other hand, if women rejected female fashion, and especially if they wore trousers, they often found themselves reviled and discredited among their colleagues and the public. It is little wonder that many women eventually ignored criticism and chose to wear knickerbockers or trousers.

The sidesaddle posed another vexing question. Like women on farms and ranches, women in the field realized that sidesaddles did little good on rough terrain for either the rider or the horse. Consequently, most women shucked formality and learned to ride astride.[34] During the 1890s, not only did Californian Kate Brandegee wear trousers, but she rode into the mountains near San Jose del Cabo astride a mule.

Equipment constituted another predicament for women. On their persons, women carried everything from canteens and lunch sacks to collecting cases, plant presses, and sketch pads. On pack mules, and later in automobiles, they transported water, suitcases, tents, cooking equipment and stoves, scientific instruments, field glasses, cameras and tripods, and food supplies. Faced with such loads, however, most women also continued to include such domestic amenities as cots, sheets, and blankets. Lilla Leach admitted that although she and her husband "reduced our load to the barest necessities," the ratio was "100 pounds of botanical equipment, mostly blotters," to "125 pounds of camp equipment, food, bed, tent and so forth."[35]

Obviously, women could reestablish homes in the outdoors, but could they do it in safety? Women's personal security *was* questionable in the field. Animals especially provided frequent threats. Although some women, notably Alice Eastwood, placed their faith in good luck rather than guns, other women naturalists assumed the responsibility for protecting themselves. During the early 1900s, Dr. Mary Sophie Young packed a .25-caliber Colt automatic in her skirt pocket. On a 1914 trip, Young confronted a black bear she considered shooting, but the bear spotted another enemy and "made tracks around the mountain side at the rate of about twelve miles an hour." On another occasion, Young proved that she was capable of defending herself by defeating a rattler with rocks instead of bullets: "as rocks were bigger than bullets, the chances of hitting him were greater with rocks." Young reached down the crack into which the dying snake had slithered and sawed off the rattlers. "The end," she wrote, "when cut off entirely, asserted its independence by waving the rattles defiantly in the air."[36]

Nor were women afraid of the dangers posed by men. Given prevailing worries about decorum and safety, it seems that women would maintain an acceptable distance from men in the field. This was not the case. Such botanists as Mary Sophie Young hired male assistants, who went into the field with them. In addition, women and men traveling together slept in the same tent, dormitory, or barracks. Nelle Stevenson recalled that the "ladies and gentlemen" in her 1907 botanizing party often slept in the same room.[37] Presumably, limited accommodations accounted for such a policy. In addition, the group would have provided chaperonage.

•

Clearly, women naturalists defied censure and solved the problems facing them. As a result, their numbers grew and their activities multiplied so rapidly that yet another controversy arose. So many botanizers, birders, and other naturalists went into the field that critics judged *them* a threat to nature. In addition, women naturalists frequently utilized harsh collection methods, which were often learned from their male mentors and associates. Female naturalists employed rifles, poison, knives, and traps to capture animals, or they hacked at the earth with jackknives, chisels, and hoes. They carried off rocks, skulls, bones, and fossils. Frequently, they bought, sold, and swapped specimens. Sometimes women naturalists even took birds and their eggs from active nests.

Yet, most nineteenth- and early twentieth-century women would have said they believed in preserving life, whether human, plant, or animal. By becoming naturalists and specimen collectors, they had to reconcile female beliefs with the demands of their work. Thus, women often borrowed from men the argument that naturalists must collect—and even kill—in order to preserve.

Martha Maxwell was one of the earliest women naturalists to

come under attack. After founding the Rocky Mountain Museum in 1874, Maxwell developed the art of presenting specimens in natural poses and habitats, often in diorama form. In her exhibit at the Philadelphia Centennial Exposition in 1876, she claimed such a diorama was "woman's work." On the one hand, then, Maxwell preached the necessity of preserving animals and their habitats. On the other, Maxwell slaughtered, usually with a rifle, animals and birds. This petite woman, under five feet in height and described as a "modest, tenderhearted woman," enjoyed posing for pictures with her rifle by her side.[38]

In response to criticism, Maxwell maintained that killing animals was an act of preservation. Everyone, she argued, consented to have animals killed for their personal consumption on the dinner table. "I never take life for such carnivorous purposes!" she added. "I only shorten the period of consciousness that I may give their forms a perpetual memory; and I leave it to you, which is the more cruel? to kill to eat, or to kill to *immortalize!*"[39]

Later generations agreed with Maxwell, seeing her as a preservationist. One biographer stated, "Colorado will ever be indebted to Mrs. Maxwell for her untiring devotion to her state in thus gathering together so rare a collection."[40]

Like Maxwell, other women naturalists wielded guns with proficiency. Crack-shot Annie Alexander learned her skills and attitudes from her father. According to him, Annie could regularly "put a ball through an animal's neck at 100 yards." On an African trip in 1904, she brought between two hundred and four hundred pounds of meat into camp each day. Her father remarked that, given the chance, she would have bagged a trophy lion or other game animal.[41]

Of course, these women lived in an era when sportsmen shot buffalo by the thousands, hunters brought back animal trophies from Africa, and people depended on game meat for sustenance. Yet, women's acceptance of such attitudes contradicts the oft-made statement that women brought a more compassionate philosophy to science.

Fortunately, by the end of the nineteenth century, technological advancements provided humane alternatives to collectors. When possible, for example, women naturalists turned to cameras as a way of collecting nature. Despite the innovations, however, thousands continued to ravage nature for their own goals. Although women naturalists contributed to the conservation ethic, they also threatened the environment in their own way.

•

The foregoing discussion indicates the existence of an important question for women naturalists: should they act like men and espouse male values, or should they infuse their own perspectives and beliefs into science and environmental conservation? At the time, no clear-cut answer existed. If women acted "female," they generated confusion among men, but if they acted "male," they received criticism for being too manlike. This conundrum was nowhere more apparent than in the scientific establishment, which held a deep-seated prejudice against women's scientific abilities.

Of course, not all female naturalists sought professional recognition or financial reward for their efforts. They regarded themselves as strictly amateurs. In June 1885, twenty-five-year-old teacher Mary Hetty Bonar signed on as a cook for a cattle drive so she could "botanize" along the way. From her home state of Minnesota to North Dakota, Bonar collected specimens of plants, soil, and rainbow-colored sands of the Badlands. She raced to the top of every butte and entered every bazaar, curiosity emporium, and taxidermist shop to see what she could learn about animal specimens. At the end of the two-month trip, Bonar was "tired," "happy," and loaded down with materials.[42]

This informal botanizing trend proved long-lived. Sometime during the early 1900s, Carrie Sweetser of Oregon joined two traveling companions, "the Misses Hunt from Pasadena—one a physician." For the next two weeks, the three women climbed the Pinnacles of Sand Creek and scrambled over Garfield Peak to locate specimens of ocean spray, phlox, veratrum, and polemonium humile, as well as "several things new" to them.[43]

Overall, such amateurs provided an important service. Had natural history depended on paid professionals to advance its cause, progress would have been slow. Because middle- and upper-class white women often derived financial support from men, they could afford to operate on a volunteer basis. Such women collected and classified specimens, lectured, established organizations, and encouraged awareness of conservation goals. In a sense, women's economic dependence gave them the opportunity to contribute to the natural sciences in a comprehensive way that would have been impossible had they needed paid employment.

Other female naturalists, however, hoped to disseminate information and derive income from their efforts. These women sought rigorous scientific training, academic degrees including the doctorate, and paid employment. Nevertheless, because of prejudice against women in science, they frequently ended up working behind the scenes: conducting research, establishing collections, cataloguing, and staffing scientific organizations and clubs.

Many of these women taught in high schools and colleges, especially during the nature study movement that emerged between 1895 and 1925. This science curriculum, which targeted elementary and some secondary schools, aimed to stimulate children's interest in the environment. Started by naturalist Anna Botsford Comstock of Cornell University, nature study provided a chance for women to teach and make scientific contributions. When the Nature Study Association formed in 1908, about 60 percent of its members were women. Unfortunately, the movement lost favor during the 1920s, when such "female" and "sentimental" techniques as nature walks, aquariums and terrariums, and recording weather data came under attack from scientists.[44]

Other women aligned themselves with various types of scientific organizations and societies. One of the best known was Mary Katharine (Kate) Curran Brandegee, who received a medical degree in 1878 from the University of California. As a dedicated botanizer, Kate joined the California Academy of Sciences the following year. In 1883, she abandoned her medical practice and became the curator of the academy's herbarium, a position she held for two decades. With the financial support of her second husband, Townshend Stith Brandegee, a civil engineer and plant collector, Kate botanized all over California. In 1891, she founded the Botanical Club and *Zoe*, a botanical journal. In 1894, the Brandegees moved to San Diego, where they developed a botanical library and herbarium.[45]

A fair number of other women found, or created, work in museums, which offered low pay and few fringe benefits. In 1926, avid collector Ellen Schulz Quillin became the first director of the Witte Memorial Museum in San Antonio. With her husband, Quillin explored southwest Texas, especially the Big Bend area. She also pursued an active writing career, during which she published *Texas Wild Flowers* in 1928 and a series of children's books during the 1930s. In addition, Quillin built the first reptile garden in the country, which was intended to promulgate the environmental benefits of snakes.[46]

•

Given the impediments, how did women naturalists integrate themselves into the scientific professions and establish their reputations? Like English women, American women recognized the importance of networks and mentors, both male and female.

Annie Alexander relied on Martha Beckwith to pique her interest and corresponded with Beckwith throughout her life. Alexander also traveled with women friends and eventually formed a partnership with Louise Kellogg. Similarly, Iowa ornithologist Althea Sherman, whose posthumously published *Birds of an Iowa Dooryard* (1952) remains an undisputed classic, regularly communicated with naturalists Alice Laskey and Margaret Morse Nice.[47]

Women naturalists also relied on men—fathers, uncles, brothers, husbands, friends, and colleagues—for training and guidance. Although some men opposed women entering scientific fields and professions, others educated, mentored, and hired women. When Annie Alexander made her first foray into Shasta County, California, in 1902, she accompanied an expedition led by Vance C. Osmont, assistant professor of mineralogy at the University of California. The group included Alexander's mentor, paleontologist John C. Merriam. Certainly, Alexander learned techniques and information from these men, but she also absorbed some of their perspectives. She explained that she earned men's respect by acting like them; on one occasion, after forcing her way through dense brush and trees, she made the discovery of the trip—three lizards.[48]

Another significant case of male mentoring—and inadvertent indoctrination—is Edith Schwartz Clements, the University of Nebraska's first female doctor of philosophy. When she married botany professor Frederic Edward Clements in 1899, he urged her to enter the botany program at the university. With his help and encouragement, Edith left home and family during graduate school to work at the University of Nebraska Alpine Laboratory in Minnehaha, Colorado. She subsequently published her research results. In 1907, Frederic moved to the University of Minnesota; the following year Edith received her doctoral degree from Nebraska. The couple became partners in the new field of ecology. Edith gained renown in a male-dominated realm and earned an entry in *Who's Who* for her wildflower books, photographs and illustrations, and contribution to the *National Geographic Magazine*. After Frederic's death, Edith continued to speak, write, and campaign for an understanding of environmental evolution and the need to treat nature with care.[49]

•

Frequently, despite such networking and mentoring, women still found it difficult to break into established science organizations and bureaucracies. Whether they succeeded often depended on the climate of the times and the area of the country.

Immediately after the Civil War, widespread prejudice in the Northeast and South discouraged many women from entering scientific fields, or at least from openly admitting their interest. One mid-nineteenth-century eastern editor explained that "if an unfortunate female should happen to possess a lurking fondness for any special scientific pursuits she is careful (if of any social position) to hide it as she would some deformity."[50]

The picture changed during the late 1800s and early 1900s, at least for white women of the middle and upper classes. In particular, women entered higher education. In the East, such schools as Barnard, Bryn Mawr, Mount Holyoke, Radcliffe, Smith, Vassar, and Wellesley not only specialized in educating women but also encouraged the work of female scientists, including biologist and environmentalist Ann Haven Morgan and botanist Lydia White Shattuck. Women also invaded the professions in growing numbers. Nationally, 8 percent of women engaged in professional pursuits. In the West, 14 percent of women entered professional fields, including science.[51]

Despite the changes, the East still held sway over the West. When Kate Brandegee founded *Zoe* in 1890, she used the name K. B. Brandegee. In her reminiscences, she wrote that she hoped to avoid eastern prejudices regarding women botanists in positions of power. Her ploy failed, however, when she wrote a negative review of the work of New York naturalist Nathaniel Lord Britton (whose wife was an accomplished botanist). Britton responded with a vitriolic attack on Brandegee by gender.[52]

The following three decades provided more changes, all chaotic. Women found themselves hired as emergency workers during World War I and then fired when the war ended. The granting of woman's suffrage in 1920 seemed a turning point toward greater gains, yet anti-feminism also persisted throughout the 1920s. When the stock market crash of 1929 plunged the nation into a cataclysmic depression, women lost jobs along with men. Women took whatever employment they could find, driving the number of women workers up 3 percent during the 1930s. Also during the 1930s, women's college enrollment dropped 3.5 percent.[53]

•

In the checkered history of female botanizers, birders, and other naturalists, one important theme stands out: most women who prized the environment also argued for its informed use. Sometimes they put forward their message in sentimental, "female" terms that ran counter to those of male scientists. As in England, most American women refused to talk in plain terms about such subjects as mating and procreation. Instead, they used nonscientific "code" words or submerged the issue under other observations. Arkansas environmentalist Ruth Harris Thomas even gave names to the birds she observed and humanized their courtships and matings.[54]

Such other women as Alice Eastwood leaned more toward the scientific side. Throughout her career, Eastwood urged Californians to preserve native species, whether they be stumpy salt marsh plants or enormous redwoods. Her advocacy of environmental preservation earned her honors ranging from local garden club awards to a citation from the Seventh International Botanical Congress in Stockholm in 1950. She also had a grove of giant redwood named after her, as well as a fuchsia, a lilac, and an orchid. Perhaps most apt of all was Eastwood's inclusion in every edition of *American Men of Science*.[55]

In Eastwood's view, nature provided everything from scientific interest to spirituality. "The feeling that comes from the order and law of the universe," she wrote, "is truly religious and I think that every scientific person must be religious without any belief in a dogma of any kind."[56] When Eastwood died of cancer in 1953, the California Academy of Sciences recognized her enormous legacy by renaming its herbarium the Alice Eastwood Herbarium.

The specimens that remained within the herbarium's walls represented Eastwood's hedge against environmental tragedy. Outside its walls lived the plants that she and others had labored so hard to save. These American women—from botanists and birders to geologists and entomologists—worked to protect the "wild" west from depletion.

4

Writers and Poets

Women writers and poets played a huge, if often unsung, role in the early conservation movement. Recently, one investigator even suggested that nature writers and poets may have influenced environmental thought more than did politicians.[1]

This study would agree that late nineteenth- and twentieth-century nature essays, books, and poems shaped public attitudes, which in turn underwrote the programs of government leaders, including Theodore Roosevelt and Gifford Pinchot. It would add that female authors participated significantly in the development of nature writing, contributing distinctive perceptions and feminized views of western terrains and often becoming conservation proponents themselves.

The work of New Mexican writer Mary Hunter Austin proved especially influential. A transplanted easterner who came to think of herself as a westerner, Austin celebrated the Southwest and its peoples in everything from essays and articles to some thirty books, which, in her own day, earned Austin a prominent place on America's literary stage.[2]

In 1903, Austin's first book, *The Land of Little Rain*, portrayed the southwestern desert as mystical, undefinable, yet seductive. She rejoiced in the desert's small pleasures, which she called "strange things" in the area's "tumultuous privacy." Austin explained, "I like the smother of sound among the dunes, and finding small coiled snakes in open places." In addition, Austin saw the desert as far stronger than southwestern migrants, who did not fully understand what desert living would demand of them. Thus, she expressed less concern about the effects of "civilization" on the desert than the desert's impact on people. As a model for those who wished to live in the desert, Austin pointed to American Indian and Hispanic peoples, who knew how to live harmoniously with nature.[3]

After *The Land of Little Rain*, Austin continued to write frequently of the Southwest. During the war years and the 1920s, the incredibly prolific Austin produced novels, children's verse, essays, and short stories. Many people saw her as primarily a literary figure. Some thought poetry to be Austin's forte; others preferred her essays. Still others judged her more of a flamboyant personality than a writer.[4]

Only a few critics recognized Austin as a nature writer and environmentalist. At least one reviewer of *The Land of Little Rain* recognized certain similarities between John Muir and Mary Austin. "What John Muir has done for the western slopes of the Sierras," a commentator wrote in the *Brooklyn Eagle*, "Mrs. Austin does in a more tender and intimate way for the eastern slopes." Critic Carl Van Doren even declared that "a new degree ought to be conferred" upon Austin, that of "Master of the American Environment."[5]

But such commentators failed to assess the differences between Muir and Austin. They overlooked the fact that Austin's feminism, notably her determination to retrieve women's relationships to western wilderness, separated her from Muir in a fundamental way. Unlike Muir and other male writers, Mary Austin advocated feminist principles throughout her work. Her white men, materialistic and exploitative, sacrificed their very souls to the desert, while her white women understood and sympathized with the land. Austin also regarded the West as an opportunity for women to "walk off" the societal values that bound them.[6]

In addition to her writings, Austin's personal life demonstrated her enduring allegiance to conserving the environment. She believed in an ethic of care or stewardship of the West, which she saw as the hope of future generations. Although she had met John Muir and claimed to "know something of what went on in Muir," Austin was more than a disciple. She had her own environmental causes. In 1905, for example, Austin protested the Bureau of Reclamation's scheme to divert water from the Owens Valley to Los Angeles. Over a decade later, she opposed Boulder (Hoover) Dam, saying it was a "debacle" reflecting the greed of its backers.[7]

Despite her writings and personal activism, however, Mary Austin gradually drifted into the shadows of the American literary canon. After her death in 1934, her short stories and many of her books went out of print. Although *The Land of Little Rain* remained available, it received less attention than deserved by this classic of early twentieth-century nature writing.[8]

•

Lesser writers than Austin shared a similar fate. Although widely read and revered in their own day, women writers were soon forgotten. These women were influential at the time, but their views of nature and its future were largely lost to environmental history.

In part, this occurred because of the dominance enjoyed by such American male nature writers as Henry David Thoreau during the early 1800s. At the time, women, who were just beginning to establish themselves as writers, were expected to confine their efforts to domestic novels and other uplifting works. These women wrote primarily for women readers, whose enthusiastic response indicated the presence of an extensive, specialized market for works that considered women's issues and employed female language and metaphors. As a result, women writers were so successful with the "domestic" genre that they often enjoyed best-seller status, publication in other countries, and multiple reprinted editions.

Still, the "domestic novelists," as most were called, commanded little respect among their peers. Author Nathaniel Hawthorne reportedly referred to them as "that damned mob of scribbling women." Neither he nor many other Americans had much faith in what women authors had to say, especially if they overstepped the boundaries into the realm of "serious" topics, including the environment.

Thus, as women authors struggled to gain professional credence, their white male counterparts wrote numerous essays and books advocating what is now called "ecological romanticism."

Well before the Civil War, this philosophy questioned the idea of nature as a resource for human exploitation. Instead of depleting nature, many male writers maintained that uses of nature should include aesthetic, philosophical, religious, and commercial considerations.[9]

But the romantic tradition has not been fully explored. Ecological romanticism was far more than the writings of Henry David Thoreau and his male cohorts. The concept of environmental stewardship had dimensions of gender, religion, and race, which remain largely unanalyzed. Although generally unrecognized, various women writers expanded and strengthened ideas of ecological romanticism.

Most significant, perhaps, was Susan Fenimore Cooper's *Rural Hours*, published in 1850, four years before Thoreau's *Walden*. In fact, Cooper helped popularize the nature essay and developed her own version of the pastoral myth. Daughter of writer James Fenimore Cooper, Susan Cooper came from a rich tradition of nature writing. As the first woman nature essayist on the American scene, she augmented other women's appreciation of nature and piqued their interest in learning more about it.[10]

In the widely read *Rural Hours*, Susan Cooper did not attempt to justify herself as a writer by rejecting things domestic. Instead, she enlarged upon the growing notion of nature as providing a family's larger home. If nature was home, Cooper implied, then women's domestic sphere included nature. Moreoever, she saw the environment as an appropriate women's concern. Thus, Cooper believed she had the right to advocate stewardship of the land. She called for laws and policies designed to protect animals and forests. "Thinning woods and not blasting them" would be a step toward conserving divinely created nature, Cooper argued, and toward regulating humankind's larger home, the outdoors.[11]

Another neglected group who contributed to early ecological romanticism were Mormon women, or members of the Church of Jesus Christ of Latter-day Saints. Like Cooper, Mormons in general argued for the biblical concept of stewardship, including care of the environment. Especially after the Mormons reached Utah in 1847, they proclaimed they could return the earth to an Edenic state only through wise usage, rather than improvident waste, of natural resources.[12] Also like Cooper, Mormon women adopted these goals as their own, incorporating environmental messages and programs into their extensive network of volunteer organizations.

Women of color lent yet another perspective to ecological romanticism—that of who "owns" nature. A few years after Cooper's *Rural Hours* appeared, Philadelphia free black Charlotte L. Forten indicated that some African-American women—at least those of the educated middle class—yearned to experience nature. In her journals, she noted that although women benefited from outdoor exercise, studying flora and fauna, and collecting plant specimens, the twin institutions of slavery and prejudice barred black women from enjoying nature. Although free herself, Forten felt she could not travel to see Kentucky's Mammoth Caves until slavery had ended. She lacked the ability to delight in nature while so many of her people suffered: "How strange it is that in a world so beautiful, there can be so much wickedness."[13]

Thus, the American tradition of ecological romanticism had wider implications than those suggested by male authors. Themes that resonated with women, religious minorities, and people of color stayed in the background. But those same themes constituted a treasure-trove of values and traditions to later generations of thinkers and writers, including such submerged motifs as Susan Cooper's and Mormon women's ideal of God-given stewardship of the land as a female duty and the kinds of relationships various sorts of people could develop with nature.

•

After the Civil War, women writers followed the traditions of ecological romanticism—and added to them. Women's nature writing generally lacked the twin themes of conquest and domination of landscapes that marked so many men's works of the same era. While others argued for "progress" and the use of natural resources, women typically emphasized the beauty and spirituality of nature. They also interpreted nature as female and employed female images to describe the environment. As a result, female nature writers perceived the environment as accommodating and welcoming, especially of strong, independent women willing to meet nature's challenges.[14]

These women writers also rejected the widespread belief that people had hegemony over nature. Instead, they emphasized the need for humans to live in harmony with the environment. Female writers focused on the necessity of living with the demands of the physical world rather than subduing them, which allowed women to perceive the violent side of nature—to be realistic—without feeling overwhelmed or threatened by the environment.[15]

As early as the 1860s, writer Helen Hunt Jackson pondered and expanded such ideas. In 1867, she moved to Colorado Springs, where she explored nature, climbed mountains, and wrote essays, poems, and travel sketches about the Colorado landscape. Jackson found the Colorado outdoors not only beautiful but accessible and spiritual as well. She described landscapes in terms of such women's metaphors as family and birth. In the December 1876 issue of the *Atlantic Monthly*, Jackson tried to convey "the silence of the wilderness." She concluded, "This is silence like that in which the world lay pregnant before time again."[16]

In 1879, Jackson published *Bits of Travel at Home*, which pointed to health and beauty in nature but also recognized its violent side. Her image of a dead tree, its body "stiffened straight in death and its myriad limbs convulsed and cramped in agony," reminded readers that the environment had unpleasant aspects as well as bucolic ones. She did not, however, suggest that people should "tame" nature for their own purposes.[17]

•

Following the lead of Jackson and others, women writers by the late nineteenth and early twentieth centuries had developed a form that might be called "women's pastoral." Although this interpretation of western landscape utilized the customary pastoral mode, it placed female images squarely at its core. Women's symbols took center stage, while the western environment became Mother Earth; she was hospitable to women, including those fleeing from difficult situations.[18]

Despite the widespread myth that women detested the West and faltered in face of many of its challenges, a number of female authors characterized the West as a haven for women, even offering them freedom and opportunity. Why has the work of such writers dropped into the background? Perhaps Americans of subsequent generations had other ideas about the "appropriate" place of women, especially in the American West.

One such writer was Marah Ellis Ryan. In 1890, she created a heroine who fled civilization for the refuge and liberty the West offered women. In *Told in the Hills*, Ryan portrayed western landscapes as welcoming and exhilarating for women.[19] The hapless female victim of the frontier, as characterized by such novelists as Hamlin Garland and Ole Rolvaag, had no place in Ryan's vision.

Meanwhile, an immigrant from Germany, Josephine McCrackin, not only participated in the movement to preserve the American West but also wrote short stories set in the Southwest. Her work often featured women leaving spouses and establishing themselves as independent women. In a career that spanned five decades, McCrackin had stories appear in such collections as *Overland Tales* (1877), *Another Juanita* (1893), and *The Woman Who Lost Him* (1913). Partly autobiographical, McCrackin's writings demonstrated that determined women could triumph over the challenges of the West.[20]

In the twentieth century, such other novelists as Willa Cather and Ellen Glasgow followed the women's pastoral format, but with a pronounced feminist bent. In both Cather's *O Pioneers!* (1913) and Glasgow's *Barren Ground* (1925), women agriculturalists rescued the land from harsh or uninformed usage. The authors also emphasized the spiritual bond their characters established with nature through the rejuvenation of the land and the freeing effects of the women's success on their inner feelings. In a sense, then, Cather and Glasgow turned the older, male-oriented pastoral interpretation on its head. In their work, women who saved a piece of the landscape reaped satisfaction and autonomy from their efforts.[21]

•

In itself, women writers' superimposition of a female culture onto the western environment is unsurprising, for authors of many different backgrounds situated their own cultures and communities in the places about which they wrote.[22] But women writers virtually reconstructed the western environment, making it appealing to women and worthy of their solicitude. They presented a West that not only welcomed women but that *demanded* women's help in saving it.

Consequently, women's stewardship of the West became a frequent motif. Novelist Agnes C. Laut's *The Freebooters of the Wilderness* (1913) demonstrated that women were indeed effective stewards. Laut's story focused on both sheep killing in the West and the destruction of timber and mineral lands. When an environmental crusader opposed "peanut politicians and public plunderers," he lost his job. But the situation was far from hopeless. A wealthy woman put up the money to continue the fight, while the crusader married the daughter of an assassinated sheep king. The new wife was a strong woman who loved the West and willingly succored her husband through all. She provided the necessary commitment, for she refused to let go of her "splendid big free life" in the West because of eastern special interests and corrupt politicians.[23]

Did such books have any impact on the developing conservation movement? In 1938, Edith E. Kohl's *The Land of the Burnt Thigh* also portrayed the West as a place where women could succeed. Basing the book on her own and her sister's homesteading experiences in South Dakota, Kohl presented a West in which women could survive, endure, and even triumph on their own. In addition, Kohl portrayed western landscapes as needing a woman's gentle touch. Her woman-focused book was credited with causing federal officials to recognize the necessity for water conservation projects on the Missouri River in South Dakota.[24]

Neither Laut nor Kohl enjoy much name recognition today, however. Perhaps the most well known twentieth-century writer to utilize such themes, and to argue for the necessity of living in harmony with nature, was Nebraskan Mari Sandoz. Although known as a novelist and a historian of the Great Plains, Sandoz infused environmental maxims into her books as well as into her articles, speeches, and dinner addresses. Because she believed in moral messages, in drawing upon the past as a guide to the future, her characters often evinced what today would be called environmentalism.[25]

In fact, Sandoz's major focus throughout her life and work concerned humankind's impact on western land and the land's effect on people. In *Old Jules* (1935) Sandoz even listed as a character "The Region: The upper Niobrara country." As in her other books, in *Old Jules* the Plains and the environmental cycle contributed a unifying motif.[26]

Sandoz's only notable deviation from the women's pastoral form was *Slogum House* (1937), in which the female protagonist exploited nature and symbolized greed, while her husband instilled their daughter with a love of nature and conserved rainwater by digging irrigation ditches and terraced pools. Still, in *Slogum House*, Sandoz indicted male politicians, financiers, and land-grabbers as the major culprits. Also, later in her career Sandoz wrote entire novels about men's senseless exploitation of buffalo and beaver.[27]

In *Slogum House*, Sandoz's primary purpose was to argue for environmental conservation. She characterized northwestern Nebraska as symbolic of the entire nation, which "was so short a time ago the land of promise." In Sandoz's view, the country now lay "paralyzed, all activity halted except foreclosure and eviction and the lengthening lines of those who had no roof and no bread." To reinforce her point, Sandoz invoked the biblical words of Jeremiah: "And I brought you into a plentiful country, to eat the fruit thereof and the goodness thereof: but when ye entered, ye defiled my land, and made mine heritage an abomination."[28]

Sandoz, a native westerner herself, was more realistic than most about myths surrounding the American West. She could see both the bright and dark sides of the region and its peoples. Even though Sandoz intended her dramatic, tense story of exploitation of the West to wake people up to the need for environmental conservation, *Slogum House* seemed to alienate many Americans instead. Perhaps her heroine, Gulla Slogum, acted in an overly "unfeminine" way, or Sandoz's charges were especially frightening in 1937. Certainly, a combination of overcultivation and drought had made such states as Kansas, Oklahoma, and Texas vulnerable to ravaging winds that stripped the soil and left in their wake the Dust Bowl. In addition, despite relative prosperity in the South-west and the Pacific Northwest, tragedy after tragedy raked the West. As a result, thousands abandoned worn-out fields, while western states applied for one federal subsidy after another. Thus, Sandoz imparted a moral message that few Americans wanted to hear.

Clearly, Sandoz and other women writers achieved much for environmentalism. Obviously, they revealed the environmental abuse occurring throughout the West. But women writers also drew women's attention to western landscapes and made women feel they had a place in the West. The western environment be-came accessible to women, who in turn recognized their responsi-bility to care for the land and its resources. Subtly yet powerfully, women writers prevailed upon women to save Mother Nature.

•

As in England, some American women nature writers appealed di-rectly to children, hoping to imbue them with a love of nature at an early age. Such ventures were often short-lived, however. In 1891, Katharine Bagg [later Katharine Bagg Hastings], a young woman living in Tombstone, Arizona, started a publication for children called the *Bug-Hunter.* She asked five cents per copy and fifty cents for a year's subscription. In the *Bug-Hunter*'s first issue, Bagg stated that her magazine would address all branches of natu-ral history and would especially offer "hints to boys and girls who would fancy collecting the members of the insect world." She promised to answer such perplexing questions as "how catch? how kill? how keep?" True to her promise, Bagg covered a range of in-sects, including butterflies, ants, spiders, and locusts, yet she did not attract enough of a readership to continue publication. In the same year, 1891, Bagg began and ended publication.[29]

A nature writer who more successfully wrote for children was Opal Whiteley of Walden, Washington. Like English writers Christina Rossetti and Margaret Gatty, Whiteley observed nature from a child's point of view, placing an eccentric female child at the center of the physical world.

Whiteley herself had an unusual childhood and adolescence. As a young girl, she read botanical works and kept extensive nature journals. In 1916, she entered the University of Oregon to study botany and eventually to write nature books for children. At the same time, she helped lead the Junior Christian Endeavor organization in Oregon. Whiteley wrote, "my nature study is of much help to me in my work with the juniors for I find that the child heart readily unfolds to the true and the beautiful in God's out-of-doors."[30]

After Opal Whiteley left college in 1918, she gave nature lectures and reconstructed from scraps of paper a diary she supposedly had written at age six. When her diary, *The Fairyland around Us,* appeared in 1920, a storm of controversy broke over it. Could Whiteley have written such a work at age six? Could she have included French and Latin names? Were her parents, as she claimed, really angels?[31]

Reviews were mixed. One called Whiteley "a master of make-believe," while others commended her for keeping "the child's point of view of nature." Yet others called her "peculiar" and her diary a "hoax." Scientists looked askance at Whiteley's book, while the public bought copies by the thousands. Despite its inconsistencies, *Fairyland* was obviously a compelling nature book. With the controversy still unresolved, Whiteley left for Europe in 1923. Some years later, London authorities judged her unable to care for herself and placed her in Napsbury Hospital, a mental asylum.[32]

In the 1990s, what is the verdict regarding Opal Whiteley and her nature diary, which was recently reprinted in paperback? On the one hand, Whiteley may have been a "mystical-natured prodigy," as at least one commentator has argued. Clearly, she left behind a paean to nature, written in the words of a child. She told of singing creeks, gray lichen people whose language she understood, and a lily that floated on a pond like "a little sky-star." Surely,

Opal Whiteley performed a service in spreading the love of nature to Americans, especially children.[33]

On the other hand, evidence exists of instability, perhaps even religious fanaticism, in Whiteley's personality. Certainly, the publication of *Fairyland* and its attendant dispute marred the reputation of amateur botanists in the eyes of the scientific establishment. Moreover, Whiteley's fanciful descriptions must have convinced many that women's view of nature was capricious and better kept separate from hard science.

•

Between 1870 and 1940, then, women nature writers fell into one of two groups. Many slipped their messages between the lines; others directly addressed conservation concerns. The first group of authors reached people who were not seeking conservation maxims and perhaps had never thought about such problems, while the latter group wrote for those already interested in the future of western landscapes.

At the same time, authors who would not have described themselves as "nature writers" at all wrote myriad works that concentrated on such specific environmental issues as protecting birds or preserving national parks. Although they focused more on specific problems, these writers, too, demonstrated a woman-centered view of nature in their entreaties for the preservation of the environment.

Some of the most eloquent of these appeals originated with women who were scientists first and writers second. Ornithologist Florence Merriam Bailey gained renown as much for her engaging writing as for her work on behalf of birds. Of her first summer in the West in 1891, Bailey wrote that although she traveled to Utah with a friend "for the birds and the climate," the summer turned into a spiritual experience as well. When the women climbed the Wasatch Mountains, a "hush" fell on their "spirits." According to Bailey, "it seemed as if the noble mountains under whose great shadow we had passed the summer had at last admitted us to their Holy of Holies."[34]

Before and after her marriage, Bailey wrote extensively about bird habits. Her early writings include *My Summer in a Mormon Village* (1894) and *A-Birding on a Bronco* (1896). In her classic study, *Birds of New Mexico* (1928), she brought together a range of sources, including the field notes of the 1820 Long Expedition, government surveys, and her own observations. Bailey's last book, *Among the Birds in the Grand Canyon Country* (1939), was written for the National Park Service while her husband, Vernon, served as the director of conservation for the American Trappers Association (ATA). Florence, pleased with ATA efforts, wrote her niece that the ATA was making "an astonishing attempt" to be as "humanitarian as they can."[35]

Scores of other women took different tacks. Rather than birds, the issue that inflamed popular writer Caroline Lockhart of Cody, Wyoming, was the Montana Fish and Game Department's policies. Lockhart railed against the agency's extermination of such species as the bobcat and editorialized in the *Cody Enterprise* against recreational hunting. In 1924, Lockhart, a staunch outdoor enthusiast, bought the L Slash Heart Ranch west of the Big Horn River Canyon, where she put some of her long-held principles into practice.[36]

Novelist Honoré Willsie Morrow championed forest reclamation and desert preservation. She set her stories in a range of western settings and, as in *We Must March: A Novel of the Winning of Oregon* (1925), used a historical approach to make her points. Although Morrow's name is largely forgotten, she gained a wide audience, especially during the 1920s and 1930s.[37]

The West in general and its national parks in particular became the soapbox topic of journalist Mary Roberts Rinehart. During the war years and the 1920s, Rinehart wrote about her travels in the American West, always with an environmental focus. Her articles and books played an important role in advertising western landscapes to the public and convincing Americans that the West was worth saving. Although she lived primarily in the East, Rinehart helped explain the West to generations of Americans.

Besides being a writer and journalist, Rinehart was a sportswoman who liked to fish and ride. Gradually, she became a naturalist of sorts, appreciating bears, trees, and rivers, but she could also be a tourist, enjoying the occasional comfort of a hotel or Great Northern Railroad cars. Perhaps most importantly, Rinehart found the West especially liberating for women who could mount horses without assistance and survey trails with clearer, calmer eyes than when they started.[38]

Rinehart especially supported the national park idea. In her *Through Glacier Park: Seeing America First* (1916) she explained to readers who had never visited a national park that Montana's Glacier National Park did not consist of "neat paths and clipped lawns." Rather, Glacier preserved the "wildest part of America." Although she objected to what she called the government's "niggardly provision" for park facilities, Rinehart admitted that she would never have seen the area without government intervention.[39]

With adeptness, Rinehart characterized Glacier National Park in a way that left no doubt as to its value: "here are ice and blazing sun, vile roads, and trails of a beauty to make you gasp." At the same time, she portrayed nature as luxuriant and generous: "red raspberries as large as strawberries served in the diner, and trout from the mountains that seemed no nearer by mid-day than at dawn!" She also equated nature with the triumph of endurance, authenticity, health, and "living."[40]

Rinehart followed her popular *Through Glacier Park* with several more volumes of similar design. In her 1923 book, *The Out Trail*, she reinforced the idea that men and women experienced disparate reactions to nature. "The difference between the men I have camped with and myself," Rinehart stated, "generally speaking, has been this: They have called it sport; I have known it was work." In her view, only one man in a thousand sought the wilderness because he loved nature. He went instead to prove his manhood, to become more fit, or to get away from women. Women, however, went to admire their menfolks' exploits and to enjoy nature. Because of lesser physical strength, however, a woman felt more vulnerable in the wilderness, her only resources being moral fiber and "nervous energy."[41]

Critics assessed Rinehart's work as dramatic, humorous, and

entertaining, but no one analyzed its effects on the burgeoning conservation movement.[42] Strictly speaking, Rinehart wrote neither nature books nor environmental literature. Yet in a sense she wrote both. Rinehart validated the national park concept and attacked such inaccurate notions as the Great American Desert. She also personalized such groups of American Indians as the Navajos and Hopis and argued for the preservation of their cultures. Ultimately, her light approach made it possible for thousands of people, especially women, to savor western landscapes secondhand or to visit the national parks in person, often becoming environmentalists in the process.

•

Also significant were nature poets. Occasionally, one would deviate from the standard interpretation. A few female poets lauded economic progress and took a typically "male" attitude. At least one advocated the conversion of the Arizona desert into a field "blooming like a rose in May."[43]

Most, however, pursued the "female" line by emphasizing the spiritual side of western landscapes. The spiritual focus proved a strong one for such women poets as popular lyricist Ella Rhoads Higginson, who in 1898 published a book of nature poetry, *When the Birds Go North Again,* in which she wrote not only about nature but about the American West. In a poem titled "God's Creed," Higginson claimed she would never worship in church again. "For I have knelt in western dawns," she explained,

> When the stars were large and few,
> And the only font God gave me were
> The deep leaves filled with dew.[44]

The spiritual emphasis continued well into the twentieth century as poets frequently reminded readers that the western landscape was the work of God. One wrote that the "patient hand of God" had chiseled the cliffs and chasms of Colorado's Mesa Verde National Park, which were marred and invaded by civilization.[45]

Meanwhile, other female poets idealized specific aspects of western nature. Some hallowed California's great redwoods. Some found merit in the Far West's chinook winds. Others even defended the unrefined desert.[46]

During World War I and the early 1920s, for example, Arizona poet Phoebe Bogan proclaimed that the desert was not a "wasteland" and wrote instead of its "untamed beauty." In "The Desert Uncompromising," Bogan recognized the ferocious side of nature but expressed no need to subdue it:

> Cacti spurning, rocks burning,
> With the hideous heat of the sun,
> And lizard starting, their endless darting
> Till a new hiding place is won.

> Cactus flowers boldly cower,
> In the midst of their treacherous nest,
> And my fingers torn by a deadly thorn
> That has put its power to test.

> Bones lying, plaintively crying
> Of that ghastly sin of old,
> When the Desert starved them, from food debarred them
> To greed the Desert is sold.[47]

Bogan admitted that although she occasionally longed to return to the East, where she could "surrender" herself to "spring moods," she always chose the desert, for it gave her a sense of peace and total satisfaction.[48]

Established "female" themes displayed great tenacity. As late as the 1920s and 1930s, a distinctly female interpretation of the physical world continued to appear in nature poetry. During the 1930s, the Mormon poet Olephia "Leafy" King combined a love of the outdoors with writing poetry. She established a reputation in Nye County, Nevada, as an adept hunter, shooter, and all-around outdoorsperson. In 1933, a local newspaper proclaimed that since childhood Leafy King had always bagged a deer on the very first day of hunting season. It was not surprising that King, who favored no-nonsense boots and trousers, wrote poetry that equated life in the West with freedom for women. She placed "cowgirls" and "cowgirl wives" in the center of her poetic dramas, noting that the West gave women the "ability to roam."[49]

King's poetry also extolled "Nature's beauty" and called for the preservation of the West and its inhabitants. In "The Coyote's Tale," she argued for the perpetuation of such creatures as the coyote. Of a coyote with three puppies King sympathetically wrote,

> So you see I have my problems too,
> three hungry mouths to feed
> That's why I prowl where I shouldn't prowl,
> That's the nature of my breed.[50]

•

Even though the names of many of the women mentioned above are unfamiliar to contemporary readers, that of Mary Hunter Austin is widely known. Because the feminist revolution of the late 1960s caused a revision of the American literary canon, Austin regained her title, "Queen Victoria of American letters," as well as her reputation as a poet, mystic, feminist, folklorist, novelist, storyteller, and nature writer.[51]

In her 1932 autobiography, *Earth Horizon*, Austin already viewed herself as a nature writer and environmentalist. "All places were beautiful and interesting," she wrote, "so long as they were outdoors." Gradually, she committed herself "to the idea that she was to write of the West" as well as to work for its conservation.[52]

Austin maintained that she differed significantly from male naturalists. In her autobiography, she admitted that she had always been fond of a bit of verse that encouraged women to "raise the world from all that's low," including despoiling the environment. In other words, Austin believed she had a duty associated with her gender. In 1918, she wrote that women had a unique way of seeing nature: "This is what women have to stand on squarely, not their ability to see the world in the way men see it, but the importance and validity of their seeing it in some other way."[53]

Austin believed that women's point of view had been too long neglected, that it was her mission to recover "the unexplored treasure of women's experience in the West." As an avowed feminist, Austin associated western landscapes with freedom for women, with the opportunity to learn about Mother Earth and become its keepers. She rejected the belief that men's perceptions constituted the norm, preferring instead to have the benefit of both male and female insights.[54]

Perhaps it was this "woman's viewpoint" and feminist perspective that explains the neglect of Austin and similar women writers during the post–World War II period. Austin's mystical approach—and her claims to have a different view of nature than men—must have alienated the male establishment. Also, in a hard-headed era dedicated to fighting the Cold War and communism, Austin's views had little appeal.

By the 1970s, when the environmental movement revitalized in the United States, Austin was all but forgotten. During this decade, however, contemporary feminism encouraged American women to retrieve their history and find female role models. In 1923, Mary Austin had said, "Not to know their own prophets is rather a serious predicament for women."[55] Feminist scholars duly discovered Mary Austin as one of their forerunners and prophets.

By the 1980s, Austin had also assumed the status of a "pioneer" environmentalist who paved the way for everything from contemporary concerns to ecofeminism. She was a maverick, a woman ahead of her times who wrote not only "of the landscape but the spirit of the West."[56]

The moral of Austin's story is that fashions change with the times. Austin was a force in her own day, both as a writer and an environmentalist. After her death in 1934, her work and views received less and less notice. Now, near the end of the twentieth century, Mary Austin is ranked alongside Henry David Thoreau and John Muir as a dedicated nature writer, naturalist, and environmentalist.[57]

Austin's roller-coaster celebrity suggests that other women writers also deserve retrieving and reassessing. The "female" approach to western nature and its preservation may offer useful insights to contemporary problems.

5

Visual Image-Makers

Far more difficult to analyze is the effect of female visual image-makers on the early conservation movement. The work of illustrators, artists, photographers, gardeners, and landscape architects—unlike that of naturalists and nature writers—was seldom intended to convey conservation tenets. Visual image-makers, however, put nature in an appealing format that, albeit inadvertently, convinced people that the environment *could* be shaped, managed, and conserved for human use, at present and in the future.

California landscape architect Florence Yoch took as her maxim that "use" by people was "the primary factor influencing design of an outdoor environment." Yoch's definition of her profession was equivalent to that of an environmentalist: "the art of fitting the land for human use and enjoyment." Also like environmentalists, Yoch was at the will of climate, water conditions, available materials, and even cultural values, for she further believed that every society created its own preferred landscapes, ranging from prim English parks to California's "natural" gardens.[1]

With the administrative talents of her partner, Lucile Council, Florence Yoch pioneered landscape architecture for women in the Southwest. Beginning in 1921, with Council's advice, Yoch devised her own designs, all with unusual innovations. She utilized seasonal color schemes, maximizing the best plants and flowers for each time of year. She always tried for a natural look—an off-center tree, a crooked walk, an overgrowth of flowers. She was the first to transplant full-grown olive trees. Yoch also converted an orange grove into a garden by preserving seven of the original trees and replanting the rest.[2]

Yoch's admirers called her an artist, but she was also a fine technician. During the early 1900s, Yoch sought training that suited her philosophy. She studied at the University of California at Berkeley, Cornell University, and the University of Illinois at Urbana-Champaign before graduating from the University of Illinois in 1914. She also read widely, observed plant life, and visited the great gardens of Europe. As a result, she designed elegant yet feral gardens so the earth would have periods of rest and could naturally replenish itself. Also, Yoch's designs always took account of what she called "California conditions," including climate and native plants.[3]

Not only did Yoch bring nature to people, but she made it usable and self-renewing. Her environments proved attractive and stable rather than threatening and degenerating. From patrician parks to country gardens, Florence Yoch's styles convinced the world that landscapes could be improved by human intervention.

Between 1870 and 1940, then, artists of various kinds interpreted nature for conservation advocates. On the one hand, nature might be wild and uncontrollable, threatening and "male" in its ferocity. Or it could appear tractable and in balance with its surroundings, totally "female" in its beauty and lushness.

The latter perception of nature promoted environmental values far more than the first. In order to support the conservation cause, one had to agree that the environment should be altered for human use. Whether landscape was to be prepared for recreation, wildlife habitats, or reforestation, it was necessary to believe that humankind had the ability to pattern nature as it chose.

·

In the hands of late nineteenth- and early twentieth-century female artists, the physical world became pliant and adaptable. Following the example set by their English counterparts, literally thousands of American women artists represented landscapes in some artistic media. Many followed a traditional line by working in such formats as needlework, while others pursued the more formal art forms, including painting and architecture.[4]

81

These numerous women artists generally enjoyed credibility with the public. American societal notions of the late nineteenth and early twentieth centuries approved of women "dabbling" in art, and most Americans believed it was "acceptable" for women to depict nature.

In 1864, for example, Helen Tanner Brodt accompanied her husband on a military expedition to California's Mount Lassen. She was the first known white woman to climb the peak, and the lake near the summit bears her name. Brodt also carried home memories that she turned into sketches and paintings. Later, she added other California landscapes and ranch scenes to her growing repertoire.[5]

During the 1870s and 1880s, "flower artists" flourished. In England, the most visible flower artist was Marianne North. In the United States, perhaps the best known was Alice Stewart [later Alice Stewart Hill], who hoped to bring the beauty of Colorado flowers to the world. Stewart studied at New York's Cooper Institute, at the New York Academy of Design, and with a Chicago floral portrait painter. On her pony Gypsy, she combed the area around Colorado Springs for floral specimens, which she painted or used in instructing her many students.[6]

Even though such women usually went unheralded as artists and, despite their talent, were largely forgotten, their interpretations of nature, notably in the American West, reached more and more Americans every year. During the early 1900s, for example, Louise Keeler of Berkeley, California, illustrated nature books written by her husband, Charles, took photographs for him, and lectured about his ideas. Although Louise received little recognition for either her expertise as an artist or her initiation of a "save-the-trees" campaign, her artistic interpretations widely influenced scientific thought.[7]

Moreover, American women increasingly developed a genius for expanding their markets. From the artist Cecilia Beaux, who illustrated four early federal land surveys, to Lillian Wilhelm Smith, who in 1913 became the first and only woman to illustrate Zane Grey's western novels, women demonstrated an entrepreneurial spirit.[8] Other women's work appeared as illustrations in books, journals, and newspapers; on greeting cards and in garden books; in art and craft exhibits; in lectures and stage shows; and in such commercial material as railroad company advertising.

Those women who sold their work to railroad companies saw their interpretations of the West appear on illustrated posters and calendars and in guidebooks and brochures. Minnesota artist Elsa Jemne painted in Glacier National Park during the summers of 1925 and 1926 in a studio provided by the Great Northern Railroad. She created high-quality landscapes and portraits of Blackfeet people that the Great Northern featured in its leaflets and guides.[9]

During the 1930s, when the New Deal's Works Progress Administration programs supported artists, women also gladly painted murals and landscapes on post office walls and in other public buildings. Women's renditions of rolling hillsides to verdant prairies greeted Americans all over the nation.[10]

But how authentic were women artists' constructed landscapes? As with the European woman Maria Sibylla Merian, nature painting for American women artists served as a function of their motivations. Some women searched for "selfhood" and autonomy, whereas others wanted to preserve the landscape and its peoples in ways available to them. Still others needed extra income. Although there is little evidence of gender consciousness, some women artists may have painted for feminist reasons.[11]

Moreover, realism was not a major trend among American women nature artists of the period from 1870 to 1940. Their approaches leaned more toward romanticism, impressionism, and abstraction. Painter Mary de Neale Morgan tucked into the background of her *Landscape* the archetypal, idyllic country cottage, while Ada Bertha Caldwell, who during the early 1900s trained well-known illustrator Harvey Dunn, produced western landscapes that gently ebbed and flowed, much like the later paintings of Grant Wood.[12]

In addition, women fell under the influence of earlier male painters, schools of painting, such popular trends as modernism, and the need to exhibit and sell their work.[13] As women, they carried with them female traditions of viewing nature as well as gender values as deep as their very psyches.

Consequently, most women nature artists of the era produced work that had certain predictable features. Generally, women presented physical environments that Americans understood, wanted to visit, and hoped to save for the future. Beginning in the 1930s, for example, the southwestern landscapes of Mary Russell Ferrell Colton, curator of the Museum of Northern Arizona, presented inviting outdoor views, as well as Hopi and Navajo scenes.[14]

Some women's compositions presented female landscapes full of fecundity and spirituality. The ultimate example was the work of western landscape artist Georgia O'Keeffe, who first visited New Mexico in 1917 but who did not locate there until after her husband's death in 1946. Although she sometimes sketched and painted from nature, O'Keeffe also collected flowers, sea shells, rocks, pieces of wood, and fragments of bones to take home. "I have used these things," she explained, to show "what is to me the wideness and wonder of the world as I live in it."[15]

O'Keeffe came to love the Southwest, particularly New Mexico. There she could have a garden and "do a lot of work outside." She especially savored the desert, which she perceived as "vast and empty and untouchable." She painted its mesas again and again, combining them into what she simply called "My Mountain." O'Keeffe also tried to capture the ethereal beauty of light, darkness, and other desert moods.[16]

In addition, Georgia O'Keeffe's controversial flowers spoke to the growing pressures of life in the United States in the early to mid-twentieth century. Although she painted what she saw in a flower, O'Keeffe magnified it so that viewers would "be surprised into taking time to look at it." She vowed, "I will make even busy New Yorkers take time to see what I see of flowers."[17] O'Keeffe not only carried her interpretation of nature to people, but she forced them to look at it and consider it.

Clearly, these and other women artists contributed a wide variety of visual images of landscapes and their resources. Such likenesses proved especially important to environmentally oriented Americans. It was through illustrations, sketches, and paintings that many Americans formed ideas of how the West actually looked. Moreover, the work of women artists also lured Americans westward to see the land for themselves, or inspired them to preserve the western landscapes they already knew and loved.

•

Meanwhile, during the latter part of the nineteenth century, the number of American women nature photographers rapidly multiplied. Their photographs brought a new dimension and firsthand feeling to viewers' understanding and experience of the outdoors. Whether people lived in the West, visited its sights, or had never seen it, they could now understand through photographs its need for preservation.

In order to produce images with such impact and immediacy, women nature photographers had to be hardy. Unlike illustrators and painters, they had to spend time in the field. Given the character of their technology, they could not bring home a flower or rock, photograph it, and fill in the background later. Also, those women who ventured forth into the hinterland to photograph wildlife and landscapes had to possess great physical stamina. Because of the rudimentary and complex technology required, especially during the wet-plate era of photography, women had to carry a back-breaking load of equipment and a darktent into the field. During the 1870s, California photographer Eliza W. Withington was even known to use her outer skirts as what she called a "dark closet" in cases of emergency.[18]

Women photographers showed little fear of the challenges the environment might hold for them. During the 1890s, another California photographer, Mary Winslow, traveled alone by buggy. The San Francisco Examiner commented that Winslow's "only arms are a revolver and a man's hat, and she goes wherever she pleases," including the far reaches of Yosemite.[19]

Despite their fortitude and hard work, women nature photographers found it difficult to gain recognition. Such organizations as the San Francisco Photographic Artists Association, founded in 1866, barred women from membership. It was not until 1890 that the California Camera Club was organized, accepted women members, and published the photographs and technical essays of women. Given this situation, it is to the credit of early landscape photographers that their work frequently brought prime prices, graced classroom instruction, and appeared in natural-science books and articles.[20]

Even though the 1890 U.S. census reported 2,201 professional female photographers, women fought uphill battles in many western states. In Minnesota, the first known photographer was a woman. Beginning in 1848, Sarah L. Judd of Stillwater produced daguerreotypes. Between 1859 and 1900, over 60 women photographers appeared in Minnesota directories or gazetteers, or signed their names to cabinet card photographs they produced. Wearing floor-length skirts, corsets, and long-sleeved shirtwaists, these women not only took a large number of the formal photographs of the era but did landscape work as well. Despite the prevalence of women photographers, not until 1889 did the *Northwest Amateur* begin publication in St. Paul, and not until the mid 1890s did camera clubs gradually organize in Minnesota with women as members.[21]

The problem was the same that many women faced when trying to break into a profession: male dominance and mistrust of women's professional abilities and women's potential willingness to accept lower pay. Male members of photographic societies and camera clubs even threatened to resign if female members were admitted. In 1889, when photographer Catharine Weed Barnes responded in print to one man who styled himself "Perplexed," she stated that camera clubs might be better off with such members "outside than inside." Yet she answered "Perplexed's" objections point by point. Barnes concluded that all societies should give women "a fair field and no favor," for the day was coming when only the question of quality rather than gender would apply to photographic work.[22]

As women proved themselves consummate professionals, suspicion of them gradually diminished. An additional factor that broke down the exclusivity of the photographic profession was improved technology. Around the turn of the twentieth century, camera equipment became lighter to carry and easier to operate.

The Kodak camera soon proved a standard accouterment for everyone, from amateur to professional nature photographers.

Sierra Club members especially took advantage of the opportunities the Kodak offered. In 1902, a Sierra Club excursion into California's Kern River Canyon included both amateur and professional photographers. The party brought back—and published in the club bulletin—photographs showing a cataract of frigid water tumbling down a mountainside, storm-beaten yet robust trees, and slim icicles dangling from ice-encrusted tree branches.[23]

With time, cameras continued to improve. In 1916, two Fullerton, Nebraska, couples and the women's mother set out in a Ford touring car, piled with food, equipment, a tent, and supplies of film. The men shot rabbits along the way, while the women shot photographs with their Kodaks.[24] The women carried their images of Nebraska scenery back to friends in Fullerton, thus influencing ideas of the western landscape and promoting interest in preserving it.

Because of better technology, nature photographers also became ubiquitous. Such women as Myrta Wright Stevens and Evelyn Jephson Cameron of Montana and Elfie Huntington of Utah proved that they could excel using modified Kodaks and other specialized equipment. They applied a female perspective to their art and were able to bring in much-needed extra income with their nature photography.[25]

Still, if a woman wanted to succeed in the rapidly professionalizing field of nature photography, she had to rise far above others. Between 1910 and 1940, distinguishing oneself increasingly depended on the amount of passion, individuality, and ingenuity found in a photographer's landscapes. Just as English women photographers modified views to suit themselves and their clients through shadows and even cutting grass and flowers, American women mastered the art of revising the physical scenes that lay in front of their camera lenses.

Moreover, some women believed that female photographers possessed more innate ability to achieve creativity, and thus prominence, than men. Women, they claimed, made the best landscape photographers because of their unique perception of nature and their particular aesthetic sense. Women also possessed special talents, such as quicker perceptions, sensitivity for colors, and unusually good taste in expressing nature's beauty.[26]

Certainly, many successful landscape photographers during the 1920s were female, especially those who leaned toward artistry rather than technical skills in their work. Anne Brigman gained a reputation as "Philistine, radical, virile, unafraid," as well as for being a "fervent feminist." According to at least one reviewer, Brigman also created photographs in which inanimate objects appeared alive; her emotions vitalized rocks and trees, and her very soul infused her environments. Another said Brigman studied composition "as carefully as the most delicately trained impressionist painter." She herself admitted that she glorified her work "with fancy."[27]

In short, according to the reviewers, Brigman's photographs were art. Moreover, unlike so many other women nature photographers, Brigman sought the dark side of nature. She preferred places like California's Desolation Valley, which she found primeval, austere, forbidding, and sinister, "and yet," she said, "with all it is most radiant and beautiful." Consequently, in several Brigman works, an aged tree extended its jagged branches against a skyline filled with clouds. In others, masses of clouds swirled over desolate landscapes.[28]

Were landscape photographs art or realistic renderings of nature? Photographers themselves had no clear answer to this question. As early as 1900, one critic noted that any person "of ordinary intelligence can produce a photograph." As a result, she argued, "our highways and byways are littered with distorted reflections of nature." The camera, which to her symbolized "degenerate art," either produced photographs having little or no intelligence behind them, or too much inspiration and idealization.[29]

In 1911, another commentator offered a more conclusive observation. She stated that "realistic" photography was impossible to attain. All photographers, she argued, grouped subjects, made a careful analysis of light and shade, and looked for local color. According to her, nature photography was "forceful realism" or "geographical art."[30] In other words, landscapes contained the photographer's perception of what nature *should* be, as well as his or her personal style and emotions.

Other people called this type of nature photography "pictorialism." Also in 1911, one authority heralded the landscape photographer Maude Wilson of Carmel, California, as a "new name" in pictorialism. Wilson, he declared, was an "extremist in elimination." Rather than emphasizing subject matter, she focused on the "lyrical vein" of things. Because she sought "impressions" of nature, she purposely underexposed her images so they would appear vague.[31]

The argument continued throughout the decade. In 1919, photographer Beatrice B. Bell recommended capturing landscapes on foggy days, for fog softened "unfavorable backgrounds." In mist, Bell pointed out, scenes that appeared unattractive in the glare of sunlight take on interesting shapes and might even produce a "pictorial gem."[32]

Such creative approaches might have served the photographic artist well, but they also skewed peoples' perceptions of nature, which in turn affected their opinions of the environment and its conservation. Moreover, photography played a crucial role in shaping environmental attitudes, not only because it was so pervasive, but also because it carried an aura of truth and reality. Although nature photography inspired viewers to adopt a conservation ethic, it is arguable just what type of environment they thought they were saving.

Women photographers themselves often became committed environmentalists. Perhaps because of their frequent contact with natural settings, they developed an interest in preserving western nature. Beginning during the 1890s, Alice Hare photographed California scenes, including parks and gardens, to preserve their beauty. She arranged her images of the Santa Clara Valley in albums and put them on public display. Soon, such magazines as *Sunset* bought and published Hare's nature photographs. By the early 1900s, she also participated in the restoration and renovation of Santa Clara's oldest plaza and helped found a park. After she moved to Merced in 1911, Hare photographed the unspoiled nature of the area and also initiated a tree-planting campaign.[33]

•

In addition to women artists and photographers who constructed their own interpretations of nature, women gardeners and land-scape architects shaped physical environments to suit human needs and expectations. Like English women, notably Jane Loudon and Gertrude Jekyll, American female gardeners contributed to environmental aesthetics as well as to the belief that nature could and should be modified for future usage.

Unlike English women, however, American women entered gardening quite early in their nation's history. After all, the agricultural base of the American economy made gardens an integral part of most homes. During the American colonial period, Martha Daniel Logan of St. Thomas Parish, South Carolina, gained acclaim as a horticulturalist. Beginning in the 1760s, Logan and Pennsylvania botanist John Bartram exchanged letters, seeds, and cuttings. In addition to managing a successful nursery business, Logan published treatises on gardening and conscientious use of nature's gifts.[34]

From colonial women to African-American slave women and women in the early West, all types of women gardened. South Carolinian Eliza Lucas Pinckney not only planted the first indigo in the United States during the 1740s but also established extensive formal gardens. Slave women not only tended field crops but also helped maintain family vegetable gardens. And western women, from American Indians to white women settlers, grew not only herbs and vegetables but flowers and trees as well. In fact, it was Indian women agriculturalists who contributed corn to the American and European economies.

By the mid–nineteenth century, however, social class and racial distinctions determined what type of American women gardened. As in England, middle- and upper-class women employed professional gardeners; all other women dug in the soil with their own hands. A number of women protested this trend. In 1849, English-woman Jane Loudon's *Gardening for Ladies* became available in the United States. Loudon pointed out that "ladies" could wear garden gloves to save their hands and could use lightweight, small spades. Twenty years later, Harriet Beecher Stowe and Catharine E. Beecher's *The American Woman's Home* included three chapters on gardening. Its frontispiece showed a fashionable and refined female gardener working under the shade of a parasol held by a servant.[35]

During the 1870s, a rash of women's gardening books appeared on the American market. From Anna Warner's *Gardening by Myself* (1872) to Louise Shelton's photography book, *Beautiful Gardens in America* (1928), these volumes urged women to take control of their gardens. These were not to be regimented, formal gardens, but natural plantings of native grasses, flowers, and trees. According to East Coast gardener Celia Thaxter, gardens integrated "wilderness" into the well-run home.[36]

Women living in the West also seized the opportunity to influence gardening philosophies. San Diego horticulturalist Kate Olivia Sessions believed in gardening with native plants. She collected and advocated the planting of the Matilija poppy, San Diego lilac, aloe, bougainvillea, and eucalyptus. Sessions, who in 1881 earned a doctorate from the University of California at Berkeley, wrote a regular gardening column in a San Diego newspaper and in *California Garden*. Each year, she planted a hundred trees in Balboa Park. Like Gertrude Jekyll, Sessions wore gardening boots and practical clothes, yet despite this flaunting of custom she significantly affected both public and private gardens in the San Diego area.[37]

Many women gardeners also participated directly in environmental activities. They often felt responsible for public green spaces as well as private. Women organized to transform parks, roadsides, and historic sites. As civilizers and conservators of home and society, women applied their gardening skills to such community, state, and national concerns as parks and public gardens, recreation areas, and forests.[38]

When the Garden Club of America was organized in 1913, its mission included environmental concerns. Under the leadership of Margaret McKenny of Olympia, Washington, the celebration of

Arbor Day and tree planting were popular garden club projects. McKenny had studied landscape architecture in New York during the early 1900s and worked as executive secretary of the City Garden Clubs of New York City. Soon, however, she returned to Olympia, where she served on the state tourism commission and traveled extensively talking about Washington's natural resources. McKenny chaired the Conservation Committee of Washington Garden Clubs and was president of the Audubon Society. Her many books, illustrated with her own photographs, included volumes on birds and flowers in gardens, on city and wild gardens, and on wildlife and wild flowers.[39]

Eventually, under the leadership of Minnerva Hamilton Hoyt, Garden Club groups spoke, wrote, and lobbied for national parks and monuments, especially Joshua Tree National Monument in Southern California in 1936. Hoyt also attempted to interest people in desert conservation by bringing the desert to them through Garden Club exhibits.[40]

Clearly, women gardeners generated many ideas and projects. But the difficult task of implementing gardeners' desire for naturalism combined with order fell to landscape architects. An early and important voice was that of New Yorker Beatrix Jones [later Beatrix Jones Farrand], who was the only woman among the founders of the American Society of Landscape Architects in 1899. Later, during the early 1900s, she established a successful practice on the East Coast.[41]

In 1913, Beatrix Jones married distinguished Yale historian Max Farrand. After he accepted appointment as director of the Henry E. Huntington Library in San Marino, California, in 1927, Beatrix extended her practice to the West Coast. In 1928, she designed landscapes for the California Institute of Technology and the Solar Laboratory, both in Pasadena. The following year she designed gardens for the residence of Roger I. Rogers in Beverly Hills, and between 1930 and 1935 she planned the renowned gardens at the Huntington Library and Art Gallery in San Marino. Later California commissions included Mrs. William H. Bliss's residence, Casa Dorinda, in 1936, Los Angeles's Occidental College in 1937, and the Palomar Mountain Observatory site in 1938. In these designs, as in her other work, Beatrix Farrand took a stand somewhere between the formalists and the naturalists.[42]

Unarguably, women gardeners and landscape architects helped shape Americans' conceptions of landscape and nature aesthetics. Most emphasized the blending of nature and the least intrusive garden designs. Typically, women preferred to use indigenous plants and natural materials. Borrowing heavily from English gardener Gertrude Jekyll, they encouraged natural gardens over the ordered and formal.[43] In women's gardens even "wild" settings were inviting and benign.

•

Between 1870 and 1940, nature-oriented architects also contributed to the social construction of nature. Although the profession of architecture was less accommodating to women than that of landscape architecture, several women who entered the field distinguished themselves.

During the mid 1880s, Arizonan Annie Rockefellow was the only woman in the architecture program at Massachusetts Institute of Technology. After graduating, she practiced in western New York and eventually relocated near Tucson. Rockefellow liked to use Native American motifs and to fit subtle buildings of local materials into their physical environment. In a 1932 radio program she said, "Any building that fits into the landscape comes nearer to true architecture than the finest design in the wrong place."[44]

Architect Mary Elizabeth Jane Colter, who created National Park Service "rustic style" designs, espoused a similar philosophy. During the late 1880s, Colter studied at the California School of Design in San Francisco (now the San Francisco Art Institute). She was sympathetic to new theories that encouraged buildings consistent with their natural environments rather than replicas of traditional European designs. In 1892, however, Colter found limited job opportunities for women architects. She took a teaching job at Mechanic Arts High School in St. Paul, Minnesota, where she remained for fifteen years.[45]

Around 1900, Colter visited a friend who worked in a Fred Harvey gift shop in San Francisco. After Colter expressed an interest in a summer job with the Harvey company, she received an offer in 1902 to design and decorate a museum, craft room, and salesroom in the Indian building next to Harvey's Alvarado Hotel in Albuquerque. Colter's success in Albuquerque led to a 1904 commission to plan the Hopi House in Grand Canyon National Park. In 1910, the Harvey company hired Colter as architect and designer of its hotels, restaurants, and railway station venues. In her years with Harvey, she worked on twenty-one projects, including the La Fonda Hotel in Sante Fe and Union Station in Los Angeles.[46]

Throughout her career, Colter maintained her belief that a building should reflect its physical environment, looking indigenous to the spot. When, in 1914, Colter planned a refreshment center known as Hermit's Rest in Grand Canyon National Park, she used stone, crude posts, and furniture of twisted tree stumps. Dingy and with cobwebs in its corners, Hermit's Rest cost $13,000 to build but looked old and authentic in its surroundings. Scattered throughout the park were other of Colter's arcadian, rustic, motifs: the Watchtower, the Lookout, and Bright Angel Lodge, which in 1985 achieved a place on the National Historic Register.[47]

Because of her skill and diplomacy, Colter wielded power with Fred Harvey, his architects, and company administrators. Officials of the Santa Fe Railway, which paid part of Colter's salary and owned the facilities that Fred Harvey operated, also found her insightful and inventive. Colter had the uncanny ability to add local color without making it appear overdone or "touristy." Even nature photographer Laura Gilpin described Colter's work as "beautiful and very authentic."[48]

Colter's environmentalist influences were found elsewhere as well. When the Grand Canyon region was about to become a national park, Colter contributed to the 1916 plan that established guidelines for future development. Her work convinced Fred Harvey to discontinue erecting Swiss chalets with gingerbread trim, as in the alpine style of El Tovar, in favor of her own basic and local styles. During the 1930s, Colter consulted with officials from

Grand Canyon National Park and from the office of Secretary of the Interior Harold Ickes.[49]

In her later years, Colter became a crusty, irascible autocrat who called workers "her boys" and brooked no objections from suppliers. If she could not find what she wanted, she had it specially manufactured. Still, through the Fred Harvey and the Santa Fe Railway companies, Mary Colter left her mark on the West, especially the tourists' West. She gave millions of visitors as authentic an experience of the western environment and its peoples as they were likely to get. For the first time, tourists saw sand paintings, or even Navajo women at their looms.

Colter also assisted the early twentieth-century conception of western nature and its aesthetics. Because of her lookout points and telescope stations, people came closer to nature, but they also viewed natural wonders from seats in comfortable dining rooms and coffee shops; they traveled on the backs of mules in the Grand Canyon by day and slept in genuine-looking southwestern beds by night; and they watched native artisans at work on wooden floors with log walls around them.

Along with other women's creations, Colter's work helped Americans understand why the West needed preserving, but it also provided them with a sanitized, especially "female" view of the West.

•

Like Colter, many women devoted their careers to providing visual images of the West. Landscape architect Florence Yoch dedicated her entire adult life to reshaping western landscapes. In 1930, she exulted that the days of "bush-whacking gardening" were on the wane. She believed the coming era belonged to the United States, where architects and gardeners took into account local conditions, materials, flora, and fauna. According to Yoch, the individual American's link to the outdoors was increasingly the patio, terrace, arbor, pergola, loggia, veranda, balcony, and garden.[50]

In her designs, Yoch avoided geometrics and rows. Instead, she drew on primitive and simple new-world architectural and landscape traditions. Despite widespread study of the world's grand gardens, Yoch came home to California and to its environmental heritage. There she planned gardens that connected Californians to the environment beyond their walls.[51]

In her later years, Yoch turned to designing sets for motion pictures. She and her business partner, Lucile Council, devised "natural" landscapes for some of the most famous movies of the 1930s. It was Yoch who created the lush, southern environment of Tara in *Gone with the Wind*. She also "landscaped" such films as *The Good Earth* and *How Green Was My Valley*.[52]

Had Florence Yoch come to see nature as so disembodied and manageable that it was theatrical fantasy? Certainly, she shared an interest in gardening and the outdoors with Polish actress Helena Modjeska, who viewed California's landscape as a stage setting. Seeking improved health, Modjeska had set off during the early 1890s for Anaheim, California, from which she issued glowing statements of the area's incomparable natural beauty. In a few years, the Modjeskas purchased a farm and named it "Arden" after Shakespeare's "Forest of Arden." Modjeska's own words confirmed her perception of nature as theater: "The whole picture looked more like fantastic stage scenery than a real thing, and looking at it, my imagination carried me far, far beyond the hills, back to the footlights again."[53]

Whether Yoch ever reached this extreme in her own perception of nature is doubtful. Although her movie sets were striking and illusory, her later gardens stood every bit as natural and enduring as her earlier designs. Still, it is more than just an interesting point. Did most Americans want to conserve nature on its own terms, or did they have in mind the saving of a feminized, constructed environment that suited their own needs?

1. An Apache camp scene in New Mexico indicates native women's daily closeness to nature and their sensitivity to usable resources, 1885. *Photo by Waldo Twitchell, courtesy of the Museum of New Mexico, Neg. No. 10238.*

2. Despite the restrictive tenets of Victorian womanhood, scores of white women went west and established homesteads on their own. Three women homesteaders near a tarpaper claim shack in South Dakota, ca. 1907. *Courtesy of the South Dakota State Historical Society, Pierre.*

3. Women from all over the world learned outdoor skills and settled in the American West. Asian settler Polly Bemis in Idaho, 6 February 1910. *Courtesy of the Idaho State Historical Society, Boise.*

4. Western women also ran ranches and participated in cattle drives. Feliz Ruelas in Box Canyon in Arizona's Santa Rita Mountains, 1920s. *Courtesy of the Arizona Historical Society, Tucson.*

5. In spite of cumbersome clothing, western women took up a wide variety of outdoor activities. Arizonan Gertrude Wein on a quail hunting expedition, ca. 1905. *Courtesy of the Arizona Historical Society, Tucson.*

6. Women of color occasionally overcame the barriers to their participation in scientific and environmental activities. Hispanic botanist Ynes Mexia on a collecting expedition, undated. *Courtesy of Special Collections, California Academy of Sciences, San Francisco.*

7. Women often led in the areas of botany and environmental conservation. California botanist Alice Eastwood collecting a grass named for her, undated. *Courtesy of Special Collections, California Academy of Sciences, San Francisco.*

8. In the Pacific Northwest, Lilla Leach became a noted botanist and active environmentalist. Leach on a winter collecting trip in western Oregon, undated. *Courtesy of the University of Oregon Library, Eugene.*

9. Ornithologist Florence Merriam [later Florence Merriam Bailey], ca. 1886. Merriam campaigned for bird preservation and wrote nature books about the Southwest, especially New Mexico. *Courtesy of Smith College Archives, Northampton, Massachusetts.*

10. Boulder, Colorado, taxidermist Martha Maxwell arranged nature as she perceived it—full of wild animals yet unthreatening to women. Maxwell stands at the center of her creation, undated. *Courtesy of the Colorado Historical Society, Denver, F33139.*

11. Many "scientific" women found employment in museums and used these institutions as a base for environmental projects. Texan Ellen Schulz Quillin, first director of San Antonio's Witte Memorial Museum and founder of the country's first reptile garden, examining a twig with a magnifying glass from her collecting case, ca. 1927. *Courtesy of the Institute of Texan Cultures, San Antonio.*

12. Iowa ornithologist Althea Sherman corresponded with, and gave support to, other women scientists. Sherman at her gate in National, Iowa, undated. *Courtesy of Oberlin College Archives, Oberlin, Ohio.*

13. Nebraska writer Mari Sandoz argued for environmental causes in her writings and speeches. Undated. *Courtesy of the Nebraska State Historical Society, Lincoln.*

14. New York journalist Mary Roberts Rinehart traveled in the West and wrote about the region's national parks, always arguing for the national park concept. Undated. *Courtesy of Glenda Riley.*

15. The Missoula Camera Club starting for the Bitterroot Valley on a photographing venture. Photo by Myrta Wright Stevens, 1890s. *Courtesy of the Montana Historical Society, Helena.*

16. San Diego horticulturalist Kate Sessions arranged nature in a palatable form and argued for the conservation of plants and trees. Undated. *Courtesy of the San Diego Historical Society.*

17. Architect Mary Colter shaped western parks, especially the Grand Canyon, to be natural yet hospitable to visitors. Undated. *Courtesy of Special Collections, The University of Arizona Library, Tucson.*

18. Mary Colter's entrance arch to Hermit's Rest. Colter's "rustic style" sites emphasized the need for buildings to remain in harmony with their environment. Undated. Colter also worked with the U.S. Park Service and other agencies on conservation projects. *Courtesy of Virginia L. Girattan.*

19. Women of color who joined clubs often tried to solve race-related problems first but increasingly found time and energy for environmental issues. Montana Federation of Colored Women's Clubs in Bozeman, 1924. *Courtesy of the Montana Historical Society, Helena.*

20. Despite the paucity of scholarly investigation on the relationship of peoples of color to the environment, sources indicate that they also enjoyed club outings. Little Flower Club of Tucson, 1935. *Courtesy of the Arizona Historical Society, Tucson.*

21. Women climbed mountains for adventure, to make a feminist statement, or to bring attention to environmental issues. Feminist Julia Archibald Holmes claimed to be the first woman to climb Colorado's Pikes Peak. Undated. *Courtesy of the Denver Public Library, Western History Department.*

22. Mountain-climbing clubs promoted the sport and undertook environmental conservation efforts. Members of the Colorado Mountain Club stop
for a rest and a photograph, 1914. *Courtesy of the Special Collections Department, University of Colorado at Boulder Libraries.*

23. Women pursued a variety of outdoor activities, including hunting. Although some opposed killing wildlife, others saw hunting as a sport.
Women hunters with their dogs along North Dakota's Red River. Photo by
F. J. Haynes, 1870s. *Courtesy of the North Dakota Heritage Center, State Historical Society of North Dakota, Bismarck.*

24. Outdoor women also liked to fish. Women fishing at Montana's Lob Hot Springs, 1890s. *Courtesy of the Montana Historical Society, Helena.*

25. Californian Lottie L. Tillotson was an intrepid traveler in an era when women were told to stay at home. Tillotson atop Arizona's Eagle Rock, 1896. *Courtesy of the Lottie L. Tillotson Collection, Autry Museum of Western Heritage, Los Angeles, California.*

26. Like Lottie Tillotson, many women sought adventure and education through travel. As early as 1878, the Miles/Hoyt exploration of Yellowstone included several women: from left to right, Mrs. Rice, Mrs. F. D. Baldwin, Mrs. E. P. Ewers, Miss Baldwin, Mrs. N. A. Miles, and Hattie Sanborn. *Courtesy of the Montana Historical Society, Helena.*

27. Victorian attire notwithstanding, women enjoyed camping. Mrs. R. C. Taylor at Yosemite Valley's Royal Arches, 1897. *Courtesy of the Lottie L. Tillotson Collection, Autry Museum of Western Heritage, Los Angeles.*

28. Women proved they had fortitude as travelers, as well as a tolerance for risk. Going-to-the-Sun Highway, Glacier National Park, undated. *Courtesy of the Montana Historical Society, Helena.*

29. By the 1920s and 1930s, other entrepreneurs created a variety of schemes and innovations to explore western landscapes. Arizona Wonder Circuit Tours "wonder bus," undated. *Courtesy of the Arizona Historical Society, Tucson.*

30. A significant number of women environmentalists also included historic structures in their conservation crusade. Woman at an unidentified Arizona site, undated.

Courtesy of the Arizona Historical Society, Tucson.

31. Women anthropologists and other scientists regularly took part in expeditions to explore western sites. Newell's Expedition down the Colorado River included Lois Jones (left) and Dr. Elizabeth Clover (right) from the University of Michigan, 1938.

32. Arizonan Grace M. Sparkes worked on behalf of the Smoki people of Prescott for such historic sites as Turzigoot national monument and for such environmental goals as water and soil conservation. Sparkes, 1958. *Courtesy of the Arizona Historical Society, Tucson.*

33. After 1940, peoples of color increasingly pursued nature travel and historic sites in the West. African Americans near Arizona's San Xavier Mission, 1940s. *Courtesy of the Arizona Historical Society, Tucson.*

34. Post–World War II women activists had myriad environmental goals. Nevadan Velma B. Johnston earned the name "Wild Horse Annie" for her efforts to save wild horse populations. Undated. *Courtesy of the Denver Public Library, Western History Department.*

6

Club Women and
Other Activists

As American women widened their spheres of activity, reform and
charitable activities increasingly engaged their energies. Typically,
between 1870 and 1940, benevolent women supported not only
one "cause" but often two or three or four. Among their crusades,
a significant number of women listed trees, birds, parks, and other
facets of environmental preservation.

Sometimes such women participated in the club movement
that rolled over America during the late nineteenth and early
twentieth centuries. Other times they chose public, professional,
or personal routes. In almost every case, such women reshaped
people's visions of the environment and enlarged their own roles
and impact on American society as well.[1]

As early as the 1870s, for example, Mary Ann Dyer Goodnight
of the Texas Panhandle developed her own crusade. Goodnight had
a lifelong interest in both the outdoors and benevolence. She often
said that her mother and father and nature had educated her. After
marrying Colonel Charles Goodnight in 1870, she spent the first
seven years of her married life in Pueblo, Colorado, helping her
husband and brothers establish the first Methodist Episcopal
Church South in southern Colorado. When she and her family relocated to west Texas in 1877, Goodnight found herself the only
white woman living within two hundred miles.[2]

Instead of lamenting, Goodnight turned to nature and expanded
her philanthropy. A biographer commented that "because there

was no one to be friendly with except her own family," Goodnight "made friends of the birds, and the wild flowers and the trees." She also helped those in need, including "orphaned baby buffaloes."[3]

Goodnight instructed her husband and brothers to collect helpless buffalo calves—more properly known as bison calves—from the canyons and bring them to her so that she could raise them by hand to preserve the breed. Gradually, her first orphans produced the Goodnight Buffalo and Cattalo Park. By the early 1930s, the herd numbered approximately two hundred animals, which each summer produced between sixteen and twenty calves. In 1931, Goodnight's niece, Annie Dyer Nunn, explained that "Aunt Mary revolted at the merciless slaughtering of the buffaloes. . . . instead of creatures fit only to be slaughtered the buffaloes were a part of the history of West Texas and the state's most valuable game."[4]

Mary Ann Dyer Goodnight was not alone. From club women to political activists, women attempted to preserve aspects of the western environment. The objects of women's preservation ranged from bison to waterfalls and streams, from mountains to forests.

•

In the United States, the first women's clubs emerged after the Civil War. Prohibited from joining most men's clubs, women took a separatist approach by founding groups of their own. In Boston in 1868, reformer Caroline Severence and poet Julia Ward Howe founded the New England Woman's Club, while in New York in the same year journalist Jane Cunningham Croly organized Sorosis. These and later groups appealed to wives and mothers, both future and present, to join together in improving life for themselves, their families, and their communities.[5]

As clubs mushroomed across the United States, they provided women with support networks and created a gradual awareness and base of action of such social programs as environmentalism. They also demonstrated a strong religious allegiance. Most groups began and ended their meetings with prayer, litany, or creed. Typically, members asked God to "guide and inspire" the work of the assembled women. Clubs also dedicated special projects, including parks and forests, with prayers and invocations seeking God's protection for such club gifts to communities.[6]

In addition, women's clubs had a clear patriotic commitment. Some used public-spirited names for their projects, such as the Utah group that founded George Washington Memorial Park. Others inveighed all good citizens to think about the nation's future and to act on America's behalf, whether concerning children and family, or rivers and forests.[7]

In planning their first undertakings, most newly formed women's clubs began with literary activities. One commentator of the 1880s described such groups as "literary, historical, and conversational" organizations that included thousands of women of every age. The Dubuque, Iowa, Ladies' Literary Association, for example, proclaimed that "we have students of all ages, from girls in their teens to grandmothers whose gray hairs have not quenched their love of study."[8]

Within a few years of founding, however, women's organizations moved into community improvement projects, including social reform and environmental conservation. Club women defined conservation in its broadest sense: children, family, schools, at-risk peoples, historic sites, and the physical environment.

Gradually, the underlying women's club philosophy decreed that any aspect of the environment affecting women and their families fell under the purview of women's clubs. Of course, this definition included virtually all aspects of the outdoors. In addition, a club's conservation policies had to be meaningful to the group's members, fulfill a critical need of the era, and have relevance to an organization's locale.

California's Ebell Club is an excellent example of such a course of development. In 1876, noted German scholar Dr. Adrian Ebell organized the first chapter in Oakland, California, to help women become "better fitted" in culture and knowledge. Ebell members aimed to advance general culture and promote the well-being of their community. They also gradually adopted environmental goals. In the late 1800s, they began by discussing travel, including outdoor destinations. By the early 1900s, the Ebell Club voted to join the Archaeological Institute of America. Next, Ebell members added the study of California nature and history. In 1905, Charles Lummis wrote Ebell chapters asking them to support his dream of a great southwest museum.[9]

Twentieth-century clubs followed a similar evolution yet moved more quickly to the establishment of environmental projects. In Nevada, for example, the Mesquite Club of Las Vegas, formed in 1911, undertook tree planting, reportedly planting more than two thousand trees in one day through its "Town Beautiful" project. In 1919, the U-Wah-Un Study Club, also of Las Vegas, devoted itself to music and literature but soon engaged in studying Indian baskets and the desert and in giving nature books to the local library. In 1928, the Goldfield Woman's Club stated its goals as the advancement of philanthropic and "reformatory efforts," as well as the betterment of its community, including the physical environment.[10]

In Idaho a similar pattern developed. Burley's Civic Improvement Association pursued a variety of activities, including publishing a cookbook and sponsoring dinner parties. It also worked for such local refinements as establishing green areas. The group's first president, Mildred Forgeon Rich, who founded the organization in 1913, said, "we succeeded in getting the city fathers to plant a few trees." From there, association members urged people to plant grass and clean up refuse.[11]

In Utah, the Aurora Club started in 1913 as a social and sewing club. Within a year, it had progressed to studying Hopi Indians and organizing an annual "lake party" at the Saltair resort. Although Aurora members continued to sew, especially during World War I when clothing was in short supply at the front, they showed growing interest in such natural sites as Zion, Grand, and Bryce Canyons. By the time the Aurora Club affiliated with the Utah Federation of Women's Clubs in 1921, Aurora members organized regular historical and natural tours.[12]

Thus, by the 1920s, most existing women's clubs had environmental agendas as a matter of course. Even in Hawaii, already well-endowed with natural beauty, club member and philanthropist Ethel Frances Smith Baldwin supported beautification projects on the island of Maui. Following World War I to the late 1920s,

Baldwin sponsored public parks and the planting of shower trees along Baldwin Avenue from Paia to Makawao.[13]

•

Generally, local women's clubs soon joined into state federations. These umbrella groups were quick to develop environmental policies and pass them on to member clubs. Such mandates often had special significance to a particular state. Also, state federations massed behind the national park concept, a unique American undertaking. Even though histories of national parks, forests, and other sites usually overlook women, they often played a critical role.[14]

During the 1880s, for example, Virginia Donaghe McClurg followed the lead of anthropologists Alice Fletcher and Matilda Coxe Stevenson by exploring Colorado's Mesa Verde cliff dwellings. During the 1890s, McClurg lectured about the cliff dwellings without eliciting much support for their preservation. In 1900, she approached the Colorado Federation of Women's Clubs, which appointed her head of a committee "to save the Cliff Dwellings." Six years later, after much campaigning and vacillating, Congress adopted a measure creating Mesa Verde National Park.[15]

Moreover, several nonwestern club women adopted western sites as their causes. In 1929, Rosalie Barrow Edge, a New York club woman, suffragist, and devoted birdwatcher, founded the Emergency Conservation Committee (ECC). As a one-woman operation, Edge wrote numerous letters, testified, lobbied, and spoke on behalf of ECC causes, which included "defending and creating National Parks."[16]

Edge was dedicated not only to the West but also to women. She believed that men, because of business commitments, found it difficult to "take a strong stand on the side of public interest." Unequivocally, Edge stated, "But women can do it, and they should."[17]

In addition, club women supported the establishment of the National Park Service and such parks as Colorado's Estes Park, California's Sequoia National Park, and Arizona's Grand Canyon National Park. Garden Club of America affiliates all over the West also joined in the effort to create reserves and green spaces.[18]

By the early 1900s, state federations claimed a wide province for themselves. The fourth president of the Nevada Federation of Women's Clubs, a Mrs. Omer Maris, argued in 1912 that "conservation is particularly a woman's job." To her, environmental conservation meant saving our national resources as well "as their proper use and development." To fulfill its vow, the federation promoted forest preservation and clean water.[19]

State federations also placed a heavy emphasis on local planning. Because the Utah Federation of Women's Clubs believed that environmental conservation constituted "a vital issue" in the future development of the state, it instructed local clubs to gain a better knowledge of Utah's natural resources and how they should be conserved. Thus, by the 1920s, club agendas included highway beautification, forest and wildflower protection, cleanup movements, and park initiatives. At the same time, the 1918–20 federation yearbook revealed a comprehensive statewide plan for the conservation of natural resources. Under the direction of a Nephi woman, the program considered forests, roads, highway markers and decorations, waterways, birds, wildlife and flowers, soil, parks and monuments, school gardens and fairs, and irrigation.[20]

By the latter part of the 1930s, the Utah Federation had also invested heavily in forestry preservation programs. In issuing guidelines to the Utah Federation, the U.S. Forest Service said, "It is only natural that the women should rise to protect and perpetuate their birthright and that of their children and children's children."[21]

The Forest Service applauded the growing interest of Utah women's clubs in forests, for it believed that "organized active interest will beget desired results through molding public opinion to help us realize our conservation objectives." It recommended specific actions for women's clubs, including sponsoring lectures and essay contests, organizing tours to such reclamation projects as Echo Dam in Weber Canyon, and fostering the proposals of county planning boards.[22]

In 1952, the historian of the Utah Federation of Women's Clubs stated that the environment had "always been a vital issue" with the federation, which had planted some three hundred thousand trees throughout the state. She pointed out that, besides the natural environment, club women hoped to conserve many things: child welfare, youth, and quality public schools. Despite this broad definition of conservation, numerous environmental imperatives originated with the Utah women's clubs. The Wasatch Literary Club of Salt Lake asked that Monument Park in southern Utah be set aside as a public facility, while Provo club women urged that Mount Timpanogos become a park.[23]

Federations in newer western states followed the lead of more established groups. "We believe in Arizona," state federation president Sue Greer proclaimed around 1930, especially Arizona's forests, birds, wildlife, lakes and streams, and "priceless trees and flora of her deserts." In Alaska, the state federation of club women preserved forests and streams, protected fish and other species, and fought highway advertising.[24]

•

At the helm of thousands of such local women's clubs and state federations stood a parent group, the General Federation of Women's Clubs. The national federation had been in existence longer than most state federations and many clubs. As early as 1890, club women who recognized the need for national coordination organized the General Federation on the basis of two hundred clubs and twenty thousand women.[25]

Frequently, the General Federation of Women's Clubs considered the programs of local and state groups and then selected some as nationwide initiatives for affiliated women's clubs. For example, in 1900, at the instigation of the California Club, the national federation introduced a national forestry program. Federation leaders urged local clubs to appoint forestry committees and to initiate such activities as planting trees, preserving wooded areas, and supporting forest legislation.[26]

Gradually, the national federation increased its environmental programs. In 1912, club woman and philanthrophist Marion Crocker addressed the General Federation on the topic of conservation. She spoke for the preservation of plant life, animals, and birds, pleading with women "to choose some other decoration" than birds for their hats. Like English women, Crocker especially urged environmental education among children to lay "the foundation of things for the next generation." She warned that misuse of natural resources would lead to disaster: "the time will come when the world will not be able to support life, then we shall have no need of conservation of health, strength or vital force."[27]

Another state initiative the General Federation supported was a clean water campaign. During the early 1900s, the Iowa Federation of Women's Clubs urged wise water usage, purity of streams and rivers, and prohibition of industrial pollution "with chemicals, refuse, or dross of any kind." The national federation adopted the priority and lobbied for clean water and water conservation.[28]

·

A brief survey of Washington women's clubs demonstrates some of the similarities and differences in club projects and priorities throughout the West. Despite its relatively remote location and distance from the centers of communication, Washington state clubs showed a remarkable similarity in most ways to other western women's clubs.

The Washington Federation of Women's Clubs, formed in Tacoma in 1896, worked toward preserving state resources, notably the establishment of Mount Rainier National Park in 1899. In fact, the influence of women's clubs in Washington State proved crucial to conservation as a whole. One Washington historian claimed that "the conservation movement took root" in the state under the inspiration of two groups: the Mountaineers and the Washington Federation of Women's Clubs.[29]

Like other state federations and groups, Washington clubs also adopted national mandates, notably the national federation's forestry program. During the late 1890s, Washington groups planted trees and spoke out against the abuses of what they called "timber barons." Forests soon became a constant concern of the Washington federation. Members spread their message through environmental education, prizes, improvement projects, campaigns for the prevention of forest fires, and celebration of Arbor Day. During the early 1900s, women's clubs began raising money to save one Washington state forest. Finally, because of the fund-raising efforts of Jeanne Caithness Greenless, in 1949 the state federation purchased a 613-acre tract on the Naches Pass Highway, which it called Federation Forest State Park.[30]

In addition, Washington women's clubs chose to pursue their own blend of projects. Nationally, in 1912, through letter writing, speechmaking, and lobbying, they supported the establishment of the Bureau of National Parks and the Good Roads movement. Statewide, during the 1920s, Washington clubs supported the Lincoln Highway and roadside beautification. The "Keep Washington Green" project of the 1930s and 1940s also met with great success on the state level.[31]

In one area, however, Washington clubs differed from the usual western women's organizations. In its original 1896 constitution, the Washington Federation of Women's Clubs stated that it welcomed African-American and Native American women as members of any women's club.

The paucity of numbers of women in the area may account for the federation's stand. If so, the admission of women of color was slow to pay off, for these women usually had their own agendas to pursue. Segregated organizations of nonwhite women (who were primarily African Americans) focused on goals ranging from arts and crafts to charitable and racially oriented programs. During the 1920s, the Independent Mothers' Club and Progressive Mothers worked to improve child welfare and extended assistance to needy children. The Booklovers Club studied the writing of such black authors as Joel Chandler Harris and W. E. B. Du Bois. The L'Allegro Club, composed of young girls, encouraged its members to go to college and raised scholarship funds to make this possible.[32]

Black club women also organized state federations, which formulated goals for affiliated groups. The Washington Federation of Colored Women's Clubs, founded at Spokane in 1917, emphasized scholarship funds for black girls.[33]

On the national level, leadership came from the National Association of Colored Women (NACW), formed in Washington DC in 1895 from a coalition of competing organizations. When the NACW incorporated in 1904, it claimed a hundred thousand members in forty states. Like individual units, the national group emphasized education, the home, and child welfare. But it also urged "the enforcement of Civil and Political Rights," including widening opportunities for black women in "all fields of human endeavor" and promoting "inter-racial understanding."[34]

Gradually, however, black women's clubs turned to environmental issues. They had long shown intense interest in such health problems as garbage collection and school hygiene. Groups often sponsored such events as the Pierian Literary Club's Clean Up Week in Spokane. Eventually, such projects grew into support of associated programs. During the early 1940s, the Washington Association of Colored Women contributed $100 toward the purchase of the Federation Forest.[35]

Similarly, women's clubs composed of American Indian women had more pressing problems than preserving nature.[36] Research is so incomplete on Hispanic and Asian women's clubs throughout the West that these groups' positions on conservation are unclear. Such organizations as Tucson's Little Flower Club, however, suggest that some significant information may lie hidden in archives, for this Hispanic church-centered group seemed very interested in outdoor outings and aspects of the natural environment.[37]

·

Clearly, the women's club movement marshaled tremendous numbers of members and an impressive nationwide organization on behalf of environmental issues. Its leaders often proved prophetic, alerting the public to a problem before most people realized it existed. As early as 1896, Amy P. S. Stacy, the first president of the Washington Federation of Women's Clubs, urged forest preservation and opposition to the incursions of the logging industry.[38]

In addition, the women's club movement provided a voice for outdoor women concerned about the environment. Nevada's Florence Humphrey Church, who scaled Mount Slide in 1901 and was the first woman to ride horseback over one thousand miles along the Sierra from Yosemite to Mount Shasta, founded the Nevada Women's Faculty Club at the University of Nevada and served as president of Reno's Twentieth Century Club.[39]

Moreover, the club movement developed a network that intensified the effectiveness of environmental programs. In a circular movement across the entire West, local and state groups fed ideas upward to the national federation, while the national organization communicated initiatives downward to other local and state groups. In 1905, for example, Topeka club women founded the West Side Forestry Club, a concept that had its roots in the forestry program of the national federation and the forestry committee of the Kansas state federation. Among other things, the West Side Forestry Club established Willow Park in Topeka and helped preserve Pawnee Rock, an Indian lookout and landmark on the Santa Fe Trail, as a state historic site.[40]

The club movement also identified environmental conservation with a panoply of cherished white, middle-class ideals: motherhood, family, community, religion, and patriotism. Club women never tired of talking about God's natural resources and American abundance, both of which were to be preserved for America's children. Thus, women's clubs lifted environmentalism above a political agenda to a sanctified American ideology.

Even by the 1920s and 1930s, when women's clubs took on political agendas, conservation remained a constant goal. For example, women environmentalists organized groups to support the work of new federal and state agencies. In 1940, the Ladies Auxiliary of the Nebraska Association of Soil and Water Conservation Districts formed "to encourage conservation and development of land and water resources, in conformance with objectives and policies of the National Association of Districts." Within the year, five hundred female members distributed conservation information to rural and urban groups, presented programs in schools and to clubs, sponsored essay and poster contests, held workshops and field trips, and assisted with the district county fair exhibit.[41]

•

Besides working within the extensive and complex women's club network, some women struck out on their own. Each in her own way, these women activists labored on behalf of the environment. Some supported the lecture, education, and lobbying efforts of such existing conservation organizations as the Save-the-Redwoods League, founded in 1918 in San Francisco's Palace Hotel. Others enrolled in female-led groups, such as the Outdoor Circle, organized in Honolulu in 1912 by Cherilla Lillian Storrs Lowrey.[42]

Those who were bolder still, and usually more feminist in philosophy, gave speeches, wrote articles, and authored books. English women's experiences, including those of suffragist and lecturer Frances Power Cobbe, had demonstrated that public speakers played a critical role in the growth of any social movement. Following the English example, American women took the platform, hammering away at the need to preserve the fragile environment. Thus, they raised people's awareness and often caused them to take action or at least support environmentalism.[43] Written pieces also proved important, often outliving speeches in people's memories and offering the possibility of rereading.

Individual women activists existed in every part of the West. During the early 1900s, Californian Josephine Clifford McCrackin not only joined such environmental groups as the Sempervirens Club to save the giant redwoods but also wrote letters, founded the Ladies' Forest and Song Birds Protective Association, and was the first woman member of the California Game and Protective Association.[44] During the 1920s and 1930s, Nebraska cattle rancher Maud Ham Schooler-Briggs-Nelson campaigned on behalf of city parks and cemetery beautification in the Sandhills region of the state, while Nebraskan Essie Buchan Davis, owner and operator of a huge ranch north of Hyannis, proved herself an energetic conservationist and, in 1939, was the first woman to receive the Nebraska Master Farmer Award.[45]

Meanwhile, still other bold American women promoted their causes by moving to, and reclaiming, land in the American West. One transplanted California ranchwoman adopted water as her issue. Harriet Williams Russell Strong, who first came to Plumas County in 1854, settled in Oakland after her marriage. When her husband committed suicide in 1883, she pulled his almost bankrupt estate out of debt and established the Strong Ranch in southern California. Strong planted citrus fruits and walnuts, and studied irrigation and flood control. In 1887 and 1894, Strong patented plans for sequential storage dams. She also advocated flood and water supply control for Los Angeles County as well as federal aid to develop the Colorado River.[46]

Similarly, Jeanne Smith Carr and her husband bought land north of Pasadena in 1877. After her husband's health failed, Carr proved herself as dedicated an environmentalist as her protégée John Muir. As a widow, she oversaw the making of a ranch out of bleak *chaparral*. Carr told writer and reformer Helen Hunt Jackson that she intended to "make a wilderness not only blossom but repay the cost of its blossoming." By 1890, Carr had two hundred varieties of trees and shrubs growing on her land. John Muir himself lavished high praise on her efforts: "I have never seen so [sic] happy flowers in any other home."[47]

•

Individual women activists gradually appeared other places as well. For example, environmentally oriented women fought both for the preservation of western lands and for the enlargement of their own roles as paid professionals in the administration of national parks. During the early 1900s, the national park system came under attack by female activists who wanted to participate in operating the parks that women had helped establish.

The U.S. Park Service traditionally avoided hiring women. A change occurred in 1916, however, when young Esther Burnell spent the winter as a homesteader in Colorado's Estes Park. After she made a thirty-mile solo trip by snowshoe across the Continental Divide, her reputation as an outdoorsperson grew. Encouraged by well-known guide Enos Mills, Esther and her sister Elizabeth took the park service examination and became licensed nature guides in Rocky Mountain National Park for the summer of 1917. For the next twelve seasons, Elizabeth directed Mills's trail school and led groups up Longs Peak. Esther married Enos Mills; after his death in 1922 she operated Mills's Longs Peak Inn for more than twenty years.[48]

Other women employees followed, partly because the Burnell sisters paved the way and partly because the entry of the United States into World War I caused a dearth of male naturalists and rangers. In 1918, Helene Wilson served at Mount Rainier National Park and Clare Marie Hodges at Yosemite. Two years later, Isabel Bassett became Yellowstone's first woman naturalist. In September 1920, the *Denver Post* reported that Helen Dove was the only woman forester in the West and claimed that "the little Sister of the Rockies" had already prevented sixteen blazes with timely reports from her Devil's Head Peak post. Accompanying photographs showed Dove, a Denver artist, operating a huge chain saw and hanging from the side of her station applying a coat of paint.[49]

After the achievement of woman suffrage in 1920, followed by a decade of optimism, women's gains increased. Between 1923 and 1930, Yosemite Superintendent Washington B. Lewis even compensated wives of rangers for working at their husbands' stations. In 1928, Rocky Mountain Superintendent Roger Toll hired Margaret Fuller Boos, a recent doctoral recipient in geology from the University of Chicago. Boos worked for two summers as a ranger, attired exactly like her male colleagues in high boots, breeches, white shirt, tie, and Stetson hat.[50]

These women proved successful and, according to one superintendent, filled "a long felt need." By the early 1930s, however, park service officials in Washington DC mandated that only men be hired. At least in part, the Great Depression of the 1930s reversed the earlier situation. Harsh economics encouraged a renewed emphasis on women's domestic roles as wives and mothers and on the hiring of men as "breadwinners."[51]

•

Eventually, as women's opportunities widened, individual activists even began to fight for conservation through politics. As conservation programs in the United States moved into the political realm, they required legislation, planning commissions, and regulatory agencies at local, state, and national levels.[52] In turn, this political structure offered additional openings to women interested in any form of conservation. Thus, similar to English women who had supported W. E. Gladstone in Parliament on the issue of animal welfare, American women seized political opportunities whenever possible.

Thousands of women supported environmentalism through state officeholding. In 1909, Sharlot Hall became the first woman to hold public office in Arizona when Governor Richard Sloan appointed her territorial historian. In 1924, voters sent Hall to Washington DC as a Republican elector. Hall also wrote about the Southwest's needs and problems in Charles F. Lummis's *Out West* magazine, helped run her family's ranch, and modeled outdoor activity for other women. Her lifelong message was that the Southwest offered irreplaceable resources that had to be preserved or else be lost forever.[53]

Other women entered—often for the first time—very different kinds of state office. During the late 1800s and early 1900s, a native Hawaiian, Emma Kaili Metcalf Beckley Nakuina, served as first state commissioner of water rights, was the first curator of the Bernice Pauahi Bishop Museum in Honolulu, and wrote on water and folklore. Later in the century, during the 1920s, Grace B. Melaven of Santa Rosa, New Mexico, acted as game and fish warden with the New Mexico Game Department. It fell to Melaven to enforce the rules protecting New Mexico's environment and to impose penalties for misuse.[54]

Women also served in state legislatures. In 1915, Arizona voters elected Frances Willard Munds to the state senate. A dedicated woman-suffrage advocate, she remarked that many "conservatives" would be "shocked to think of a grandmother sitting in the state Senate." Grandmother or not, Munds chaired the state central committee, where she fought corporate abuses in the state, and served on the land committee, which established policies regarding the management and sale of all state-owned land.[55]

Virtually every other western state had its women politicians. In Utah between 1899 and 1901, Alice Merrill Horne served in the state house of representatives, where, among other things, she tried to solve Salt Lake City's smoke-pollution problem. Between 1921 and 1925, state senator Antoinette B. Kinney, a longtime advocate of planting trees and establishing parks, pushed policies to support Memory Grove, a canyon near Salt Lake City that had been a dumping ground for rubbish before women converted it to a park.[56]

Western women also went to Washington DC as elected members of Congress. Beginning in the mid 1930s, Oregon's Nan Wood Honeyman supported a Works Project Administration endeavor for a foot, cycle, and bridle path in the Lake Oswego district of Clackamas County. More importantly, Honeyman influenced members of the House of Representatives to study and evaluate the Columbia River, the Sandy River, and the Columbia Gorge. With the assistance of Gertrude G. Jensen of Portland, who chaired the "Save the Columbia Gorge" committee and helped prepare the first Columbia Gorge commission report in 1937, Honeyman opened the question of preserving the Columbia Gorge to national scrutiny.[57]

In addition, women served in such environmentally sensitive departments as the Department of the Interior. Under Secretary Harold L. Ickes during the early 1930s, Isabelle F. Story, chief of the public relations division, studied the national parks and the question of conservation. In 1933, she published *The National Parks and Emergency Conservation,* which explained the evolution of the park idea and argued for such programs as the Civilian Conservation Corps.[58]

•

It is significant that many women activists frequently came from a club background, bringing with them long-held environmental philosophies. From Hall and Munds in Arizona to Horne and Kinney in Utah, all were former club women. Obviously, the women's club movement planted many seeds: a willingness to speak out, the ability to take action, an ongoing concern for the physical environment, and a desire to expand their own roles in American society.

Still, despite the energy that American women expended, the programs they planned, and the speeches they made, their efforts often met with indifference or attribution to someone else. Mary Ann Dyer Goodnight's bison herd is an excellent example. Although Goodnight took the fate of the buffalo into her capable hands after her husband's death in December 1929, the future of the vast Goodnight holdings (which subsumed Mary Ann's property after her death) was unclear. Because the Goodnights did not have children, no direct heirs claimed the ranch or the buffalo. The estate went onto the auction block.

By 1931, rumors flew. One reported that the Goodnight herd faced imminent sale and slaughter. In November a hunt would be held on the herd's twelve thousand grazing acres. Expert cowboys would guide big game hunters, while Kiowa Indians would also be invited to attend. Only young animals would be saved for zoos, parks, and "old time ranchmen." A public outcry ensued. Mounting pressure on the state game commission and on the legislature, which had listed environmental conservation as one of its priorities, created a standoff between the present owners of the Goodnight properties and proponents of preservation.[59]

Fortunately, the deceased Mary Ann Goodnight had her niece to speak for her—and for the herd. Annie Dyer Nunn declared, "the revolting cruelty of the hide-hunting years was shocking in the extreme. . . . on every hand there was evidence of the merciless destruction." Certainly, Annie Nunn knew how to sway the public and threaten state officials, for she added: "It would be much easier for the state to save them than it was for the lone woman. But will it be done?"[60]

Eventually, a combination of state support, public subscriptions, and a donation of former Goodnight land rescued Mary Ann Goodnight's bison herd. By the mid 1930s, the bison, now named the Colonel Charles A. Goodnight Herd (rather than the Mary Ann Goodnight Herd), roamed the Palo Duro Canyon. Although the colonel always gave his wife full credit for rescuing the Texas bison herd from annihilation, her name was lost to history.

Thus, Mary Ann Goodnight serves as an example of the typical fate of women's conservation efforts. She was a woman ahead of her time; not until 1886 did the Smithsonian Institution first warn westerners regarding the imminent disappearance of the species. But neither Goodnight nor many other Texas women appear in contemporary histories of either Texas or U.S. conservation.[61]

7

Climbers and
Other Athletes

Even though mountain climbers and other athletes do not spring to mind as obvious environmentalists, they often enlarged the ranks of the early conservation movement. Especially in such western states as Colorado, California, Oregon, and Washington, nineteenth-century women not only scaled every summit in sight but typically became environmentalists, either by example or advocacy. By the turn of the century, women from all over the United States and Europe also journeyed to the American West to partake in the daring undertaking of climbing and to publicize the wonders of the region.

As in any other sport, a variety of types of women climbers emerged. There were Sunday afternoon climbers as well as dedicated, conservation-oriented climbers. There were also the "fire-eaters," who, bright-eyed and energetic at five in the morning, fed their sleepy-eyed companions dried fruit and gave a peptalk about the climb ahead. One Denver climber, Agnes Vaille, was of the latter variety. By the mid 1920s, she established—and accomplished—one goal after another.

In 1924, Vaille set her sights on a winter ascent of Longs Peak. With other climbers, she was unsuccessful in several attempts at the feat. Although fellow climber Carl Blaurock finally gave up, Vaille found a young Swiss guide named Walter Kiener, newly arrived in Denver, who claimed to have scaled the Alps under similar conditions. On 10 January 1925, Vaille set out from Denver with Kiener and her friend Elinor Eppich [later Elinor Eppich

Kingery], hoping to set a record as the first mountaineer to conquer the perilous East Face of Longs Peak in winter.[1]

When the attempt went awry, Vaille gave her life to her avocation. After blowing snow and jagged ice caused Vaille to fall one hundred and fifty feet down an ice-glazed rockface, Kiener showed incredible stamina in locating a rescue party and leading it to Vaille. But the rescue arrived too late. Even though Vaille, one of the most proficient climbers in Colorado, had mastered all but sixteen of Colorado's fifty-four peaks over fourteen thousand feet, she lay frozen to death in the snow.[2]

Agnes Vaille's calamity revealed that a woman's commitment to the outdoors could prove demanding, even life-threatening. For climbers, an interest in outdoor sports and the conservation of mountainous areas and other natural arenas could prove to be serious and sometimes perilous.

•

Long before Agnes Vaille's tragedy, white American women discovered the joys of mountain climbing. Although no records exist, it is likely that early American Indian women climbed western mountain ranges. Legends suggest that native women living near California's Sierra Nevada range incorporated the mountains into their religious and ceremonial practices. One story says that a woman named Tee-hee-neh rappelled to the Lost Arrow Spire to retrieve the dead body of her lover, Kos-soo-kah.[3]

Later, white American women followed the lead of such Native American women and also gained inspiration from the widely publicized feats of their English counterparts. As early as 1858, twenty-year-old feminist Julia Anna Archibald Holmes ascended Pikes Peak wearing what she called the "American Costume"— bloomers. After traveling with her husband and brother by ox wagon and on foot for more than eleven hundred miles from Kansas to Colorado, this determined woman scaled one of Colorado's most impressive elevations.[4]

Holmes, who on the westward journey wore a knee-length calico dress, "pants of the same," moccasins, and a hat, was an early feminist. She believed women who wanted equal rights should share hardships with men. Thus, she walked much of the way to Colorado, stood watch with her husband, and hoisted a seventeen-pound pack on her back for the ascent of Pikes Peak.[5]

On 5 August 1858, Holmes finally stood on the summit. "Nearly everyone tried to discourage me from attempting it," she wrote, "but I believed that I should succeed; and now here I am and I feel that I would not have missed this glorious sight for anything at all." After Indian guides assured Holmes that no native women had ever reached the top, she concluded (not necessarily correctly) that she was the first woman, white or otherwise, who had "ever stood upon the summit of this mountain and gazed upon this wondrous scene which my eyes now behold."[6]

Clearly, feminist principles inspired Julia Holmes, just as they had many English female climbers. In Holmes's letters and other writings, she attempted to give insight into women's overland journeys and to reveal the rigidities of a male-dominated culture. She grumbled when the men confined her to the wagon, criticized her clothing, and objected to her taking a turn at standing guard. Conservation of an environment she so admired was probably the farthest thing from Holmes's mind as she prepared to climb Pikes Peak.[7]

Thirty-two years later, however, another "bloomer girl" made a similar incredible climb, this time for the purpose of exciting interest in the sport of climbing and publicizing the Pacific Northwest's highest peak, Mount Rainier. On 4 August 1890, schoolteacher Fay Fuller, also twenty years old at the time of her feat, donned a "thick, blue flannel bloomer suit," heavy boy's shoes, a loose blouse with pockets, and a straw hat, and mounted her horse astride. Unlike Holmes, Fuller immersed herself in nature along the way. Despite fourteen hours in the saddle, she recalled "a beautiful ride through the wilderness, alone with nature and her wonders."[8]

When she reached Rainier, Fuller ascended its slopes in the company of four men, including a photographer whose shots later played a key role in the movement to create Mount Rainier National Park. Before beginning, Fuller shouldered a canteen, grabbed her alpenstock, and "resolved to climb until exhausted." After vaulting across crevasses, trekking on glaciers, and scaling walls of solid ice, Fuller's party stood on Mount Rainier's summit. "It was a heavenly moment," she later wrote. "Nothing was said—words cannot describe scenery and beauty, how could they speak for the soul!"[9]

That night the members of Fuller's party satisfied themselves with boiled-beef soup made from a packet of beef extract. They slept little because of the intense cold and the roar of avalanches hurtling down the mountainside. The next morning they had to melt their frozen shoes by placing them in the stream before putting them on. Even after the climbers descended, such symptoms as swollen faces, peeling skin, and sensitive eyes bedeviled them with what Fuller called "intense pain." Despite these aftereffects, she advised anyone who wanted "to begin life anew" and "to fall in love with the world again" to spend a few days on Rainier's slopes. Subsequently, Fuller's reputation and frequent writings helped popularize climbing and secure support for the creation of Mount Rainier National Park.[10]

•

Even though the nineteenth-century bloomer girls, Holmes and Fuller, did a great deal to arouse public interest in mountainous regions of the West and to demonstrate that "weak" women were capable of making demanding climbs, lesser-known or unknown women also should be credited for developing the sport and drawing attention to the western environment.

Accounts of such women are sometimes discovered in local newspapers. In 1863, the *Virginia Evening Bulletin,* published in Virginia City, Nevada Territory, reported that four unnamed women scaled Mount Davidson in the company of one man. The women's ascent of this "lofty craggy peak," the short article commented, demonstrated that "west coast females" were courageous and daring, and possessed great endurance. Similarly, accounts of Addie Alexander's ascent of Longs Peak in 1871 lay buried in old copies of the *Boulder County News* and the *Greeley Sun,* which referred to Alexander and her female companion as "well-muscled females."[11]

What these and other commentators did not mention was that

women usually climbed in constrictive clothing, used equipment designed for men, and proceeded at the pace and direction of men. This was certainly the case for Anna Mills when she climbed California's Mount Whitney in 1878. Whereas the men wore trousers and sturdy boots, Mills wore an ankle-length skirt that impaired her climbing ability and prohibited her riding astride.[12]

Even in 1903, the first Sierra Club women's team to ascend Mount Whitney did so in skirts, albeit ankle-length and without ground-brushing dust ruffles. A member of the Mount Whitney group, Marion Randall Parsons, recalled, "We all climbed Whitney in skirts." Later, after the hem of her stout denim skirt caught on a boulder, suspending her head downward until a helpful passerby set her free, Parsons converted to knickerbockers (knee-length trousers).[13]

Besides such problems, early women climbers encountered harsh situations that sometimes claimed their lives. In 1884, Caroline (Carrie) Josephine Welton from Waterbury, Connecticut, successfully scaled Pikes Peak and then decided to attempt Longs Peak. Described as "a true lover of nature," Welton was determined to experience the spectacular scenery that Longs Peak offered. Wearing a man's suit under a dress, she covered her face with a yellow-silk sun mask. Despite rising winds and dangerous gusts, she and her male companion reached the summit. On her way down, she weakened and took a chill. Although her guide went for help, Welton died before he returned. This marked the first recorded death of a woman climber in the United States.[14]

In spite of Carrie Welton's tragedy, women persisted in climbing Longs Peak and other summits. In 1906, Victoria Brougham from Michigan made a solo ascent of Longs Peak. High winds assaulted her, but she kept going. Although she reached the top, Brougham got lost on her way down. She spent a miserable night with Scotch, a dog belonging to the guide Enos Mills, until rescuers found her. Although Brougham almost lost her life on Longs Peak, she appeared for lunch looking relaxed and quite fit.[15]

Despite the perils, early twentieth-century western women continued to set records for "firsts." In 1913, the *Humboldt (Nevada) Star* reported that a Mrs. Fred T. Dull of Elko was the first woman to climb Mount Ruby, the "home of perpetual snow." In 1924, a divorced homesteader named Geraldine Lucas became the second woman to scale Wyoming's imposing Grand Teton. Fifty-eight-year-old Lucas was, however, the first local woman to reach the Grand's summit.[16]

Obviously, undeterred by opposition and danger, a significant number of American women climbed mountains. Why did they do so? Probably for many of the same reasons as men: exercise, excitement, achievement, adventure, and a love of nature. But women climbers also exhibited a decidedly feminist bent. Julia Archibald Holmes was an outstanding example, climbing Pikes Peak to show that a woman could achieve such a feat. Subsequent women climbers spoke in favor of woman's suffrage and let their pictures be used in conjunction with the suffrage campaign.

In 1910, writer Esther Merriam proclaimed—more hopefully than accurately—that the feminist crusade had been won, at least in mountain climbing. In *Harper's Bazar*, Merriam declared that "women no longer require a separate record, devoted to the exploitation of the feats of *women*." She added that American women climbers "compete successfully, with climbers of note, regardless of sex, in all parts the world."[17]

Women climbers also loved the natural environment. They hoped to show others its glories and teach judicious use of nature. Some also wished to revise masculine values of exploiting western landscapes. Typically, unlike most men, women climbed more to savor nature rather than to conquer it. Thus, most women athletes gradually developed a strain of environmentalism based upon such often-stated female values as cooperation and preservation for future generations.

During the early twentieth century, women guides exhibited a combination of female and environmentalist philosophies. Guides Anne and Isabel Pifer led male and female hikers up Longs Peak and other slopes, instructing the climbers to "look while you're hiking" and to "enjoy" nature.[18]

Meanwhile, Alma Wagen relocated from her native Minnesota to Tacoma, Washington, where she climbed the Olympic and Cascade Mountains and reached the top of Mounts Saint Helens,

Adams, and Hood. In 1918, with many men serving in World War I, Wagen was successful in obtaining a job as a guide in Mount Rainier National Park. There she encouraged men and women to climb, instilling a love of nature in the climbers she guided and helping them appreciate what she called "life on the world's top side." Still, Wagen could not escape the competitive nature of male climbers. On one occasion, she overheard a male climber admit that he had achieved the summit only because he had a woman guide: "I simply couldn't let a girl see me quit."[19]

•

So many women and men scrambled up the West's mountain slopes that climbing clubs soon organized, notably the Sierra Club in California in 1892; the Mazamas in Portland, Oregon, in 1895; the Mountaineers in Washington State in 1907; and the Colorado Mountain Club (CMC) in 1912. These groups spawned local clubs in such places as Tacoma and Everett. Unlike climbing clubs in England, these organizations welcomed women members and devoted themselves to environmental programs.[20]

The earliest of these, John Muir's Sierra Club, accepted women from its inception. Women were involved in club outings, membership, leadership, and environmental projects from the beginning, although the Sierra Club did not have a woman president until Aurelia Harwood was elected in 1927.[21]

So that successful climbers could record their names, dates, and elevations climbed, the Sierra Club placed "Summit Books" at the tops of mountains. These registers indicate that large numbers of women, married and single, climbed during the 1890s. But how did the books get positioned on the summits?

Sierra Club members, both male and female, climbed the mountains, register books in their backpacks. In 1897, for example, Robert Martin Price, a charter member of the Sierra Club and on its board of directors, spent from 14 July to 6 August hiking and camping in Yosemite to place Sierra Club registers on peaks.[22]

What is seldom mentioned about Robert Price's trip is that his wife, Jennie Ellsworth Price, accompanied him throughout the entire journey. His account took little notice of Jennie's prowess, although it did indicate that she climbed alongside him. He remarked instead that the climbs were dangerous and the equipment carried was sizable: bedding, food, an ax and other tools, fishing tackle, cooking utensils, linens, medicine, clothes, photograph plates, tinned foods and condiments.[23]

Jennie Price's narrative of the Yosemite trip, which appeared in the 1897–99 *Sierra Club Bulletin*, revealed that the party consisted of three men and herself. She noted that she carried a nine-pound pack of cooking utensils, clothing, and toilet articles. Price also wrote of steep, smooth rockfaces; impenetrable brush; "immense granite stairways"; and "dashing, whirling, foaming" cascades. She added that she slept on sand banks, fought off wasps, and dodged forest fires, bears, and snakes. When the journey ended, Price felt "regret and gladness mingled." She urged "anyone who is anything of a mountaineer" to journey through the entire length of the Tuolumne Cañon, "a scenic wonderland, with never a dull step in the whole distance."[24]

At the conclusion of Jennie Price's essay, John Muir remarked that Yosemite's Tuolumne Cañon was "perhaps the roughest of all the Sierra streets, and her [Price's] quiet walk through it was a fine, notable performance." Muir could think of no other woman who had traveled its entire length. Calling Jennie Price a "capital mountaineer," Muir recommended the establishment of a trail through the cañon so other people could experience its beauty and understand its needs, just as Jennie Price had done.[25]

Despite Muir's praise, Price's achievement is essentially lost to history. How many other women's stories lie buried in archives or dusty attics? Fortunately, climbing club records have preserved evidence of a pervasive female presence in all their activities.

Washington State's Mountaineers also placed summit books on mountain peaks. These registers offer a wealth of information. From 1907 to 1932, numerous women, many of whom were members of Mountaineer organizations, climbed Mount Christie. Some women hiked with husbands; many more climbed on their own. Some groups were totally female in composition. Although most hikers originated in Washington and Oregon, some traveled from as far away as Chicago and New England.[26]

Between 1917 and 1924, Mount Adams, at 12,307 feet, attracted women from Connecticut, New York, Ohio, and Montana, many of whom commented that they camped and climbed on a weekly basis. Between 1925 and 1940, Little Tahoma, at 11,117 feet, drew fewer women, probably due to its poor visibility and difficult climbing. Still, one early group consisting of two women and two men noted that they made the climb in five hours and forty minutes, while later all-male groups logged six hours and upward.[27]

Between 1915 and 1924, Mount Rainier, which stood 14,408 feet high, also lured fewer women climbers than men. Of the women climbers, some were married and climbing with husbands; others were single and ascended with Mountaineer groups. In 1919, Georgia Lyon traveled from Chicopee Falls, Massachusetts, to climb. The following year, Marjory Seale came from Auburn, California. In 1927, Dorothea Dickinson recorded Utica, New York, as her point of origin.[28]

Mountaineer club records also indicate that the groups targeted a different peak each year; Mount Olympus in 1907, Mount Baker in 1908, and Mount Rainier in 1909. Hikers traveled by foot or horseback to trailheads, where they loaded supplies and equipment onto pack animals. The Mount Baker expedition involved packing over thirty miles without trails. To reach Rainier's peak, club members often had to cut their own trails. Understandably, women members often abandoned hampering skirts at the trailheads and adopted trousers instead.[29]

In 1911, Anna Newman of Evanston, Illinois, kept a detailed account of one such Mountaineer trip. She recorded that sixty-four Mountaineers, "about equally divided as to men and women," participated in the club's fifth annual outing. The expedition, which cost $45.00, included food prepared by three cooks and transportation to the Cascade Range. Pack horses carried provisions and equipment weighing approximately two tons. Newman noted that the Mountaineers had multiple goals: to study the Northwest's environment, to preserve the area's natural beauty, and to "encourage a spirit of good fellowship among all lovers of out-door life."[30]

Newman enjoyed the trip. Although it was the first time she had camped outdoors, she slept soundly in the open. She found the "girls' camp" informal, even "gypsy-like," and appreciated what she called "the botany bunch," hikers who preserved and studied the specimens they collected during the day. All in all, Newman judged the outing a "tremendous success."[31]

Naturally, the mighty Mount Rainier proved a perennial favorite with the Mountaineers. In 1924, the group's brochure stated that "any person of normal health and strength who is a good walker, and willing to sleep in the open air," would enjoy the outing. "It is not an endurance test, but, it is a camping, tramping and climbing trip," the bulletin added. It further assured Mountaineers that the cost of the three-week trip would not run "more than $67.50 or less than $62.50."[32]

"For Men and Women," the Mountaineeers advised bringing such items as tents, sleeping bags, and stout shoes. The only place recommendations differed by gender was in the matter of clothing: "woolen knickerbockers suitable to be worn without skirts on trail and climbs" for women and "outing suits, preferably of wool" for men.[33]

Obviously, the main purpose of the Mountaineers was to climb mountains, but members placed a heavy premium on protecting the environment as well. As early as 1916, Mountaineer meetings were concerned with such issues as the Permanent Wildlife Protection Fund, the National Parks Conference in Washington DC, and the protection of Chinook language and culture. In following years the group considered the establishment of public camps, studied the wisdom of allowing sheep grazing on public lands, and erected markers along trails. In addition, Mountaineer organizations cooperated with local units of the Federation of Women's Clubs to promote environmental programs and establish national parks.[34]

A similar pattern emerged in Colorado. On 3 April 1912, four women and three men met in Denver to establish the Colorado Mountain Club. Among the founding members of CMC was Denver librarian Lucretia Vaile. She explained that the group's charter not only brought together climbers but promised "to stimulate public interest in our mountain area" and "to encourage the preservation of forests, flowers and natural scenery."[35]

Three weeks later, on 26 April 1912, twenty-five members—

nearly half women—ratified the constitution. Shortly thereafter, twenty-one hikers spent $10.00 each to participate in the club's first one-week outing. Vaile remarked that the club later held larger, longer outings that cost more and involved rugged scenery. "But I doubt," she wrote, "if there have been any richer in delight than the first."[36]

Lucretia Vaile initiated many other women into the sport of mountain climbing. Sometime between 1910 and 1920, she and her sister Gertrude, head of civilian relief for the Rocky Mountain division of the Red Cross, tramped seventy-two miles to assist Leila Kinney and Agnes Hall in their qualifying climb for CMC membership. The organization's rules required ascent of a peak of at least 14,000 feet principally on foot, so the women chose Pikes Peak. Although they encountered everything from an enraged bull to getting lost in the dark, all four returned to Denver unscathed.[37]

Membership in CMC grew rapidly and soon included clubs that ranged in locale from Denver to Chicago. In August 1914, a CMC expedition of about fifty people included thirty Prairie Club members from Chicago. Pearl Turner of Colorado Springs remembered that the outing started inauspiciously. Drenching rain and cold winds made her pull her old woollen dress closer around her body. When conditions improved, about twelve people, including Turner, climbed Ute Peak.[38]

On subsequent days, Turner and the other women created a female enclave by camping in tents or under the stars in a "ladies' camp ground." While in camp, wearing either her woollen dress or a skirt, Turner endured rain, hail, lightning, and an accidental fall into a creek.[39]

For climbing, Turner donned "tramping togs," presumably knickerbockers or trousers, and even scaled what she termed "Richthofen the terrible, Richthofen the difficult, Richthofen of the dangerous rockslides." On 28 August, she concluded "a glorious and never to be forgotten two weeks in the mountains."[40]

Turner later joined other climbing jaunts, including a 1919 CMC trip. Although the outing enrolled nearly ninety people, only about thirty-five of these came from Colorado. The rest hailed from Illinois, Missouri, Virginia, and Wisconsin. In addition, approximately sixty-five of the participants were women, including Elsie Seelye Pratt, M.D., of Denver.[41]

Turner soon broadened her geographical horizons. In 1922, she responded to what she described as "the wanderlust that is in me" by making a two-week horseback trip into the High Sierras. Two years later, Turner traveled to Seattle to join the Mountaineers on their 1924 excursion to Mount Rainier.[42]

Turner felt at home on the Rainier trip, at least at first. A woman identified as Mrs. Nash from Seattle mentored Turner, and three previous acquaintances from the Chicago club appeared. Then the eighty hikers divided into "ladies'" and "gentlemen's" camps, where they battled mosquitoes and mountain rats that ran over the campers' faces as they slept. Turner's sight of her first glacier intimidated her more, however. She staggered through snow and crawled over ice. She appreciated the help of male climbers who "handed" her around a sheer rockface. Despite raw blisters, she joined the main climb toward Gibralter Rock, where a hiker had perished only five days earlier. Although two women and two men had to be rescued from a fall into a crevasse and fog obliterated the party's trail, Turner's group made it back to camp safely.[43]

Pearl Turner's experiences make it clear that the CMC's primary objective was to bring together climbers, campers, and hikers. Certainly, such groups as the CMC proved especially helpful to women climbers. Club activities encouraged the participation of women who had neither husbands nor brothers as climbing partners. Clubs chaperoned and safeguarded women, while creating a relatively nonsexist atmosphere. They also provided organized and safe excursions at reasonable cost. Moreover, climbing organizations pioneered the social and professional acceptance of women climbers. When thousands of women proved themselves as climbers each year, critics found it difficult to maintain that women were incapable of such exploits.

But climbing clubs also proved instrumental in providing opportunities for women to protect the environment they enjoyed and loved. A charter member of the Fort Collins CMC, Laura Makepeace, pointed out that the organization had a growing commitment to preservation of nature. According to Makepeace, CMC members saved individual trees, built nature trails, and established bird sanctuaries. Harriet Vaille Bouck, the older sister of Agnes Vaille, the Denver climber who perished on Longs Peak in 1925, supported the founding of Rocky Mountain National Park. Also, CMC members advocated the establishment of Dinosaur National Monument, the removal of billboards in Denver Mountain Parks, and a campaign to "Save the Wild Flowers."[44]

•

Just as English women entered a wide variety of sports other than mountain climbing, American women living in all parts of the nation experimented with sports of all kinds. East of the Mississippi River, the 1870s and 1880s saw women's growing participation in such sports as tennis, aquatics, field hockey, rowing, track and field events, and winter sports. During the 1890s, Smith College sponsored basketball for women, while golf achieved popularity because it seemed well suited to women's "delicate" nature.[45]

At the same time, individual women also provided prototypes for women interested in sports. When shooter Annie Oakley, who hailed from Ohio, joined Buffalo Bill Cody's Wild West exhibition in 1885, she faced what she termed "prejudice" against women. But Oakley persevered to become a star shooter, a record-setting competitor, and a skillful hunter. Because she decided to maintain her dignity and what she called her "ladyhood" by wearing skirts and riding sidesaddle, Oakley wooed fans to her side. Between 1885 and her death in 1926, she opened sports of the rodeo arena to other women.[46]

Other women from east of the Mississippi River hunted, camped, and rode, and they urged other women to try such activities. In 1905, New Yorker Grace Gallatin Thompson Seton published *A Woman Tenderfoot*, which strongly recommended the joys of seeing the "wild" west closeup. In 1900, Seton had spent four months in the Rocky Mountains "learning how to ride, how to dress for it, how to shoot, and how to philosophise." She passed her experience on to other women in hopes of tempting "some going-to-Europe-in-the-summer-woman" to travel to the West instead. On that all-important matter of attire, Seton recommended a smart outfit of a wide-brimmed hat, a short buttoned jacket, snug bloomers, and a skirt that could be fastened with front and back hooks for walking and unfastened for riding astride.[47]

In the West, women adopted sports popular in the East. In Nebraska, Louise Pound, who in 1900 earned a doctorate from the University of Heidelberg, distinguished herself first in lawn tennis during the 1890s and then in golf between 1900 and 1927. Pound explained that "most women at that time would use their husbands' clubs cut off." When she got her first set of matched clubs, she claimed that she cut six strokes off her game.[48]

Other western women liked to play a diversity of sports, including tennis and golf, and to enjoy such pastimes as picnicking, riding, and camping.[49] Some women even regarded riding and camping as the ultimate vacation. In 1913, ranchwoman Virginia Martin set off with a woman homesteader friend, four children, a male cook, and a male guide for a four-week horseback trip in Arizona's Apache National Forest and White Mountains. Wearing split skirts, the women rode astride. Wide-brimmed hats with veils shielded their faces from the sun; pistols protected them from more immediate dangers. Along the way, they fished and hiked to the top of Mount Baldy, 11,590 feet high.[50]

As growing numbers of women took up riding and camping, commercial providers catered to the new market. American entrepreneurs, always alert to economic potential, developed unparalleled opportunities for women. During the early 1920s, Eaton's Ranch in Wolf, Wyoming, invited "ladies" to join its riding, fishing, and pack trips. Eaton's brochure recommended "a riding suit for ladies—who all ride astride." Later in the decade, photographs from Eaton's Ranch pictured women wearing a more relaxed outfit composed of knee-high boots, tight-fitting pants, white shirts, and a cloche hat with a wide band.[51]

Resorts and tour companies also offered horseback trips exclusively for women and girls. In 1924, the Valley Ranch in Wyoming advertised a "Horseback Trip in the Rockies for Young Ladies." Beginning in 1911, the Valley Ranch had offered a similar trip for young men, aimed at students from Andover to Harvard and Yale.

By the 1920s, it cost men $850.00 round trip to ride horses specially assigned to them in order to see "big game" and "wilderness areas." The women's trip cost the same amount and targeted "young women from select families," meaning students from such schools as Abbot, Farmington, and Wellesley. Like the men, the women would each have a horse, would see "big game," but could sleep in tents "as they choose."[52]

Meanwhile, still other western women pioneered additional sports for females. Around 1900, Kathleen Mitchell Newton of Eugene, Oregon, enjoyed a hunting trip to Swift Creek Camp. In 1915, a Tonopah, Nevada, teacher named Ida Brewington won Tonopah's First Turkey Shoot for Women. Between 1923 and 1925, a Mrs. S. E. Webster of Kearney, Nebraska, earned three consecutive state titles as trapshooting champion and subsequently appeared in DuPont Powder Company and Remington Arms Company advertisements.[53]

Western women also learned to ski. After Scandinavians introduced skiing into the United States during the mid and latter nineteenth century, Americans gradually adopted the sport. During the early 1900s, Borghild Marie Bergstedt [later Borghild Marie Bergstedt Paulsen] helped promote skiing in Utah. Bergstedt, who had brought skates and skis with her from her native Norway, skated in Salt Lake City's Heath's Park and skied down Main Street to the Brigham Young statue. In 1915, she was the only woman to ski with a party on Ensign Peak. Shortly afterward, she helped organize the Utah Ski Club, of which she served as secretary. Bergstedt also claimed to be the first woman in Utah to ski down a "take-off" (ski jump).[54]

Around the same time, Denverite Marjorie Perry, who graduated from Smith College in 1905, founded the Perry-Mansfield Camp for Girls near Steamboat Springs in 1914. She spent part of every winter skiing in Steamboat Springs, at first in the customary long skirt and later in an imported red ski outfit. As a CMC member, she also hiked and skied on club outings, usually in Rocky Mountain National Park. Perry remained an active skier until 1968, her eighty-sixth year.[55]

By the end of the 1920s, American sportswomen had gained a

measure of acceptance. Although criticism of women athletes, especially mountain climbers, continued in Europe, there was somewhat more willingness in the United States to accept women's growing proclivity to participate in sports. In 1929, the *Sportsman's Encyclopedia* declared that "American girls are noted the world over as participants in all kinds of healthful, enjoyable outdoor sports." It also urged women to "insist on going along" on men's expeditions, promising that they would "have less doctor bills" and would want to make many more outdoor trips.[56]

As women began to follow such advice, they recognized the fragility of the environment and the need for improved user practices and policies. Like English women, American women gradually championed animal rights and rejected trophy killing as a desirable goal. By the early 1900s, even Annie Oakley, who once took pride in shooting energetic, English blue-rock pigeons, switched from live birds to clay pigeons.

In Montana, also during the early 1900s, ranchwoman and rodeo performer Fannie Sperry Steele developed a similar awareness. Working as a hunter, outfitter, and guide in the Blackfoot Valley, Sperry claimed, "I think like an elk so I know where to find game." She had gained sympathy for such animals as elk, as well as enormous enmity toward people who misused the environment, especially trophy hunters who simply wanted animal heads for their walls. "I will prosecute them every chance I get," Steele proclaimed at age seventy-four.[57]

•

During the early twentieth century, support for women who loved the outdoors and hoped to preserve nature came from an increasing number of sources. Barred from most male associations, American women appeared more willing than English women to form their own organizations, both for adult and young women.

In 1912, Juliette Gordon Low founded the Girl Scouts of America. Although its headquarters were in Washington DC, Girl Scout groups soon spread westward. Because American girls frequently resisted playing the role of "proper" young ladies, Low's emphasis on outdoor activities elicited a wide response. By 1919, Girl Scout troops existed in every state except Utah. The Girl Scouts even extended across the Pacific Ocean to the territory of Hawaii.[58]

The Girl Scouts taught a combination of domestic and outdoor skills to their members, including girls of color and from impoverished backgrounds. Drawing on volunteer help, the Girl Scouts reached millions of young women with such messages as the value of sports for women, the advantages of outdoor exercise, and the wisdom of preserving the environment. Among other things, Girl Scout troops taught nature study, organized hikes, and established camps for girls.[59]

Soon, founder Juliette Low became a role model for young women interested in the outdoors. From articles in such magazines as *Good Housekeeping* in 1927 to a biography written for young adult readers in 1996, a variety of authors commented that Low provided an inspiration for American girls as well as those in other countries, notably England. Her most recent biographer argued that because Low threw her own cloak of respectability and propriety around such outdoor undertakings as hiking, camping, and studying nature, thousands of girls had outdoor experiences and developed an environmental awareness.[60]

But the best-known supporter of the Girl Scouts, as well as an advocate of the group's emphasis on outdoor endeavors, was Lou Henry Hoover, wife of President Herbert Hoover. As a young woman, she loved to ride, hunt, and camp. She met "Bert" Hoover at Stanford, where both matriculated as geology majors. After Lou married Bert in 1899, she accompanied him on trips and participated in his mining and other ventures. She became known not only for her work with Girl Scouts but her support of environmental goals as well. As the first First Lady in the twentieth century to deliver speeches and broadcast over radio, Lou Hoover had tremendous influence. After the Hoovers left Washington, they donated Camp Rapidan, the rural Virginia getaway Lou had designed, to the National Park Service.[61]

During the early 1900s, private girls camps also appeared in the American West. Of course, boys camps already existed, thus giving sports-minded young men an advantage over women. During the early 1900s, Foxboro Ranches of Flagstaff, Arizona, opened one such "ranch camp" for boys. The camp managers pledged to provide boys of preparatory school and college age "the sort of living that prepared Theodore Roosevelt for the most strenuous political career of history."[62]

Even though it was harder to make a pitch for camps for girls, who at that time would not aspire to the presidency, a few organizers entered the field. In 1927, teachers Ethel Pope, trained at the University of Nebraska, and Mabel Winter, from the University of Wisconsin, announced that Camp Chonokis, "an organized summer camp for girls over twelve years old," would open on the shore of Lake Tahoe for a term of six weeks. Activities included water sports, hiking, archery, dancing, and horseback riding. For $3.00 per day or $20.00 per week, Camp Chonokis's brochure promised to provide girls with "all the joys and advantages of outdoor life" and to promote an interest in health, cooperation, sports, and nature.[63]

Chonokis required its campers to bring limited clothing and personal articles. Policy required that girls wear "the Chonokis uniform," consisting of dark green poplin or corduroy knickerbockers with a tan cotton broadcloth blouse. Shoes could include high-topped tennis shoes, boots, hiking shoes, and low-heeled oxfords. Riding breeches were also acceptable, as were riding boots.[64]

By 1930, California teacher Gladys G. Gorman, a Wellesley graduate, had replaced Ethel Pope as camp codirector. Gorman and Winter expanded the summer camp sessions and added a winter term during Christmas vacation. The women's records, camp logs, and photographs reveal a well-run camp that remained true to its original ideals.[65]

In particular, Gorman and Winter, who believed the outdoors could accommodate feminine behavior, expected their staff to model a combination of sporty and ladylike conduct for their campers. "Let us keep our manners high," they enjoined their counselors, because "parents judge the camp by the habits the girls acquire while here." Moreover, the directors took great interest in nature education and appreciation. Among other things, their files overflowed with suggestions for establishing nature trails.[66]

Gorman and Winter also supported conservation, which they

defined as "the wise use of nature on the part of man." One of their directives warned, "To use nature unwisely means death to man, to use it wisely means everlasting life." Chonokis campers learned about the environment in many ways. They made plaster casts of flowers, stems, and leaves, prepared ink and smoke prints of leaves, and studied the stars. They also read widely in the camp library, which included Florence Merriam Bailey's *Handbook of Birds of Western United States,* Maud G. McClurg's *Our Field and Forest Trees,* and Florence Grondal's *The Music of the Spheres.*[67]

Undoubtedly, Chonokis and other girls' camps reached a limited number of young women. Yet, by their very existence, such camps sanctioned women's love of sports and the outdoors. Camps also taught some young women the necessary camping and athletic skills. Furthermore, they implanted an appreciation for nature in women and inspired them to support conservation ideals in their lives. Thousands of young women carried these ideals with them into adulthood as they undertook club work and political activism.

•

Women climbers and other athletes left a dual legacy. For one, they proved the outdoors accessible to women. Even nineteenth-century "ladies" could climb or ski a mountainside without loss of decorum. For another, whether or not they were active environmentalists (most were), women in outdoor sports drew the attention of the American public to nature and the wisdom of safeguarding the physical environment.

Often, however, women's efforts were overlooked, forgotten, or discounted. Although female climbers and other athletes gained support in some quarters, many people held female climbers and other athletes to a separate—and often harsh—standard.

This was the real tragedy of Agnes Vaille, who perished on Longs Peak in 1925. Had it not been for antagonistic attitudes toward women climbers, Vaille might have become an instant martyr for outdoor women. She could have been idealized as an athlete who dared all and gave all—the ultimate sportswoman.

Instead, even during the relatively liberal 1920s, Vaille fell victim to the controversies that plagued women competitors. Because of misinformation, sexist assumptions, and unfounded charges, Vaille became the kind of woman climber so many Americans had long feared. Although she was one of Colorado's most proficient climbers, after her death Vaille was condemned as rash, impetuous, and foolhardy.

Some of the responsibility for this outcome falls on Roger B. Toll, a charter member of CMC and superintendent of Rocky Mountain National Park, who compiled the official report on the Vaille disaster. He wrote in haste and without interviewing Elinor Eppich Kingery, who traveled part of the way up Longs Peak with Agnes Vaille that fateful night. Because Toll was Vaille's cousin and friend, he perhaps wanted to close the case as quickly as possible. As superintendent, he had also actively promoted the park as a place for climbers, a stance that might prove embarrassing given the Vaille disaster. Toll did take immediate action to forestall further accidents, including having two sections of steel cable installed on Longs Peak where Agnes fell and closing the rundown and inadequate Timberline Cabin, the launch point for Vaille's trek and the rescue attempt.[68]

Another part of the accountability rests on the shoulders of journalists, who repeated slim conjectures as fact and often joined in denouncing Agnes Vaille. As late as 1959, Elinor Eppich Kingery excoriated a reporter at the *Rocky Mountain News* for telling the Vaille story in an unsympathetic way and with factual errors. Kingery wrote that Vaille had never intended to climb by night and that she came down the North Face rather than the West. Kingery added that Vaille had not "persuaded" the guide to come with her, that he, Walter Kiener, was actually the leader of the expedition. Perhaps most telling of all, Kingery pointed out that the guide did not spend his later years as a fire-lookout as the reporter had said; instead, Vaille's family paid his medical bills and helped him earn a doctorate in botany.[69]

In 1963, Elinor Eppich Kingery wrote that "the final decision to make the climb on that day was not Agnes's, and the judgment of Walter Kiener was not necessarily infallible or even good." Because Vaille was a rational person and an experienced climber who shunned unnecessary risk, Kingery fought "the general assumption of the world . . . that it was all Agnes's stubborness and poor judgment that were responsible for the whole tragedy." Despite Kingery's valiant efforts to revise Agnes Vaille's story, however, a 1980 article described Vaille as "an early women's liberation advocate" and Walter Kiener as an unmitigated hero, while a 1984 piece on Rocky Mountain National Park repeated the error-filled version of Vaille's story.[70]

Whatever the facts of the Vaille calamity, it is instructive in several ways. Agnes Vaille's accident warned other women that a commitment to the outdoors could involve danger. Moreover, ruthless judgments of Vaille demonstrated that different principles applied to sportswomen than to sportsmen. Finally, the story of a supposedly reckless Agnes Vaille was dredged up again and again, while the records of millions of other achieving women disappeared into the dustbin of history. Given that situation, it is hardly surprising that we seldom think of late nineteenth- and twentieth-century women as either accomplished sportspeople or active environmentalists.

8

Travelers and Tourists

The influence of women travelers and tourists on the growth of the conservation movement, even more than the impact of other types of women, has gone unrecognized and unanalyzed. First by wagon, horseback, and stagecoach—and later by railroad, steamship, and automobile—women participated in jaunts to the Far West, the Southwest, Alaska, and Hawaii.[1]

Such women raised public awareness of the western environment and its need for preservation by giving club reports, writing travel books and articles, delivering talks and lectures, and sharing a plethora of snapshots. They also helped feminize the West, assuring other women that they faced little danger and that western travel would bring them great adventures, incomparable experiences, and improved health. Rather than being dangerous, western travel would free women, who could tour on their own, modify customary clothing to some degree, and take home daring tales that would make their friends swoon with envy. The more feminist a woman's sentiments, the more likely she wanted to explore the West for herself.

In 1890, Margaret Long found herself enthralled by both touring and the environmental cause when her family journeyed from Hingham, Massachusetts, to Yellowstone National Park. On 5 July 1890, the Long clan assembled in St. Paul, Minnesota, to visit the local sights before their departure to Yellowstone. Although a young and inexperienced traveler, Long noted the inroads of early tourism on the West. "How the advance of modern civilization had divested this spot of most of its romance!" she wrote after viewing the Falls of Minnehaha.[2]

On 11 July, Long and her family turned their faces toward what she called the "wonders" of the West. They traveled in the relative ease of a tourist car, first through the Badlands of South Dakota and finally to the Yellowstone River. After dining in a hotel, which Long found "characteristically western in its lack of ornamentation" and "the brusque ways of its proprietor," the Longs bounced in horse-drawn wagons through Yellowstone Park, sleeping in tents and eating by firesides. From Mammoth Hot Springs to the Norris Geyser Basin to Old Faithful, Long "beheld everywhere evidence of the presence of Nature's most terrific force!"[3]

Like so many other women travelers and tourists, Long felt a spiritual connection to the grandeur that lay before her, a "strong feeling of worship for the great God of nature." Her discovery of the ethereal side of the environment caused Long to decry the desecration she saw at every turn: "we find names, initials with dates, cut into the yielding rock, even visiting cards, and placed in spots one would consider inaccessible, but all fulfilling their purposes admirable, namely advertising in full the folly of their owners." Long had little sympathy with people's need to leave their marks on sites that should, in her view, remain pristine for others to delight in.[4]

Even after Long returned to the East to graduate from Smith College in 1895 and Johns Hopkins Medical School in 1903, the lure of the West tugged at her. In 1905, Dr. Margaret Long relocated to Denver, where she directed a home for destitute tubercular women and later worked at Denver General Hospital and the Florence Crittenden Home. She took quickly to automobiles, using a variety of touring cars to roam the surrounding prairies and desert. "I am not a good joiner," she explained, "but I do belong to medical societies and motor clubs."[5]

In 1918, Long drove alone from Colorado to Nevada, where she chauffeured her friend Anne Martin from ranch to ranch, seeking signatures on a nominating petition for Martin's U.S. Senate bid. Flat tires and car breakdowns failed to deter Long. She reveled in "the great adventure into a new country." In addition, Long flaunted her freedom: "Nobody knows where I am." She also basked in the beauty of Nevada and Utah, at the same time realizing that more action was needed to save the West before it disappeared under a wave of tourism and urbanization.[6]

Spurred by her own travel experiences and the writings of such other women travelers as Mary Austin and Edna Brush Perkins, Long ventured into Death Valley in 1921, again with Anne Martin as her traveling companion. Because the women's "first trip served not at all to still the Valley's voice which called so irresistibly to us," Long returned to the desert many times, often accompanied by Martin.[7]

While continuing to practice medicine, Long also followed the Oregon and Old Spanish Trails, especially researching the "forty-niners'" crossing of Death Valley. In 1941, she published *The Shadow of an Arrow*, a combination history, travel guide, road log, and plea for conservation. She praised Death Valley National Monument and called for widespread appreciation of the valley's "wonderful and terrible beauty."[8]

In one way, Long got her wish. Her writings, maps, and speeches helped generate interest in Death Valley and its further preservation. During the 1920s, 1930s, and 1940s, the number of Death Valley tourists grew. Preservationists restored such old ghost towns as Rhyolite, while such entrepreneurs as "Death Valley Scotty" built luxurious resort hotels.[9]

In another way, however, Long was disappointed. As tourists came to the valley, ecological damage increased. As early as January 1930, the *Los Angeles Times* warned motorists they could expect traffic in Death Valley to be heavy during the coming week, partly because of the ideal summerlike climate found there and partly due to the excellence of the Stove Pipe Road.[10] Within a few years, Long decried the number of beer bottles along roadsides, the erection of unsightly billboards, and stock car races across the desert floor.[11]

Initially, Long found in the Southwest a beauty that satisfied her spiritual side as well as health-restoring conditions for her patients and a sense of freedom that confirmed her feminism. Gradually, she also became a dedicated environmentalist, first by protecting the land itself and next by shielding the desert from the very people she urged to visit it and glory in its spectacle.

John Muir hardly stood alone in dealing with a similar conservationist quandary. The difference between the two is that John Muir received excessive attention, whereas Margaret Long slid into oblivion. Like thousands of other women travelers and tourists, Long's voice, a strong one from the 1920s to the 1940s, has since been forgotten.

·

Well before Margaret Long, a number of other American women saw opportunities in travel and in writing about it. At the same time that English women began to widen their perspectives through travel, a few daring American women undertook journeys as well. From 1817 to 1831, Anne Newport Royall traveled from the eastern coast of the United States to the Mississippi River, subsequently producing twelve volumes of spicy, highly graphic travel writing. In 1852, when transcendentalist Margaret Fuller went abroad, she described such Italian lakes as Como as an expression of nature's "full heart."[12]

Later American women travelers focused their attention on the American West. Taking pleasure in unspoiled nature, those women who could afford the time and expense escaped to the West. During the 1870s and 1880s, for example, Colorado's Rocky Mountains attracted more women than just Englishwoman Isabella Bird, whose writings did a great deal to draw women to the Rockies. As in England, a plethora of accounts resulted from American women's travels. S. Anna Gordon's *Camping in Colorado*, published in 1879, emphasized the state's beauty as well as its health-giving qualities.[13]

As the beginning of the twentieth century neared, more American women published travel observations. Almost all of those accounts that sold widely described the West as glorious, picturesque, and divine. In 1903, for example, two women set out from San Francisco alone. They later reported that although they drove a horse and buggy three hundred miles, climbed mountains, forded streams, and camped along the way, they had not encountered a tramp or a robber—or even a rattlesnake. To them the "wilderness" was "a changing poem of marvelously beautiful scenery, kind faces, and willing hands, always ready to make us happy."[14]

•

Given the generally exultant female rhetoric concerning tame and welcoming western landscapes, it is little wonder that between 1870 and 1940 growing numbers of women—largely white women—ventured into the western "wilderness" in unprecedented numbers and played a crucial role in the rise of western tourism.[15]

As in England, American women travelers assisted in the widespread development of landscapes as objects for viewing, scenic tourism, and nature appreciation. But in the United States, women literally reshaped images of western scenes. As speed, luxury, and convenience increased, women's perceptions of western terrain became more benign. These women constructed a new western vista, free of log cabins, chicken houses, and storm cellars. This West offered relaxation, sport, and edification, at least to those who visited it as tourists.[16]

At the same time, women travelers characterized the West as amenable to females. Women said they found it easier and safer to roam there, especially given the growing number of resorts and tourist destinations that willingly catered to them. In 1888, Serena J. Washburn, a widow who homesteaded in Kansas, joined a friend for a railroad trip to Manitou Springs, Colorado. She stayed at the Sunny Side Hotel, where she could look down into "streets gay with pleasure seekers, those in quest of health, and the money makers." Predictably, she visited such sights as the Garden of the Gods and Pikes Peak. Like so many others, Washburn felt incapable of describing the "sublimity and grandeur" of the place: "It must be seen to be appreciated."[17]

Even women journeying to difficult and far-flung destinations claimed that hardship was minimal. Of course, transportation had improved so rapidly that women often traveled by such innovations as steamships, on which they were safe and had generous provisions. In 1890, Septima M. Collis declared that she sailed the Sitkan Archipelago without the "slightest fatigue or discomfort."

Collis advised other women to "postpone Paris and London, Rome and Vienna, the Rhine and the Alps, to some future day."[18]

As transportation improved, people founded clubs to facilitate their outings. Sometimes a group of friends formed a club and built camping facilities to accommodate summer excursions. During the 1890s, one Colorado club constructed a log house on government land near Antonito in the Conejos River Canyon, which they visited each summer. When a homesteader filed a claim on the land, club members traveled in wagons farther up the canyon, where they camped in tents.[19]

Soon more formal types of travel organization developed to help people with their journeys. One was the Minneapolis Tourist Club, founded in 1891 with the goal of preparing its members for "intelligent" travel. Although the tourist club first concentrated on travel to countries other than the United States, members soon recognized the potential of the American West. The tourist club also distributed information about travel to future travelers. By the early 1920s, tourist club members—overwhelmingly female—presented children's "picture hour" programs at schools, churches, and neighborhood centers. In addition, during the 1920s and 1930s, the club gradually adopted conservation causes, such as contributing to Minnesota's Superior National Forest reforestation program and offering such public programs as "Physical Environment as It Affects Human Progress: Erosion and Flood Control."[20]

Still other travel clubs had a commercial purpose. During the 1920s, the Los Angeles Chamber of Commerce sponsored the All-Year Club of Southern California, which gave away booklets and maps, answered questions, and arranged itineraries. The All-Year Club's goal was to reveal to the "the nation through advertising the wonders which Southern California offers to all." In so doing, the club recruited not only families but also single women.[21]

American women further feminized the West by proving themselves intrepid campers who appeared to enjoy their new experiences. No place in the West seemed too harsh for them. Contrary to the widespread belief that women naturally preferred safety and total comfort, virtually all the women who penned accounts recorded pleasant journeys.

Of course, a growing variety of modern conveniences increasingly cushioned their discomfort. As early as 1879, an army officer's wife, May Humphreys Stacy, planned a vacation around her husband's expedition to Graham Mountain near Tucson, Arizona. She, her children, and their nurse camped out for nearly a week. While the children had a separate campfire and played "emigrant," Stacy collected flowers and shot at targets with a "rifle, soldier's revolver and my own littler revolver." Despite illness, insects, clinging dust, and riding thirty-five miles over rutted roads the last day, Stacy concluded that the trip was well worth it.[22]

Because May Stacy's social position entitled her to benefits, she carried the feminization of roughing it to a high art. From the fort commissary Stacy obtained all the necessary provisions. Once in camp, a sutler cooked and washed up, while enlisted men built the fire and took care of her tent. Stacy said that the tent, with its canvas floor, a cot with a hair mattress, blue-bordered mission blankets, and clean white sheets and pillows, "looked quite like living and very cosy [sic]." A Brussels carpet, camp chairs, a trunk, and a hanging mirror completed the decor. The children and their nurse inhabited a separate tent next to Stacy's.[23]

Other women took fewer accouterments than May Stacy yet still managed to establish a comfortable presence in the outdoors. A turn-of-the century woman remembered that "Mama was always ready to pack up and tie the bedding in big canvas rolls" in preparation for a trip in "two big tents." For amusement, "Mama" fished for trout and tanned the hides of the game her husband brought in.[24]

Even in remote locations, women campers found a way to minimize their housework and maximize their pleasure. In 1907, Nellie Martin Wade claimed she was the first white woman to explore the Alaska Range near Mount McKinley by horseback. Although Wade and her husband had few luxuries, she commented that camping in the "wonderful country" of the Pacific Northwest cut down her housework, while simple eating freed her from the task of menu planning.[25]

•

Gradually, women travelers came to view western travel as liberating them from female "rules." For a late-nineteenth-century woman, a little physical discomfort or occasional danger was a small price for a sense of freedom and autonomy. In truth, such women usually were well protected in their travels by cumbersome Victorian clothing, comprehensive rules of etiquette, and membership in the dominant white culture, all of which allowed them to journey westward without excessive fear of degradation or peril.[26] Many women travelers reveled in the resulting feeling of independence they experienced.

By the beginning of the twentieth century, transportation added a sense of ease and security. Vacationers switched from horse-drawn wagons and steamships to railroads and ocean liners. Railroad companies especially competed to offer the traveler the best. Everything from the Pullman standard sleeping car and the less expensive tourist car to observation and dining cars made a cross-country journey palatable, safe, and affordable to even the most fastidious travelers. In 1901, the average round-trip fare from St. Paul to Yellowstone National Park was economical, at least for those in the middle and upper classes, at about $50.[27]

During the early 1900s to the 1930s, however, women seeking true adventure and latitude were more likely to find it through automobile travel. Although hotels, tourist camps, and lunch counters were plentiful, they often proved inadequate and expensive. In addition, such factors as unpaved, muddy roads, rainy or snowy weather, being pulled by mules across a river or getting stuck in the mud in a stream, and dirty accommodations might deter the most stout-hearted, feminist-thinking woman. As one commentator noted, even the celebrated Lincoln Highway of 1913 was "little more than a cow path."[28]

Despite the difficulties, the desire for freedom and autonomy drove women onward. During the late 1930s, Evalyn Bentley of Tucson explained that "letters, maps, and travel articles" inspired her to explore Arizona by automobile. In 1938, Bentley and four female friends decided to venture into what she called "the wilds" of northern Arizona and southern Utah. When she told her women friends she had added a shovel and tow rope to her Ford's gear, she recalled that "those strong-hearted ladies did not even smile but turned pale as possible." The women persevered, however, and returned in good health, having snapped photographs of everything from Bryce Canyon to Zion Canyon.[29]

•

Meanwhile, the growing association of western locales with improved health further stimulated western tourism. Americans came to believe that western air and water promoted health, or could cure whatever already ailed them. During the 1870s and 1880s, easterners journeyed to Denver in search of relief from tuberculosis, while some Californians headed for the Nevada mountains hoping to cure catarrh. Between 1880 and 1930, the American Southwest in particular gained a reputation as a health-seekers' paradise.[30]

Entrepreneurs quickly responded to this new interpretation of western landscapes by founding a series of spas, resorts, and sanitariums. When Boulder's Colorado Sanitarium opened in 1896, it welcomed people "suffering from any chronic disease" as well as those "weary and worn" with responsibilities and stress. The sanitarium offered the best of Colorado nature—pure air and clean water—supplemented by efficient nurses and well-trained doctors. Stating that the Colorado Sanitarium "is not a money-making enterprise," the institution's brochure promised to use its profits "in caring for the worthy poor who are sick."[31]

Despite such assurances, the Colorado Sanitarium provided facilities designed for the well-to-do: a four-story main building with verandas on every floor and several smaller, yet similarly styled, auxiliary structures and guest cottages. Basic rates, which ranged from $15 to $35 weekly, included meals with soup, meat, vegetable, beverage, bread, grain, and dessert. One midwinter menu offered five desserts: coconut custard, apple pie, roasted almonds, watermelon, and cantaloupe. Such items as examinations, nursing care, treatments, and physicians' advice incurred additional charges.[32]

Within a few years, the Colorado Promotion and Publicity Committee listed the Colorado Sanitarium as one of the state's many health resorts. "If you wish to breathe air that is death to the bacilli of tuberculosis, come to Colorado!" the committee's publication added.[33]

As a result of such claims, people flocked westward from as far away as Chicago, or even Europe. Especially in the Southwest, many visitors stayed on as residents and sometimes as proprietors of health resorts of their own. Typically, they touted the Southwest as a Shangri-la for the ill.[34] But it was not *just* the Southwest that created opportunities—economic and otherwise—by defining natural environments as health-giving. Throughout the West doctors began prescribing "health cures" for their patients, even recommending such unlikely destinations as North Dakota and Montana.

In July of 1922, on their physician's advice, Pearl Peterson, her husband, their eight-year-old son, and a dog left Minneapolis in a wagon. They spent a memorable night on 5 August in a South Dakota "tourist camp" on a farm, while chilly rain dampened their tent and their spirits. In early October they sighted a "band of Indians" on a hillside in North Dakota near Bismarck. By 14 October the weather had grown so frosty they resorted to hotel lodgings. In 1923, when the health of Peterson's husband improved, the family returned to Minneapolis. Because the health results of their trip proved short-lived, the family soon set off to Glendive, Montana. Although Peterson's husband did well on the trip, he died shortly after their return to Minneapolis.[35]

Eventually, even Minnesota itself, a land of frigid winters and humid summers, touted its lakes as health restorers that were absolutely free "of the faintest suspicion of malaria." Abetted by such businesses as the Chicago and Northwestern Railway, Minnesota agencies offered brochures, maps, and a wide variety of "health" resorts. Similarly, the Dakota Hot Springs in the Black Hills guaranteed spring waters "truly wonderful in their curative and health-giving qualities."[36]

Even though medical claims often proved far-fetched, the interpretation of western landscapes as healthful provided yet another rationale for their conservation. In an era before wonder drugs, what American would want to see pollution destroy a hot springs, or land developers despoil pure-aired mountains?

•

Of all western attractions, the national parks proved a perennially popular draw. An amazing number of travelers—Americans and others—found their way to Yellowstone National Park in particular. These expeditions often included women, who in turn encouraged other women to make the trip. As early as 1878, the famous Nelson Miles and Colgate Hoyt party, which made a late summer journey through Yellowstone, included several women, especially wives and daughters anxious for edification and adventure.[37]

A scant decade later, Edna Fay Kaiser of Montana claimed to be the first white woman to make a camping trip by horse-drawn wagon through Yellowstone Park. Despite Kaiser's declaration, many women's diaries, letters, and memoirs included a description of a Yellowstone sojourn sometime during the 1870s and 1880s.[38]

The number of women visitors increased during the 1890s when railroad companies, hotels, chambers of commerce, and the U.S. Park Service combined their efforts to promote national parks in the United States and abroad. Especially after 1900, a variety of brochures, travel posters, free maps, and works of art lured tourists to the parks and also attempted to convince them that the preservation of national park lands was a sound idea. "See America First" became a rallying cry, particularly during World War I, when travel to Europe became difficult or impossible.[39]

Thousands responded to the publicity. In 1913, the family of Nell Buchan of Powell, Wyoming, took four weeks to traverse Yellowstone's loop. The group journeyed in a lumber wagon drawn by two work horses, with a saddle horse trailing behind the wagon as what she called a "spare." Because no stores, restaurants, or lodging were available in the park, the party brought food, fished, and slept on the ground "under tarps."[40]

By the 1920s, Yellowstone was crowded, and park guides soon grew slightly disillusioned with the average tourist. Such questions as "Where do the bears go in winter?" "Do geysers freeze up in winter?" and "Did the government plant all the trees in the park?" amused Yellowstone guides.[41] But such queries also revealed tourists' meager knowledge regarding nature and the need for environmental education if conservation was to become a long-term reality.

To keep such "dudes" from meeting with disaster in the nation's parks, a profusion of camping manuals appeared. One unusually complete 1903 manual aimed at male campers included everything from camp recipes to such common-sense rules as "don't sit or lay on the bare ground" and "no loaded firearms in tent." A 1907 handbook reached out to male and female campers, even suggesting that women would enjoy fishing although attired in long skirts and corsets, and that small children and babies flourished in a camp setting. Scanning the list of apparel recommended for women, however, makes one wonder how freeing the early camping experience could have been:

> A complete golf or bicycle suit; an extra skirt, dark and heavy, walking or bicycle length; two pair stout, heavy-soled shoes; one pair canvas leggins [sic]; medium-weight underwear; a jacket, golf cape or wrap; a common shawl or blanket for shawl use; a soft felt hat; a heavy veil; two or three pair gloves; one pair extra heavy gloves; several outing flannel shirt waists; one leather belt; handkerchiefs, hosiery, neckwear, etc., etc., as suits the individual fancy. Also take a stick of camphor ice in case of chapped lips—and on account of the bright sun a pair of blue, smoked or colored spectacles often adds to one's comfort.

A last-minute caveat for females: "Don't forget your sewing bag."[42]

In a sense, such campers' manuals provided environmental information and education. People who had not seen the great outdoors for themselves had little personal interest in, or understanding of, the need for such entities as national parks. Getting travelers into the environment was a first step; helping them enjoy the experience a second step; getting them to understand environmental needs a third.

For instance, as a growing number of women descended along Hance's Trail into the Grand Canyon, many of them expressed the sentiment that the area should be a national park. As early as 1891, European women visited the canyon as part of the International Geological Congress. Two years later, Arizona preservationist Sharlot Hall made her way down Hance's route. In 1895, a bicycle party that included women made the journey.[43] These are just a few of the women tourists who returned to their institutions, agencies, or clubs with the conservation message.

Still other women kept journals, made drawings or took photographs, and told stories of their travel experiences in such a magical place as Yosemite. Although they might have been naive enough during the 1890s or early 1900s to bring home a piece of a California redwood tree or a rock from Yosemite's Inspiration Point, they also assured others that only in "wild" western nature could one find "Tongues in trees, books in running brooks, Sermons in stones, and good in everything."[44]

These women went back to their clubs with renewed enthusiasm for conservation mandates, sponsored environmental education programs, and lobbied for the establishment of additional national parks. In particular, in 1911 women's tourism and its far-reaching effects helped the establishment of Glacier National Park, which, in its first year of operation, proved itself a major western resource by attracting some 4,000 visitors. This figure rose to over 15,000 in 1917, to nearly 20,000 in 1921, and to over 63,000 in 1941.[45]

In turn, national park promoters appealed to female tourists, including single women. A 1922 Yosemite leaflet assured "women guests" that "thousands of women annually visit Yosemite National Park and enjoy Yosemite Tours without escort." The flier added, "Do not hesitate about coming to Yosemite alone." A mid 1930s Estes Park brochure went so far as to picture women riding horseback, playing tennis, and hiking. In one illustration a woman wearing jodhpurs and a shirt stood admiring the scene, while a man knelt by the campfire cooking.[46]

Whatever women wanted, from a rustic hotel to feminist freedoms, park officials appeared increasingly willing to give. In return, park boards hoped for expanded usage and continued support from women.

•

Besides national park advertising, the western tourist industry in general wooed women travelers. American entrepreneurs quickly perceived the benefit of encouraging female tourism. From railroad companies to such investors as Fred Harvey to dude ranches, entrepreneurs modified tourism—and the western landscape—to fit women's wants and needs.

As early as the 1880s, the Chicago and North Western Railway emphasized that the West was changing. Such states as Minnesota had made the transition from isolated lumber and hunting camps to an "enchanted summer land," compete with resorts designed to relieve fatigue and stress. In fact, the West was now not only welcoming but female; it offered the "queen" of mineral waters, the "queen" of resorts, the "queen" of lakes.[47]

Brochures and other advertising utilized female images. In 1910, the Southern Pacific Railroad issued a slick pamphlet clearly aimed at middle- and upper-class tourists. On the full-color cover a woman in a hat and long skirt stood on the seashore gathering lush yellow flowers. In the background, a black-robed priest ambled under the ruins of a Spanish mission, while lazy white sails dotted the horizon. Within the pamphlet's pages, photographs showed long-skirted women strolling on docks, picnicking, and golfing.[48]

One could reach such hospitable landscapes simply by boarding the latest in touring and sleeping cars. By the early 1930s, railroad companies, now challenged by automobiles for tourist business, claimed to offer the fastest and most carefree travel available. The Union Pacific Railroad even supplied new observation cars with leaded glass windows, drapes, and original paintings. Oddly enough, seats faced the interior of the car so that passengers viewed each other instead of the scenery passing outside the windows. For costs of travel one had to mail the coupon in to the Union Pacific agent in Omaha, but the brochure assured "the same as, or less rate than a similar vacation taken by any other means."[49]

Further revising and sanitizing of western landscapes came from such individual entrepreneurs as Fred Harvey, who helped "civilize" railroad travel. During the 1880s, his company—which called its employees "excursion agents"—organized tours that offered "dining cars" and "eating houses along the line," or advised travelers to bring their own blankets, pillows, towels, and lunch baskets. Female travelers who wanted to bring trunks full of long skirts, corsets, and other sartorial finery had no problem; each full ticket entitled its bearer to one hundred and fifty pounds of luggage checked through to the final destination.[50]

As travel changed, so did Fred Harvey and Company. Employing a fleet of pink-cheeked young women, the company soon provided everything from restaurants to resorts. When automobiles revolutionized travel, Harveycars offered motor drives, Indian detours, and motor cruises. The company maintained that the automobile had "let down the last barriers of time and distance, discomfort and inconvenience" for the tourist. Harveycars' all-female Courier Corps consisted of "young women, attractive and refined," who wore "outing uniforms" set off by Navajo jewelry. The women, who served as hostesses as well as guides, were well informed and even had established "friendships with representative Indians in many pueblos."[51]

What did Fred Harvey's schemes mean to women? Clearly, Harvey and Company offered employment and travel opportunities to many women who would otherwise have gone without. For women tourists, the company supplied a nonthreatening travel experience that allowed women to experience western nature and perhaps develop some stake in its future. Although it was not what Harvey and Company intended, its tours also alerted many women to the plight of the western environment. During the early 1900s, former Harvey Girl and Arizona club woman Amy Cornwall Neal helped establish the Mohave Museum of History and Art to preserve local lands, art, and culture.[52]

Of course, Fred Harvey did not have the field to himself. Hundreds of other tour companies not only supplied travel packages but shaped them to suit women tourists. During the 1920s, Arizona Wonder Circuit Tours made available a "carpeted and cushioned" Wonderbus along either a southern or a northern loop. A guide, driver, cook, and supply car were part of the deal. The travelers inhabited the back of the bus—a kitchen, bathroom, sleeping quarters, and living room outfitted with window screens, closets, a writing table, four wicker chairs, reading lights, a radio, electric fan, and "sundry other gadgets."[53]

Other entrepreneurs bought up portions of western landscapes and opened them to tourists. In Manitou, Colorado, a private company purchased the Cave of the Winds, built a "beautiful scenic auto road" to the cave, provided a guide, and charged $1.00 for admission. Other individuals bought, or already owned, picturesque spots that they turned into a particularly western phenomenon—dude ranches or resorts. As a Northern Pacific Railroad brochure put it, "Deep-rooted in the heart of every man, woman and child is a strong desire to be a part of the healthy, free, interesting life of a western ranch."[54]

In such controlled and supervised settings, couples and families could enjoy a "wilderness" vacation together. Husbands ventured out from camp on packing and hunting expeditions, while wives savored such in-camp activities as riding and fishing. Or men and women might pack and hunt together. At the Bar BC Ranch in Victor, Idaho, a married couple could even save money by sharing one big-game hunting guide.[55]

Dude ranch advertising leaflets indicate that these venues provided the most freeing travel experience to women. The evolution of the opportunities that dude ranching offered women proceeded rapidly. In 1913, the Frost and Richards Ranch in Wyoming had liberal policies for the era. Women set off for Yellowstone riding sidesaddle and wearing white shirtwaists, dark ties, ankle-length skirts, and straw skimmers. For swimming, women donned a dark dress with a full skirt reaching below the knees, tied decorative scarves around their necks, and finished off the outfit with dark hose and white shoes. Pompadour hairdos were the norm for women. Only men, who also dressed formally, were allowed to hunt.[56]

By the early 1920s, however, similar brochures advised women to bring limited clothing besides a felt hat, a neckerchief, a riding suit with breeches or a divided skirt, a raincoat, heavy boots, a sweater, a coat, wool stockings, and a bathing suit. "Any clothes will do," women were told, "provided they are sufficiently old, and comfortable." Women, who were assigned their own horses and saddles, could ride astride, hunt, shoot, and participate in back-country pack trips.[57]

By the mid 1920s, women dude ranchers routinely wore trousers or breeches, white men's-style shirts, vests, loose ties, and cloche hats. They held their own horses, wielded rifles, fished, and packed into the backcountry. In 1928, one guest ranch assured its female guests, "There is little style about a guest ranch and the atmosphere is essentially democratic." Women could avoid numerous changes of clothing; they needed only riding suits, riding boots, walking skirts, and other outdoor clothing.[58]

During the 1930s, dude ranches relaxed even more. The Four Bear Ranch near Cody, Wyoming, proclaimed itself "distinctively western and democratic." It recommended riding breeches, flannel shirts, western hats, warm hose, sturdy boots, slickers, leather jackets, and sweaters for both its male and female guests. The Pierson Dude Ranch in Del Piedra, California, suggested "breeches or frontier pants for women." By the end of the decade, a resort near Santa Fe, New Mexico, issued a pamphlet picturing women guests wearing shorts and playing cards with men.[59]

Obviously, western dude ranches offered women certain freedoms and also provided the opportunity to relax in a protected atmosphere. Women dude ranchers might, for example, choose exclusively female resorts. The LX-Bar Ranch of Hayden, Colorado, offered fishing, riding, and cattle drives. Owned by two women, one a Wellesley graduate and the other from Vassar, the LX-Bar listed among its staff experienced cowboys as well as "lady dude wranglers" who added "final touches" to picnic lunches and saw to it that "no one is lonely or over-tired."[60]

Whether at a gender-specific or an integrated resort, one could almost certainly stay within the bounds of his or her social class. One pamphlet assured its readers that at dude ranches a guest would find "the sort of people most desirable—business and professional men, artists, and men and women of letters . . . college folk . . . women and children."[61]

Even though western dude ranches and resorts sound like co-coons that could not possibly have forced anyone to think about environmental needs, they were successful in doing so. In 1926, the Dude Ranch Association was organized and quickly proved an active force in the conservation movement. In addition, individual facilities promoted environmental policies. Using a velvet touch and a subtle approach, numerous dude ranch owners informed their guests of environmental issues. At Wyoming's Valley Ranch during the 1930s, owners Larry and Irma Larcom urged visitors to enjoy nature, while observing the Larcoms' techniques of land preservation, controlled hunting, and protection of game.[62] Thus, the woman guest who proudly posed for a photograph holding her day's catch, a string of fish, might also return home to urge her club colleagues to undertake a conservation project or join in lobbying for the establishment of a national park.

•

American women travelers and tourists had an unrecognized impact on people's attitudes toward the future of western landscapes. In her day, the writings of traveler and writer Margaret Long received positive reviews and sold widely. In addition, the work of one of her favorite authors, Edna Brush Perkins, who published *The White Heart of the Mohave* in 1922, garnered such praise as "full of the atmosphere of the real desert."[63] Yet, environmental historians and other scholars generally overlook such women's influence on people's attitudes toward western lands and resources.

Why? Partly because during the 1950s and early 1960s, standards of criticism changed. Desert bibliographer E. I. Edwards condemned Perkins's book as "relatively trivial experiences and impressions." True, she was capable of turning an abstract "feminine" phrase that might raise some readers' ire. Perkins believed that the White Heart might be not only the climax of the Mojave Desert but also the ultimate experience of the outdoors: "We were going on a pilgrimage to that!" Edwards expressed far more approval of Long's "scientific" approach, which produced an "orderly and meticulous" book. He declared Long's treatise "carefully-written and authentic."[64]

Despite Edwards's endorsement, Long's book, along with Perkins's book, gradually slipped into the shadows of history, partly because women's experiences aroused little interest. Soon, dozens of books replaced those by Long and Perkins on Death Valley and the "forty-niners" who traversed it, most of which slighted women's observations and experiences. In those books that covered the "forty-niners," for example, just four women received any attention to speak of: Juliet Brier, Sarah Bennett, and Sarah's daughters, Melissa and Martha.

Only in the late 1980s and 1990s have scholars enlarged the number of female names in desert history and historiography, resulting in the reprinting of some of the writings of Perkins and Long. As the pendulum swings toward an appreciation of women travelers and tourists, it is time to recognize them as a source of energy and an impetus for the conservation movement between 1870 and 1940.

These women helped authenticate the West as a real and often glorious place, encouraged hundreds of others to follow their westward footsteps, helped identify the West with improved health, and assured a growing number of feminists that western travel would offer them certain freedoms unknown at home. In effect, women travelers and tourists recruited potential supporters for the conservation ethic.

Moreover, numerous women travelers and tourists developed into outspoken environmental proponents themselves. Because of their experiences in the West, they came to advocate environmentalism. Even finding oneself caught on the horns of a dilemma, such as Margaret Long's discovery that increased travel in the West led to beer bottles and car races, could cause a woman to renew her dedication to environmental reform.

Such women represented huge numbers. Because of their crucial impact on others, they can no longer be dismissed.

9

Beyond the Land

When contemporary Americans hear the phrase "conservation movement" or the word "environmentalism," they tend to think of land and its natural resources. For nineteenth- and early twentieth-century women, however, these terms implied far more than that. Although "conservationism" is not widely used in contemporary literature, conservation certainly became an "ism," or comprehensive philosophy, for many women. Because women accepted society's charge that they serve as "natural conservators" of family, society, nature, and life itself, many enlarged their environmental ideas into a truly encompassing ideal that included native peoples living on the land as well as historic structures.[1]

Even though one does not usually think of human beings as an object of conservation, by the late nineteenth century female environmentalists had added American Indians to their roster of causes. Unlike contemporary Americans, most late nineteenth- and early twentieth-century women would not have found the idea of "preserving" human groups an anomaly. They seemed as determined to protect the endangered Indians as California's redwoods.

This occurred, in part, because many women thought of native peoples as genuine and pure, or even as earthy and rustic, as was nature itself. Many also believed that Native Americans, as well as Hispanics, understood western landscapes. From deserts to forests, these people preserved age-old knowledge that could help all people live in harmony with their environment. Women environmentalists felt that if native cultures were destroyed, such understanding would be lost forever.

As a result, nineteenth-century white women often included people, notably American Indians, in their definition of nature. Consequently, just as they opposed the exploitation of such elements of nature as mountains or rivers, they also resisted the exploitation of people. After the Civil War, numerous white women blamed men for damaging native cultures. They especially maintained that men should stop seizing native lands, for such unfair appropriations condemned native inhabitants to a life of poverty and virtual homelessness. At the height of westward expansion—with its accompanying disparagement and removal of Native Americans—this would hardly have been a widely popular sentiment.[2]

Also, the more women environmentalists emphasized the preservation of native peoples and their cultures, the more these women found themselves embroiled in an escalating national debate regarding the path Indian reform should follow. By the early 1900s, a rhetoric of Indian reform developed, and suggested remedies multiplied. Confusion reigned. Should Indians' original heritage be restored, or should welfare programs be the order of the day? Or, one skeptical woman asked, was the Indian already what she termed "the favored child" of the nation?[3]

For women environmentalists, "Indian reform" held a number of perplexities. For one, numerous adult Indian women already lived close to nature. Although it is impossible to categorize all Indian women as having the same beliefs and experiences, Pretty-Shield, a Crow medicine woman born in 1850, indicated that she, at least, spent most of her life in close communion with birds, animals, and other aspects of the environment.[4]

Another paradox was that women environmentalists frequently participated in education programs for native youth. Thus, they wrested young Indians away from nature by forcing them into white-style classrooms and dormitories.[5]

The lack of evidence suggests that few women environmentalists examined—or perhaps even recognized—such dilemmas. As a result, the Indian "problem" grew more complicated, while much of the public discussion about it was based on a white worldview. When people asked for Native American ideas, they heard about

Indian nationalism, American citizenship for native peoples, or the desire simply to be left alone to live according to native cultures.[6]

In 1924, nature writer and Indian reformer Mary Austin tackled some of the issues. She especially attempted to clarify the connection between Native Americans and environmental programs. Austin wrote that an important factor "that the Indian Bureau has utterly failed to reckon with is the rapidly growing appreciation of such Indian culture as remain to us, as a National Asset, having something [of] the same valuation as the big trees of California and the geysers and buffaloes of Yellowstone."[7]

Austin's concept that the American public had a stake in American Indian cultures explains the notion of preserving native peoples and their ways. Americans believed they "owned" Indians as an important part of American history and the nation's environment. As a result, it was incumbent upon conservators of American society—women—to preserve not only Indians but perhaps people of Spanish heritage as well.

Of course, not all women who tried to protect Indians did so because of environmental values. Clearly, Congregationalist missionary Mary C. Collins had religious motivations for her work with the Sioux in South Dakota between 1895 and 1910. Also, groups like the Women's Baptist Home Mission Society and the Women's National Indian Association had a strong missionary bent.[8]

Many women reformers, too, had a specific goal in mind, that of "civilizing" Indians into pseudo-whites. A New Mexico field matron admitted that Indians "are learning fast," but she recommended that it was best to relocate young Indian children from their families to boarding schools, for the young "do not have so much to unlearn." Sarah E. Abbott, who labored with native people at First Mesa, Arizona, during the early 1900s, was less hopeful. She lamented that, despite her efforts, the "people of Hotevilla still maintain the same obstinate determination to go their own way."[9]

But numerous other women reformers gradually came to recognize the importance of native cultures and their preservation for future generations of Americans. Such women as Elaine Goodale Eastman, who taught botany to Sioux Indians in Dakota Territory during the 1880s, advocated a thorough rethinking of the so-called Indian question.[10]

Far less embattled an issue was the saving of historic sites. Many women agreed that historic aspects of the built environment must be saved. Fortunately for historic preservationists, the American public's growing thirst for knowledge of its past abetted their efforts.

Entrepreneurs also saw advantages in historic preservation. In particular, railroad companies were quick to exploit the growing interest in historic sites. One focus was California's Rancho Guajome, purported in 1894 to be the real home of Helen Hunt Jackson's character in her best-selling novel, *Ramona*. Based on an actual person, Jackson's Ramona reportedly lived near the San Luis Rey Mission. But in 1903, others thought Ramona probably came from the Camulos Ranch in the Santa Clara Valley. The Santa Fe Railroad happily serviced the Rancho Guajome site, whereas the Southern Pacific took passengers to the Camulos Ranch.[11]

Meanwhile, some women purchased and converted into resorts such places as the Gold Hill Hotel in the old mining town of Gold Hill, Nevada. Subsequently, additional preservation-oriented women bought and restored homes and businesses in Gold Hill, making the area a summer tourist attraction.[12]

As a result, a growing number of tourist maps listed historic sites as part of the western "landscape" that every traveler should see. By 1920, California's Mount Shasta and its Lassen, Yosemite, and Sequoia National Parks were conflated with Spanish missions and even Hollywood. As the automobile freed people to probe every aspect of urban and rural environments, folks wanted to see it all: Indian villages, Spanish missions, the Wild West, parks, and mountains.[13]

•

Of the various types of women environmentalists, women nature writers showed great interest in native cultures. In a quest to understand the means by which people learned to live in peace with such western areas as deserts and mountains, women nature writers and poets often studied Native American, and sometimes

Hispanic, peoples. They gradually came to the conclusion that the wisdom of native peoples, like western landscapes, was endangered. Because women typically envisioned the land and its peoples as a unified whole, women writers called for the preservation of indigenous inhabitants as well as what such people had learned about the environment.

The best known volume about Native Americans was Helen Hunt Jackson's *Ramona*. Although born in Massachusetts, Jackson moved west during the late 1860s and became sympathetic to the situation of Native Americans. In 1879, she visited Boston and heard Standing Bear, a Ponca leader, speak on behalf of his people. For the last six years of her life, Jackson devoted herself to the cause of Native American preservation. Her *Century of Dishonor* (1881) exposed the U.S. government's treatment of American Indians, while *Ramona* (1884) told a romantic tale of a young woman who defied her family by marrying a native man. Jackson also chronicled the theft and misuse of Indian lands in *Ramona*, but the love story overshadowed this message. Although the book became wildly popular, it failed to achieve Jackson's purpose.[14]

During the late nineteenth and early twentieth centuries, Marah Ellis Ryan took a wider view. She published idealized tales of southwestern Indians and of *Californios*, including *Indian Love Letters* (1907) and *The Flute of the Gods* (1909). Like Jackson, Ryan aimed for accuracy in her depiction of religious practices and beliefs, and she pointed out the need to preserve native cultures before they disappeared entirely.[15]

Farther west in Hawaii, Martha Warren Beckwith, who received a doctorate from Columbia University in 1918, distinguished herself for her work on the islands' native peoples. Her first book, *The Hawaiian Romance of Laicikawai*, appeared in 1919. Others followed, including her landmark work, *Hawaiian Mythology*, in 1940. Working from headquarters in the Bernice Pauahi Bishop Museum in Honolulu, Beckwith showed great respect for Hawaiian traditions, even learning to read the language like a native.[16]

Writer Mary Austin also became deeply interested in the situation of native groups and outlined meaningful goals for preserving Indian civilization. She believed that a combination of public health programs, education, and enlightened officials who recognized that "Indians do not belong to them, but to us" would be a "starter" for a new policy.[17]

To help bring about such objectives, Austin studied American Indian cultures and blended them into her writing about the Southwest. Although she was a realist who saw the harshness of the desert and the hard life it provided its inhabitants, Austin also wove people and land into an appealing tapestry. In her *Land of Journey's Ending* (1924), for example, she portrayed the area between the Rio Grande and the Rio Colorado as a place where plants, animals, and humans adapted to climatic and topographical "peculiarities and fashioned for themselves features, habits, and forms of living, suited to their environment." To Austin, Native Americans treated the Southwest as sacred ground, a view far superior to white men's concept of land as an exploitable resource.[18]

Austin's insightful essays also urged the recording of native southwestern history and culture. These included the creations of American Indian storytellers and poets, whom she considered a "neglected race of artists." Moreover, Austin tied both Indian and Hispanic stories and verse to the landscape. Through folk tales and arts, she believed, people could experience the environment and learn its secrets.[19]

Austin portrayed Indians for young readers as well as for adults. Like English women writers, she saw the importance of shaping children's views early in life. Thus, she appealed to children in such works as *The Basket Woman* (1904) and *Children Sing in the Far West* (1928). For adults, Austin collected almost forty Indian tales and legends in *One Smoke Stories* (1934), many of which concerned native women, so these stories were often left out of collections of Indian lore.

Whether writing for children or adults, Austin always included environmental messages. In *The American Rhythm* (1923 and 1930), she maintained that climate and environment created the religion, philosophy, habits, stature, and appearance of American Indians. Austin declared that the loss of native knowledge of the land would prove perilous to whites who wanted to live on the land without altering it unduly.[20]

During the 1930s, Ann Nolan Clark picked up where Austin left off. While working as a teacher and administrator for the Bureau of Indian Affairs, Clark wrote many articles, especially for *New Mexico Magazine*. She took as her topic the dilemma of the Navajos of New Mexico caught between cultures. As a teacher in a large Indian boarding school, she "saw something awful happening to Indian children." In her judgment, assimilating native children into "American" culture destroyed ancient cultural patterns and an ability to live harmoniously with New Mexico's natural environment.[21]

To help remedy the situation, Clark also wrote books for children, especially Indian boys and girls. Her works included a geography book and poetry reflecting the lives and beliefs of native children. In her poems, respect for the natural environment held a central place, as shown in this excerpt from "Fields":

> Brown fields,
> With ground all broken,
> I walk softly over you.
> I would not hurt you,
> While you keep
> The baby corn seeds sleeping
> See, brown fields,
> The sun will shine for you;
> The sun will warm you,
> And make you happy.

Because Clark's poems caught the attention of the American public, they appeared in book form in 1941. Although she did not write during the World War II years, Clark produced many books later in her life. She was also an active club woman in Santa Fe and a popular speaker who always emphasized the importance of preserving Indian cultures.[22]

Predictably, women's writings about native peoples produced contradictory results. From the white point of view, women writers drew public attention to the Indians' situation and recorded valuable information. From the Native American perspective, however, such attention was not always welcome. Between 1910 and 1930, Sioux writer and reformer Zitkala-Ša, also known as Gertrude Bonnin, argued that Indians had needs that whites were unwilling to fulfill, including respect and American citizenship. Other native women harbored unhappy memories of Indian schools that wrenched them away from parents and siblings and of prejudicial treatment by Anglos.[23]

Still, if women writers had ignored native peoples, some of these problems might have gone unnoticed. As painful as it was, women's writings brought to the American public's attention a number of serious predicaments endured by peoples living in the western environment. Furthermore, women's writings helped preserve native environmental practices and attitudes.

•

Besides writers, women visual image-makers soon became interested in native peoples as well. Because American female artists and photographers seemed incapable of exploring just landscapes, they turned their easels and lenses toward indigenous western peoples, especially American Indians and, to a lesser extent, Hispanics. More than men, women envisioned a future in which both the land and its peoples had to be preserved. Thus, they painted and photographed western peoples to conserve native cultures and ways of life, as well as to show the harmony between landscape and its inhabitants.[24]

Women's paintings of Indians not only disputed old stereotypes but also emphasized women and children, family life, and the interaction between individuals and nature. Such work enjoyed wide dissemination. Beginning in 1889, Californian Grace Carpenter Hudson reaped awards, and subsequent sales to such major collections as the National Gallery in Washington DC and the Royal Gallery in London, for her compassionate and astute studies of Mendocino County's Pomo Indians.[25]

Photographers soon recognized opportunities in portraying the West's native peoples. A significant number of women photographers attempted to depict Indians in the context of their environments. As early as 1905, Mrs. Edward H. Kemp and her husband journeyed into California's Mojave Desert, New Mexico's mesas, and Colorado to photograph the Hopis and Navajos. Later, the Kemps showed their colored stereoptican images at San Francisco's Orpheum Theater. The program, the content of which ranged from the Grand Canyon to the Mojave Desert, concluded with Navajo snake dances. Although her work respected Indian cultures, Kemp unwittingly conflated some native ceremonials with theater. According to one reviewer, "No stage setting could be made half so spectacular, with the high walls of the canyon about us and with other camp fires above and below."[26]

At the same time, Arizonan Kate Thompson Cory lived with and photographed the Hopi people in a way that revealed their grace and dignity. Rather than warriors, the Hopis in Cory's photographs were village folk living their daily lives and surviving as best they could, given a challenging environment and a limited amount of land. One critic remarked that Cory's work was the result of personal "trust" that she established between herself and the Hopis during seven years of living in the villages of Oraibi and Walpi between 1905 and 1912. Even Hopi men, who excluded their own women from certain ceremonies, invited Cory into their kivas, or chambers.[27]

Was Cory's success with the Hopis a consequence of her gender? In 1924, Mildred Ring, who photographed American Indians living in the Klamath River area of northern California, would have said yes. Ring maintained that she raised less suspicion among her subjects because she was a woman. Native Americans, who wanted little more than a sympathetic portrayal, believed she was capable of giving it. Laura Gilpin, however, who photographed southwestern landscapes and peoples during the 1920s and later, would have disagreed. "Either you're a good photographer or you're not," Gilpin declared. She believed that her knowledge and love of the Navajo people had far more impact than her gender.[28]

Unfortunately, some women photographers were not as sincere as Cory and Gilpin. They responded to the temptations of commercial gain. During the early 1900s, Emma Belle Freeman specialized in romanticized portraits of Indians in northern California and even became an official U.S. government photographer. Free-man, who had a sales room in San Francisco, had her photograph taken dressed as a Yurok Indian. In 1917, she reportedly said, "I love my Indians."[29]

Meanwhile, Kodak and Brownie cameras became so convenient and relatively inexpensive that Indians had a difficult time escaping photographers. Few whites asked permission from their subjects or understood that many Native Americans believed that the reproduction of their images on paper would lead to death. Worse yet, numerous photographers grabbed the expected view and thus produced stereotypical images.

Still, women artists and photographers introduced a slightly different perception than the standard male view of American Indians to a widely varied viewing public. During the 1920s, Kathryn Woodman Leighton sold her perceptive paintings of the Blackfoot Indians, including children and families, in Glacier National Park to the Great Northern Railroad as well as to a Paris art critic.[30]

Similarly, Laura Gilpin, who sold her work to the Library of Congress during the 1920s and 1930s, produced a lecture set of seventy lantern slides during the early 1930s and took photographs of the Pueblo people for a 1941 book, characterized Native Americans as likeable, even endearing, human beings. In addition, Gilpin often saw things others missed. Although other photographers passed by a remarkable petroglyph, probably the only portrayal of the Indian creation figure Changing Woman, Gilpin spotted it. Later, Navajo Dam submerged the petroglyph under water, so Gilpin's photograph remains the only extant record.[31]

The work of Gilpin and others reflected an interest in the domestic, the daily, the "real" American Indian behind the stereotype. Although tinged with placid romanticism and perhaps even tranquil pictorialism, such portrayals did preserve aspects of native cultures. Moreover, these representations of American Indians presented the public with the image of Indians as "deserving" of conservation, rather than the stereotype of fierce, threatening Indians who, in many people's minds, seemed to warrant extinction.

At the same time, such artists as Eva Scott Fenyes, Euphenia Charlton Fortune, and Mary de Neale Morgan captured Spanish missions and other historic sites in their paintings. Sculptor Maud Maple Miles even crafted a series of panels that were installed along the Santa Fe Trail.[32]

Others combined an interest in American Indians with enthusiasm for historic sites. Landscape architect Mary Elizabeth Jane Colter admired and respected the work of Indian artists. In 1923 in the El Navajo's Lodge at the Grand Canyon, she received permission from Indians to use their art, including sand paintings, which were traditionally reserved for ceremonial use rather than public viewing. Colter demanded that the sand paintings be authentic, for she intended to preserve the art for future generations.[33]

Colter was also a historic preservationist. She saved both the first post office at the Grand Canyon from destruction by converting it into one of Bright Angel Lodge's cabins and a former Rough Rider's cabin by incorporating it into a seventeen-room lodge bearing the man's name.[34]

Routinely, Colter studied the history and culture of places in which she was to build. West of Grand Canyon's Watchtower, built in 1932, Colter constructed a "ruin" so visitors would understand the actual condition of most native buildings and the sites on which archaeologists worked. The Watchtower itself was what Colter termed a re-creation rather than a replica. Made with specially selected natural stones, the Watchtower included genuine petroglyphs and provided a huge observation room that gave visitors a splendid perspective on the Grand Canyon.[35]

·

Club women, too, contributed much to the saving of native cultures and the built environment. In 1924, Mary Austin declared that "public consciousness" regarding Indians was growing, thanks in part to the women's club movement, composed of the "better educated half of such American women as have been accustomed to use their leisure for purposes of public and personal improvement."[36]

During the 1920s, for example, the Utah Federation of Women's Clubs expressed deep interest in the welfare of American Indians, especially those living on the Goshute Reservation at Ibapah. Club women helped alleviate the Indians' poor standard of living and lobbied the Bureau of Indian Affairs in Washington DC for reform. In the case of the Goshute Reservation, women achieved the arrest and conviction of a corrupt Indian agent and his wife as well as the dismissal of an inept teacher.[37]

Other club women collected and preserved Indian artifacts, which often became the basis for museums. In Arizona, philanthropist and club woman Maie Bartlett Heard assembled a fine collection of primitive art, including Hohokam artifacts, which became the Heard Museum in 1929.[38]

At the same time, numerous other club women focused their efforts on rescuing and restoring historic features of the built environment. During the early 1900s, the California Federation of Women's Clubs launched a campaign to save natural and historic sites across the state. These spots ranged from Long Beach's Signal Hill to Mount Saint Helena at the head of Napa Valley. California club women also recognized the importance of preserving such Hispanic sites as the original Monterey, General M. G. Vallejo's "Old Adobe" in Petaluma County, and two ancient palm trees planted at a Spanish mission outside San Diego.[39]

During this era, historic preservation came to the attention of women's clubs in all parts of the West. In Kansas during the early 1800s, Grace Meeker campaigned for markers along the Santa Fe Trail. During the early 1900s in Hawaii, club woman Elizabeth Carter Bogardus lobbied for the preservation of the Queen Emma Summer Palace in Honolulu and Hulihee Palace in Kailua Kona.[40]

Later, during the 1930s, Reno's Alice Baltzell Addenbrooke urged the Nevada legislature to save a historic home, Bowers Mansion, near Franktown, and succeeded in preserving the Fort Churchill ruins. Meanwhile, Denver's Caroline Bancroft preserved aspects of Colorado's built environment, including the grave of former slave Jennie Golden near Blackhawk.[41]

•

Perhaps the women who made the most critical difference to the preservation of Indian cultures, however, were individual activists, especially scholars. Following the lead of such English women intellectuals as Mary Wollstonecraft and Beatrice Webb, who probed the broader human meanings of environmental ethics, American female scholars, including anthropologists, archaeologists, ethnologists, and ethnobotanists, concerned themselves with western peoples.

Quietly and without fanfare, these women did the field work that retrieved bits and pieces of native cultures and ways of life. Because they were female, these investigators had an interest in family, kin, children, and household practices. They asked unusual questions, collected atypical artifacts, and unearthed and preserved a part of Indian life previously overlooked.

One of the earliest was ethnobotanist Matilda Coxe Evans Stevenson, a transplanted Texan who accompanied her husband on U.S. geological surveys during the late 1870s and early 1880s. In 1883, Stevenson was the first to report on Zuñi children for the Bureau of American Ethnology. Two years later, she founded and served as the initial president of the Women's Anthropological Society. After her husband's death in 1888, she enlarged her investigation of western pueblos, especially Zuñi, which culminated in a massive study released in 1904. Stevenson was also one of the first to argue for the integrity of native cultures rather than the imposition of white ways. In her later years, Stevenson lived among the Tewa Indians near New Mexico's San Ildefonso pueblo.[42]

Later, dedicated club woman and Indian reformer Alice Cunningham Fletcher studied western Indians. Although her home was in New York, she conducted research among Nebraska's Omaha Indians, where she lived in their tepees and ate their inadequate diet. After Fletcher involved herself in controversy by vowing to save the Omahas' endangered lands, she wrote in 1894, "I felt that I had found the work which the Creator intended me to do." She also studied the Omahas and collected native artifacts. Her massive study, *The Omaha Tribe*, appeared in 1911.[43]

Both amateur and professional women ethnologists and ethnobotanists increased in number during the early twentieth century. In Arizona, an Indian agent's wife, Louisa Wetherill, researched Navajo blanket designs, translated native legends and songs, collected herbs and sand paintings, and identified fifty-six clans. Besides preserving Navajo culture, Wetherill, who spoke Navajo, served for nearly twenty years during the early 1900s as intermediary between the Bureau of Indian Affairs and Navajo leaders.[44]

In Nevada, ethnobotanist Edith Van Allen Murphey worked on Indian reservations in the intermountain area during the late 1930s and early 1940s. She studied Indian food, medicine, and stock-poisoning plants. She also researched the Nevada "Grass Tribes," who lived in areas of Indian rice grass, or *wey*, as the Indians called it. Murphey argued that this grass, which provided the best stock feed in Nevada, should be conserved through regulated consumption and replanting.[45]

Women archaeologists also worked in the field throughout the West. In 1931, New Mexican Ruth Laughlin published *Caballeros,* which incorporated years of archaeological work with American Indians. During the 1920s and 1930s, University of Arizona archaeologist Clara Lee Fraps Tanner excavated Hopi ruins. Many of the artifacts unearthed by these investigators found a home in such institutions as the Museum of New Mexico and Museum of American Archaeology at Santa Fe.[46]

In addition, women anthropologists working in the Southwest made important contributions. The names Elsie Clews Parsons, who wrote about Pueblo mothers and their children in New Mexico and Arizona, and Ruth Underhill, who studied Papago Indians, are well known. During the 1930s, often with support from the New Deal's Works Progress Administration, Underhill and others researched Pima and other Indians and wrote numerous reports.[47]

But hundreds of other anthropologists are virtually forgotten. Among the lesser known were Sophie B. D. Aberle, Florence Hawley Ellis, and Gladys A. Reichard. During the 1930s, anthropologist and physician Sophie Aberle served as superintendent of the United Pueblos Agency of the U.S. Indian Service. Living in Albuquerque, Aberle also directed the work of the Commission on the Rights, Liberties and Responsibilities of the American Indian. Meanwhile, University of New Mexico professor Florence Ellis began anthropological investigative work and archaeological digs in

Chaco Canyon, and in 1939, Gladys Reichard's *Dezba: Woman of the Desert* revealed the author's sixteen years of experiences as an anthropologist among Navajo peoples.[48]

There were scores of others; women who labored among the Indians and argued for their "conservation." In reports, articles, books, and speeches, women concerned about American Indians tried hard to succor, educate, and "preserve" them, often with mixed results.[49]

•

As one might expect, travelers and tourists showed great interest in the American West's native peoples and historic sites. Many felt a sense of obligation to learn about, and preserve, both human cultures and historic sites. As a result, travelers and tourists sought out native peoples and historic structures, displaying in the process everything from intrusive curiosity to enlightened observation.

They soon discovered that not all native westerners welcomed such incursions. During the 1870s, incidents occurred where Indians attacked tourists in such places as Yellowstone National Park, which became the first national park in 1872. Native Americans apparently believed the "wilderness" belonged to them, while whites claimed it as their own.[50]

Gradually, the sheer numbers of tourists and the economic benefits they brought to western areas quelled most defiance. Even though many westerners distrusted and disdained the tourists who flocked over their fields, congested their roads, and pulled fish from their mountain streams, they also realized the economic boon tourism brought to the West.[51]

Perhaps Indians resisted because they foresaw what was in store for them. As automobiles grew in numbers and efficiency, it became possible for tourists to view Indians close up. During the 1920s, Harveycars of Santa Fe offered an "Indian Detour" itinerary. Fred Harvey and Company utilized a fleet of touring cars to help tourists "feel the lure of the real Southwest that lies beyond the pinched horizons of your train window." The company chose to send women as female "couriers" or guides with every party. These women provided "interesting and authentic information on the archaeological and ethnological history of the Southwest."[52]

Thus did Native American villages and reservations become transformed into tourist destinations. Although Hopi potter Nampey-o first marketed her distinctive wares through reservation trading posts, by the turn of the century she sold directly to tourists and collectors. During the early 1900s, she demonstrated her techniques at Fred Harvey's Hopi House in the Grand Canyon.[53] In this way, women like Nam-pey-o brought income into their villages and helped whites develop an appreciation of Indian arts.

Not all effects of increased tourism proved so beneficial, however. Tourism reshaped the human landscape of the West. It also created a need for preservation. Someone had to prevent unwitting tourists from destroying the remnants of native cultures. A woman on an 1871 outing recalled that when she found some poles from an "Indian wigwam," a friend suggested she take them home as "relics." She concluded they would make better fire wood and duly used them for that purpose, an action that would horrify proponents of preserving native cultures and artifacts. On another occasion, however, she followed English women's penchant for collecting specimens and artifacts. At an equally deserted encampment, she acquired what she called a "wigwam memento" from a structure adorned with deer horns and strips of buffalo skin.[54]

Tourism also revised cultural practices. Because travelers were awestruck when curious blanket-covered Native Americans crowded around the windows of their Ford or Buick touring cars, Indians who saw potential profit in the situation often adapted themselves to meet tourists' expectations.[55] These Indians assumed garish beaded outfits and performed "war" and "rain" dances.

Similarly, other groups of peoples made themselves, or found themselves made into, caricatures to attract the tourist dollar. Hispanic men wore exaggerated vaquero and gaucho apparel, while "señoritas" donned dramatic mantillas and petticoated skirts and, of course, tucked flowers behind their ears. In addition, "real" western cowboys affected high-heeled boots and jangling spurs, all to impress tourists.[56]

•

Obviously, women environmentalists' ideas about preserving native groups, as well as the built environment, had a dark underside. Because some women recognized the potential harm that could occur, they created innovative programs to prevent, or at least offset, the damage.

During the early 1900s, Arizona booster Grace M. Sparkes established and managed Prescott Frontier Days rodeo. She also helped raise funds for a first-class resort hotel. Working for the Yavapai County Chamber of Commerce, Sparkes helped define the terms "development" and "tourism" in Arizona.[57] She also had a strong environmentalist side, which she initially focused on Arizona Indians. In 1921, she helped organize the Smoki People of Prescott, a local group committed to the perpetuation of native cultures. With historic preservationist Sharlot Hall, Sparkes worked to establish a reservation for the Yavapai Indians near Prescott. During the 1930s, Sparkes campaigned for the addition of more land to Montezuma Castle National Monument. The following decade she sought a National Monument designation for the Coronado Entrada area in Cochise County.[58]

Gradually, Sparkes turned her attention to the natural landscape. On the one hand, she encouraged tourists to visit Verde Valley guest ranches, and she created such tourist activities as fairs and rodeos. On the other, Sparkes cooperated with the U.S. Park Service in the careful administration of such sites as Tuzigoot, initiated U.S. Forest Service programs in the country, and was the first to draw attention to the need for flood control and soil conservation districts.[59] Sparkes, and other women like her, maintained that tourism and environmentalism could work together.

Grace Sparkes was perhaps the embodiment of what a white woman environmentalist *should* be. She, and others like her, sought a way to combine increased usage with sound environmental and cultural values. That was, after all, the goal of the early women activists and social conservators who had developed environmentalism into a far-reaching philosophy that included American Indians and historic sites.

10

Since 1940

How have women environmentalists fared in the contemporary United States? Since 1940, although environmentalism in general took a backseat to such momentous questions as the Cold War and U.S. involvement in Vietnam, women's enthusiasm for conserving the environment has continued and even accelerated. Given the "back-to-the-home" movement that followed World War II, women's commitment is even more remarkable. Despite being told to return home and raise families, American women found ways to pursue both their volunteer efforts and professional involvement.

In spite of these developments, too many scholars continue to plod along the old, worn trail by omitting women from their accounts. Only a few include women environmentalists.[1] Although these same researchers are quick to recognize other important issues, such as the multiplication of conservation solutions and shifting societal attitudes toward wilderness, they tend to overlook women's roles. Whereas many go to great lengths to define such terms as "wilderness" and "conservation," they fail to explore the meaning of "gender." Even psychological studies and those claiming to be "state-of-knowledge" disregard women and the influence of gender.[2]

Not only do scholars and others ignore the environmental involvement of contemporary women, but most appear oblivious to the expanding role of women of color. Although democratic principles have been slow to infiltrate the environmental movement,[3] race no longer constitutes the obstruction it once did. As a result, even though women of color still focus much energy on race-related issues, a growing number also manifest an accelerating environmental awareness.

Women of color have special stakes in environmental reform. In California, for example, because of the location of toxic waste plants near their neighborhoods, people of color experience more toxic contamination than whites. On an entirely different front, such sports as skiing remain hostile to athletes of color, denying them access to a certain part of the western environment.[4]

Besides expressing concern about such specific issues, women of color are raising larger questions. A contemporary Hispanic observer, Sandra Lopez, maintains that books should pass on multiple views of nature, including those of peoples of color.[5] At the same time, Chickasaw poet, novelist, and essayist Linda Hogan argues that "wilderness" has not yet been defined. "I'm not sure we can preserve it until we find the language for it," she adds.[6]

Ecofeminism, or ecological feminism, also garners slight attention. This philosophy emanated from women who believed that men generally exploited and damaged nature, whereas women viewed nature as a mother demanding respect and consideration.

In a sense, ecofeminism is the gradual projection of a female presence onto nature. As early as 1873, traveler Grace Greenwood wrote: "Nature, being feminine, was bursting with the secret [of summer] . . . but stupid man was long enough in taking the hint."[7] Subsequent female observers explored and developed this dichotomy. Approximately one hundred years after Greenwood's book, Susan Griffin's *Women and Nature* (1978) was the first to state explicitly the bond between feminism and environmentalism. Since then, many other writers of diverse backgrounds—such as the Japanese-American writer Janice Mirikitani—have investigated the theory's possibilities and ramifications.

Because of the unparalleled energy of ecofeminism and its unique insights into U.S. environmental problems, this theory has become one of the most important environmental trends of the late twentieth century. During the 1980s and 1990s, ecofeminism generally maintained that modern science and technology damage the environment and that humanistic, and traditionally female, principles are needed for the survival of the earth and its peoples.[8]

Contemporary ecofeminists usually indict the white patriarchy and its values for dominating and damaging both women and the physical world. To them, the environmental crisis is also a crisis of the dominant (male) ideology.[9] In 1983, writer Linda Hogan stated this position in verse:

> Men smile like they know everything
> but walking in slant heel boots
> their butts show they are tense.
> Dark shirt.
> Blue fire
> puts out the sun. Rock bits
> are clenched metal fists.
>
> The earth is wounded
> and bleeds.
> Pray to Jesus.[10]

Also during the 1980s and 1990s, theorist Carolyn Merchant added a larger dimension. She espoused "radical ecology," which called for an end to the separation of humans by race, class, and gender; that is, people are connected, and no one group has the right to exploit nature at the expense of others. According to Merchant, radical ecology sought "a new ethic of the nurture of nature and the nurture of people" according to a "new social vision and a new ethic."[11]

In the mid 1990s, ecofeminist Charlene Spretnak expanded some of these ideas by casting the "green" movement in the context of both ecofeminism and women's spirituality. She maintained that, to succeed, environmentalism had to be egalitarian— free of the hierarchies of command, power, and status to which most men were accustomed. Spretnak explained, "The path I would like to take" leads to an "ecological postmodernism," based on "the sense that our social construction is grounded in the fact that we are embodied organisms embedded in subtle processes of nature." Much like Merchant, Spretnak asserted that humans "exist in profound interrelatedness," a state of being no one could afford to ignore any longer.[12]

Some observers believe that if ecofeminism's inherent gender struggle can be managed and controlled, the philosophy offers much to contemporary Americans.[13] They maintain that if women's modes of operation, including nonhierarchical organization and awareness of interconnectedness, can bring progress in solving environmental predicaments, they are worth exploring and perhaps adopting.

·

In addition to these new developments of diversity and ecofeminism, since 1940 earlier patterns of women's involvement in the environment have accelerated, thus swelling the ranks of women interested in nature and its preservation.

As happened before 1940, women entered the sciences and worked to preserve the environment, including the American West. At first, they faced hard going. During the post–World War II "back-to-the-home" movement that advised women to stay home and have children, scientifically oriented women encountered restrictive attitudes and policies in education, employment, and their professions. During the 1960s and 1970s, however, leaders of the developing feminist movement in the United States attacked narrow ideas and the barriers they produced. In particular, feminists refuted the old-fashioned belief that women were inept in scientific fields, and they campaigned for the opening of all scientific endeavors to women.

Even as recently as the 1980s and 1990s, however, female scientists have struggled to break down societal sentiments against women in science and to find their place in a field long dominated by men. Despite the help of supportive fathers and husbands, as well as the assistance of female networks, women achievers still are often disregarded.[14]

Although these changes have occurred slowly, post–World War II women scientists have followed an easier path than the birders and botanists who preceded them. For one thing, the old controversy about women's "proper" attire and behavior had died, proba-bly during the 1920s. Moreover, during the post–World War II era, the number of women in paid employment and the professions, in-cluding the sciences, generally rose in the United States.

During these years, Rachel Carson became the most well known female ecological scientist and environmental activist of the postwar period. Hers is the one name that appears in every article, book, and lecture about the contemporary conservation movement. Working in Massachusetts and Maine during the 1940s and 1950s as an aquatic biologist, Carson wrote a number of books about sea life. In 1962, she published her major work, *Silent Spring*, which alerted people to the effects of pesticides on them and the environment and which touched off an international de-bate on environmental pollution.[15]

But other seldom-mentioned women also combined scientific research and environmental activism. For her work and member-ship in various Minnesota conservation organizations, biologist and writer Helen Hoover received numerous awards, including a 1971 honor from the American Association for the Advancement of Science and a 1973 ecology citation from Minnesota's Blue Flame gas company.[16]

Since 1940, the work of amateur natural scientists has also gar-nered more acceptance. During the 1950s and 1960s, Texan Con-nie Hagar contributed to ornithology as an amateur bird watcher and bird protectionist. As a member of the Texas Ornithological Society, Hagar made field trips and compiled "nature calendars," twenty-five volumes of notes, photographs, and other documents, which now are available at the Texas A&M University Archives.[17]

Amateurs in other scientific areas also published their findings for receptive audiences. In 1947, Leonora S. M. Curtin wrote *Heal-ing Herbs of the Rio Grande*, the first ethnobotanical account of New Mexico. In 1986, Barbara Davis's *Birds of the Southwest* ap-peared. Moreover, such women were also devoted environmental-ists. Davis, for example, actively participated in the work of the Audubon Society, Arizona-Sonora Desert Museum, Defenders of Wildlife, National Wildlife Federation, Tucson Mountain Associa-tion, and Nature Conservancy.[18]

•

After 1940, female nature writers also became more numerous. Although they eventually dominated best-seller lists, change occurred slowly.

During the 1940s and 1950s, women nature writers were still primarily white, with most writing graphic yet lyrical descriptions of every part of the American West. Rather than offering explicit environmental messages, these writers frequently buried their pleas between the lines. For a nation caught up during the 1940s with wartime and postwar problems, and next with the caution and fear of the 1950s, a subtle, covert approach to environmental issues had widespread appeal.

In 1944, Minnesotan Florence Page Jaques won an award for *Snowshoe Country*, the poignant story of the northern Minnesota winter she spent living in a cabin. Her statement that "I shall always think of green ripples and gold sun when I remember this forest lodge" touched the souls of readers who could wrest their attention away from wartime problems long enough to read about the merit of Minnesota's north woods and to wonder, with Jaques, about its future.[19]

By the 1960s, however, the American public seemed increasingly aware of environmental questions and wanted to know what nature writers had to say about these issues. This occurred, in large part, because the protest movements of the 1960s forced Americans to think about a range of problems, including environmentalism.

Consequently, a growing number of magazines and book publishers sought environmental and nature writing. In 1967, *Daedalus* devoted an entire issue to "America's Changing Environment." In addition, established journals recast their focus and sometimes adopted new names. In 1968, the *Scientist and Citizen* magazine became the *Environment*. The following year, shortly after the U.S. Congress approved the National Environmental Policy Act, *Time* magazine initiated a section on the environment, while the *New York Times* hired an environmental reporter.[20]

During the 1970s, especially after Earth Day on 22 April 1970 raised people's awareness of continuing problems, the topic of the environment appeared everywhere. In 1971, newscaster Walter Cronkite added an environment report on the CBS evening news. In 1972, a team of sociologists concluded that the issue of "environmental quality" had entered public awareness as a social problem. In 1972 alone, a number of environmental journals began publication, including *Environmental Quality and Safety, Human Ecology, Journal of Environmental Quality,* and *Man on Earth.*[21]

The markets for the work of nature writers grew rapidly. Furthermore, Americans' expanding interest in the environment encouraged nature writers to explore larger issues ranging from arguments for enhanced conservation policies to abstract analyses of human perceptions of nature. From Annie Dillard to Sue Hubbel, female nature writers conveyed a complex sense of landscapes and wildlife to their readers.[22]

A number of these writers focused on the American West. In nature polemics, essays, nonfiction books, short stories, and novels, women writers revealed the natural beauty of—and the human damage done to—western marshes, trees, deserts, mountains, prairies, and plains. Some struggled to define such terms as "wilderness" and "wise use," and put forth recommendations for "management" and "recreation." Like their predecessors, most imposed female terms and values on nature, as well as placing women squarely at the center of the physical world.[23]

Naturalist and writer Ann Zwinger published many books celebrating from a woman's point of view the Rocky Mountains and their aspens, Utah and its Green River, and the Southwest's four great deserts—Mexico's Chihuahua and Sonora Deserts, California's Mojave Desert, and Nevada's Great Basin. In addition, Zwinger combined a close scrutiny of plants and animals with appeals for their informed use.[24]

Meanwhile, the number of women writers of color grew. Especially during the 1970s to 1990s, as Americans' appreciation for multiculturalism expanded, women of color gradually proffered their impressions of nature to a once hostile or indifferent public. During this time period, American Indian women writers in particular gained credibility with a large reading audience. Such writers as Joy Harjo, Leslie Marmon Silko, and Luci Tapahonso presented native women's views of nature as well as demonstrating that not all Indian women saw things the same way. The fact that they were American Indians did not cast them into one simple mold. Perhaps the one constant in their work was an ongoing awareness that women revered and needed nature. In 1978, for example, Joy Harjo wrote:

> a woman can't survive
> by her own breath
>   alone
> she must know
> the voices of mountains
> she must recognize
> the foreverness of blue sky
> she must flow
> with the elusive
> bodies
> of night women
> who will take her into
> her own self[25]

Often, nature writers of the 1970s to 1990s, whether white or of color, shared kindred perceptions of women and nature and used similar metaphors. In 1984, Paula Gunn Allen, a writer of Laguna Pueblo, Scots-Irish, and Lebanese-American heritage, maintained that women could reach out to nature by performing "the dance of feathers, the dance of birds." Five years later, Terry Tempest Williams, a white woman, similarly wrote about a woman who experienced the desert through dance, thus creating "a landscape where lines between the real and imagined were thinly drawn."[26]

There were, of course, and still are, themes that separated white writers and those of color. One was place. White women frequently wrote about nature as seen from their farms, ranches, and cabins. They divulged justifiable concerns: the preservation of wildlife pastures, the damage done by nearby missile bases, the erosion of hills and mountains. Women writers of color, however, more often viewed nature from reservations, hogans and shacks, or urban ghettos. They, too, fretted—usually about the survival of themselves and their cultures.[27]

•

In addition to nature writing, visual images of nature increased and became more complex after 1940. This occurred, at least in part, because of the growing societal acceptance of women artists and the refinement of photographic and other technology.

At first, female artists tended to follow traditional forms. Flower artists, more properly known as botanical illustrators, continued to produce delicate work that offered a highly feminine interpretation of this aspect of nature. Only a few experimented with technological innovation, including flower artist Jeanne Russell Janish of Nevada, who took photographs of the specimens she wished to paint.[28]

During the 1950s and 1960s, however, the advent of highly illustrated magazines and newspapers, motion pictures, and television encouraged Americans to become more visually oriented. In turn, female nature artists became more aggressive in both their art and their environmentalism. Iowan Shirley Ann Briggs studied art and botany, which led to jobs during the 1940s as an environmental illustrator and chief of the graphics section for the U.S. Bureau of Reclamation. Briggs also taught a course on American conservation philosophy, conducted bird-population studies in Iowa's Glover-Archbold Park, and participated in such organizations as the Rachel Carson Council and the Natural Resources Council of America.[29]

Another innovation occurred when motion picture and television producers pioneered the "nature special." Women stood in the forefront. During the 1950s, naturalist Lois Crisler lived in Alaska's Brooks Range for a year and a half to film wildlife, especially wolves and migrating caribou. With her husband, Crisler returned again and again to camp, track, photograph, and film animals. She contributed a particularly female interpretation of wolves: "the wolf had read my eyes! . . . your true feeling looks out of your eyes, the animals read it." During the 1960s, Crisler sold film footage to Walt Disney Productions, which gave her a major role in the preservation of such species as the wolf.[30]

Recent women artists have also proved enterprising in developing new forms of nature art. In California during the 1970s and 1980s, Japanese-American artist Mineko Grimmer chose a holistic approach to the landscapes she re-created in sculpture, while Korean-American artist Jungran Shin gained notice with her landscape-abstractions titled "Mindscapes."[31]

Often, such women advocated subtle environmentalism by depicting unpolluted skies, streams, deserts, even fields of crops. Women artists intended such representations as an environmental warning that natural areas were decreasing in the United States.[32]

•

After 1940, women environmentalists also remained active club members. In fact, many women held membership in more than one group. During the 1940s, Kansas native Annette Flugger helped organize the International Conservation Foundation (chartered in 1948), which was dedicated "to the protection of our renewable life-supporting resources." Flugger, who characterized environmental conservation as "one of the most vital needs" of the day, also participated in the Wildlife Society, Wilderness Society, Soil Conservation Society, Outdoor Writers Association, and Preservation Education Association.[33]

From one end of the West to the other, club women initiated environmental programs and projects. In Arizona during the midtwentieth century, attorney and active club woman Nellie Bush rose to the presidency of the General Federation of Women's Clubs. Bush also served sixteen years in the Arizona House of Representatives and was a member of the Arizona River Commission and the Basin States Committee, where she demonstrated her abiding interest in the environment and preserving it for outdoor enthusiasts like herself.[34]

Minnesota club woman Edith Herman would have agreed with Bush's priorities. Herman opened her farm to youth campers, designed a course of environmental education for the Minnetonka schools, and helped expand the University of Minnesota's arboretum. Among the honors she won during the 1960s and 1970s were the Senior Forester Award, the Minnesota soil and water conservation districts Woman of the Year award, and the *Carver County Sun* Man of the Year award. Herman used the last honor as an occasion for stating that "it is high time POW (the power of women) was recognized, encouraged and appreciated" by environmentalists.[35]

Of American women's clubs, garden clubs in particular flourished after the post–World War II era came to a close. Nationally, garden club officials instituted an environmental program dedicated to the informed use of the nation's remaining natural resources. Lilly Starkweather chaired this division from 1949 to 1953 and helped found Tucson's Rose Society and its Desert Garden Club. In a series of impassioned articles and speeches, Starkweather tried to save the desert's ivory-cupped "spoon flowers" (*Dsylirion Wheeleri*), partly by moblizing the National Council of State Garden Clubs, the Arizona Federation of Garden Clubs, and the Arizona Cactus and Native Flora Society to help defeat unscrupulous collectors and merchants who exploited the spoon-flower craze.[36]

Starkweather proved an effective advocate for other environmental causes as well. In her 1952 address to the National Council of State Garden Clubs, Starkweather urged what she termed "good management" of forest and soil. She branded the American public "a lot of economic idiots in the way they waste our natural resources," and she posed a hypothetical question: "What will the historians writing a hundred years hence say of our generation? Are we striving to become well-informed on the issues of our day, or are we relying on the next generation to do what we should be doing now for this country of ours?" To Starkweather, education and legislation provided key solutions.[37]

In addition to these women's groups, a perhaps unexpected entrant into the environmental fray was the League of Women Voters. Although one may think of the league as a political organization, it was dedicated to improving American society in general. Thus, such leaders as Mildred Hargraves of Rochester, Minnesota, led league members in adopting a strong environmental stance.

During the early 1960s, Hargraves urged league officials to move environmentalism "to a more active place on the current agenda." Due in part to her efforts, in 1964 the league's national convention voted on behalf of "long-range planning for conservation and development of water resources."[38]

Besides working through volunteer groups, female environmental activists utilized such forums as political involvement, lobbying, economic schemes, and labor protests. For instance, some highly visible women in the political realm used their position to achieve environmental reform. During the late 1960s, Lady Bird (Claudia Alta Taylor) Johnson initiated a highway beautification program. During her tenure as First Lady and well into the 1970s, Johnson reminded Americans that environmental quality affected their daily lives. Although she was frequently criticized for her efforts, Lady Bird is now heralded as a forerunner of the ecology movement of the late 1960s and early 1970s.[39]

Among women environmentalists elected to office in their own right was Maurine Neuberger of Portland, Oregon. As U.S. senator during the 1960s, she introduced a bill to establish the Oregon Dunes National Recreation Area. A longtime environmental proponent, Neuberger hoped to save this stretch of the Oregon coastline from oil and gas exploration. In the Southwest, Arizona state legislator Clara Botzum promoted a double-edged plan: development of the town of Parker and preservation of the Colorado River valley. For six terms during the 1940s, 1950s, and 1960s, Botzum lobbied for a wildlife area near Lake Havasu as well as for recreational and environmental projects along the Colorado River.[40]

Other less prominent women used the political system as citizen advocates. In Goose Prairie, Washington, during the late 1950s and 1960s, the owners of the Double K Mountain Ranch, a dude ranch, wrote, lobbied, and spoke on behalf of a Cougar Lakes wilderness area. In submitting the Double K Plan to government agencies, the two women explained that they had taken "the landscape of the Bumping River Watershed pretty much for granted until 1957," when a timber sale on American Ridge "obliterated" a magnificent stand of ponderosa pine. The two soon became vitriolic opponents of the logging industry in Washington State.[41]

The most colorful political activist of the period, however, was lobbyist Velma B. Johnston, who earned the nickname "Wild Horse Annie" by championing Nevada's wild mustang population. Johnston began her crusade during the early 1950s by informing state legislators that mustangs were sold for pet food as well as hunted from airplanes for entertainment. When her proposed bill to protect mustangs passed in Nevada in 1955, Johnston turned her attention to the U.S. Congress, declaring that the horse had played a crucial role in American history and still symbolized the American West "as all people like to think of it." As a symbol of "wild freedom," Johnston maintained, the mustang deserved a "right to survival."[42]

Wild Horse Annie hoped for federal protection of wild horses in the West. In Nevada, where approximately four thousand head of wild mustangs lived in a state composed of 70,273,280 acres, Johnson said she "did not feel that the four thousand head of horses presented a threat to the rangelands by creating a grazing shortage." She also pointed out that wild mustangs provided such ecological benefits as opening frozen water holes for other animals. Even with worldwide support and eventual legal protection, Johnston discovered that her battle had to continue, for illegal hunters evaded the law at every turn.[43]

At the same time, other women fought along economic lines, especially by seeking jobs with the U.S. Park Service and Forest Service. Although forestry had remained a male-dominated field since its emergence as a profession around the turn of the twentieth century, after 1940 women gradually gained employment as naturalists, rangers, foresters, and fire lookouts.[44]

Barriers fell—sometimes rapidly, other times under pressure. By the early 1980s, female forestry workers decided they had to fight. Although affirmative action plans aided them in obtaining Forest Service jobs in two of Oregon's national forests, resistance from male workers continued. In response, these women utilized informal organizing and formal grievance procedures to hold onto their own positions and open the way for other women forestry workers.[45]

Clearly, women activists wanted access to all aspects of nature and its preservation. Most believed that the stresses of the battle were worthwhile. Californian Margaret Owings, who developed a wildlife strategy to save birds, mountain lions, and otters, spoke for many women activists when, during the 1980s, she said: "True, I've been caught up in the grinding wheels of government, of man's ways, of human problems and prejudices. But it's been worth it. For me wilderness is an escape and a freedom to discover and rediscover."[46]

·

In addition to the progress that the above club women and other activists achieved, outdoor women also grew in number and range of interests. To do so, they had to combat a longstanding prejudice: that women naturally fear—and thus avoid—the outdoors. Despite the fact that nineteenth- and early twentieth-century women mountain climbers and athletes contradicted outdated notions about women and nature, the myths hung on. In 1969, American climber Arlene Blum received the following rejection of her application to join a climbing expedition: "One woman and nine men would seem to me to be unpleasant high on the open ice, not only in excretory situations, but in the easy masculine companionship which is so vital a part of the joy of an expedition. Sorry as hell."[47]

On a subsequent expedition a guide told Blum, "Women climbers either aren't good climbers, or they aren't real women."[48] Real women or not, Blum and hundreds of others continued to climb rather than cook. Although change came slowly for them, they persevered.[49]

Meanwhile, other outdoor women took up skiing, both at the amateur and professional levels. In Utah, just as Norwegian immigrant Borghild Marie Bergstedt predicted during the early 1900s, champion women skiers appeared. Shortly after the end of World War II, between 1947 and 1949, Suzanne Harris Rytting skied for the University of Utah team. She joined the women's Olympic team in 1952 and won the Pacific Northwest Ski Association championship in 1960 and 1961.[50]

No outdoor sport seemed to daunt postwar women. Whether it was hunting, fishing, whitewater rafting, kayaking, backpacking, or guiding, they gave it a try and succeeded. Not even long-distance arctic tracking and mushing discouraged women. In Alaska, Sara Machetanz camped, kayaked, tracked, and wrote a series of books. With her husband, Machetanz visited Inuit villages and learned to mush. In 1954, the couple filmed a documentary about sled dogs, which also contributed to Americans' understanding of the Alaskan landscape and the need to preserve it. Later, Susan Butcher won the Iditarod dog sled race so often that she inspired a tee-shirt slogan: "Alaska. Where Men are Men and Women win the Iditarod."[51]

But could all outdoor women be considered environmentalists? No. Some women hikers and horseback riders littered trails with bottles and cans. Others who professed to love the environment took advantage of natural resources to build fortunes based upon the exploitation of such mineral assets as uranium.[52] Still, it appears that a vast majority of outdoor women believed in, advocated, and lived environmentalism.

Sometimes these women worked on their own. For instance, isolated ranchwomen tried a variety of methods. One South Texas ranchwoman and active garden club member experimented with crops and breeds of stock. Another, a New Mexican rancher named Agnes Morley, wielded her pen to fight for the West. As early as 1948, she asserted that twentieth-century activities, especially atomic testing, were more "savage" than any that had gone before. According to Morley, even though Oklahoma's Cimarron Territory had its own "ferocities," modern Americans were creating "ferocities" and "wildness" that outdid anything the desert had to offer.[53]

In other cases, outdoor women preferred to work through such organizations as the Alpine Club. The Sierra Club in particular launched conservation projects and published such books as Debbie Miller's *Midnight Wilderness* (1990). After exploring parts of Alaska's nineteen-million-acre Arctic National Wildlife Refuge, Miller wanted to help protect "the extraordinary wilderness, wildlife, and recreational values of this world-class arctic refuge for future generations." By publishing her *Midnight Wilderness*, the Sierra Club helped Miller demonstrate the uniqueness of the area and warn against the destruction caused by oil exploration and development.[54]

SINCE 1940

Similarly, the Federation of Western Outdoor Clubs, which listed environmental conservation as one of its goals, campaigned, lobbied, and otherwise supported environmental reform. As early as 1944, a year before World War II ended, the California branch of Western Outdoor Clubs urged the establishment of the Jackson Hole National Monument in the Grand Teton area. In later years, Western Outdoor Clubs opposed the opening of national park land to cattle grazing, supported U.S. Forest Service postwar plans to preserve timber lands, and lamented the entry of jeeps and airplanes into former wilderness areas. If the shrinking of wilderness lands continued, the Outdoor Club's journal declared in 1945, "none of them will be large enough to get lost in, or even slightly bewildered."[55]

During the 1950s, Pauline (Polly) Dyer, past-president of the Federation of Western Outdoor Clubs, continued the crusade. In particular, she supported the establishment of the Glacier Peak Wilderness Area in Washington State. Through lobbying, court testimony, and speeches, Dyer prodded the U.S. Forest Service to protect one of the West's "last wilderness areas." Besides Sierra Club and Outdoor Club members, Dyer marshaled Mountaineers on behalf of Glacier Peak.[56]

Apparently, numerous women loved to play in the outdoors—and hoped to protect it. Whether they utilized western landscapes for recreation or practiced their professions in them, most women who were active in the outdoors also promoted its preservation.

•

After 1940, travel attracted huge numbers of American women. As before, they camped, visited western resorts, and stayed at dude ranches, returning home to promote the marvels of the West and their need for preservation. But women travelers also increasingly supported the emerging concepts of adventure and environmental travel. In 1941, the year the United States entered World War II, *Life* magazine featured a canoe trip down Minnesota rivers by two young Midwestern women. For dinner, the women caught fish and cooked them over an open fire. Furthermore, they not only paddled their own canoe but carried it as well.[57]

Farther west in Hawaii, Audrey Sutherland made similar solitary canoe trips along Molokai's northeast coast. In her 1978 autobiography, she explained, "on a solo trip . . . life becomes simple and deeply satisfying." Sutherland returned year after year to Molokai until it became part of her, a reassurance of her own confidence and strength.[58]

In addition, more women traveled in the company of female outdoor guides. Minnesotan Justine Kerfoot ran Gunflint Lodge for fifty years and was one of the first canoe provisioners and wilderness guides in northern Minnesota.[59]

As female travelers saw more of the West and its physical wonders, the majority became staunch environmentalists. One traveler in the early 1990s commented, "I now realize the vast beauty—and the vulnerability—of the West. I've joined everything from the Sierra Club to a local lobbying group. I hope it helps."[60]

•

After 1940, white women also worried about the preservation of native cultures and their knowledge regarding the physical world. Although such writers as Chickasaw ecofeminist Linda Hogan decried the tendency to conflate American Indians with endangered wilderness—"Indians have been called 'wild' and seem to represent an unfathomable mystery to Christians"[61]—many white women continued to argue that Indians came under the American women's mandate to conserve not only western land but the people who lived and worked on it. In 1941, club woman and amateur ethnologist Clarissa Brown Winsor founded the Territorial Prison Museum in Yuma, Arizona. For this and her work as curator of the museum, in 1961 Winsor received a Man of the Year award.[62]

As they had done before 1940, postwar anthropologists also took an active part in collecting and analyzing Indian lore. Problem-oriented fieldwork became popular, raising questions about everything from the nature of adolescence to a potter's feelings about her work.[63]

Most women anthropologists were also dedicated environmentalists. Until the late 1980s, for example, geologist and anthropologist Margaret Wheat's work for the U.S. Geological Survey and the Nevada State Museum gave her the opportunity to research Northern Paiute Indians. Wheat soon established herself as an expert on what she called "survival" arts of the Paiute in northern Nevada. Through her service on the Nevada State Parks Commission and the Nevada Ichthyosaur Park board, Wheat also advocated the preservation of native-related landscapes and resources.[64]

But it was not only researchers and preservationists who showed concern for contemporary Native Americans. Women in politics and the professions also championed American Indians. One was Utah lawyer, judge, and member of the U.S. House of Representatives Reva Beck Bosone, who sponsored a bill to release Indians from government wardship. Bosone also spent years, in Congress and in a fifteen-minute weekly radio broadcast, supporting such conservation causes as land reclamation and water conservation, especially the Columbia Valley Authority and the Central Utah Project.[65]

At the same time, native women took a growing part in preserving their cultures and environments. After 1940, native women gradually reshaped their role in the environmental movement from objects of preservation to initiators of programs. By the 1970s, healer Brooke Medicine Eagle emphasized the need to safeguard customary ways of knowing nature in the contemporary technological age: "Our dominant society and education give us the way of the Mind, but the way of the Heart is being born from the very land itself."[66]

Native women also offered themselves as models and leaders for other women environmentalists. In 1990, Anishinabe leader Winona LaDuke called upon white women to spread the Anishinabe way of living as "an integral part of the creation" through the nation and the world.[67]

•

What is one to make of this cornucopia of post-1940 women's names and information about their involvement with western nature?

For one, as the twenty-first century nears, it is clear that women are an integral part of American environmentalism. The numbers of female advocates—as well as their types and origins—have multiplied. Neither age nor class, race nor ethnicity, education nor lack of it, limits women's participation in environmental efforts in the way it did prior to 1940.

For another, feminist sentiments have exerted an important influence. Although "back-to-the-home" propaganda urged American women to give up their public involvement, a significant number ignored the message. They continued to volunteer and to seek paid employment in environmentally related areas. More recently, feminist thinkers have applied their philosophies to environmentalism. The result, ecofeminism, suggests other than the traditional ways of implementing environmental programs.

Another conclusion might be that future environmental survival demands such diversity. As ecofemnist Starhawk has pointed out, trends toward globalism connect all peoples and places. "There is no isolated part of the world anymore," she stated; "there is no isolated biological system." In Starhawk's view, everyone must work together to save the earth: "That's what environmental science is really about . . . different ways of going about the same understanding."[68]

Lastly, if cooperation between all types of people is critical to preserving nature, then women's contributions and perceptions must be taken into account. Not only have women given support, effort, and energy to the growth of environmentalism in the United States, but they have also developed alternative ways of viewing landscapes and their use. As they continue to be active into the twenty-first century, women will change the face of environmental history and transform environmental policy.

Conclusion

•

Rethinking
Environmental
History

Despite the pleas of such scholars as Carolyn Merchant, Janice Monk, and Vera Norwood entreating environmental historians and other researchers to incorporate women into their studies and to include feminist analysis, both suggestions remain long overlooked.[1] Yet the foregoing pages demonstrate that numerous white, well-to-do women not only participated in both the early and the contemporary conservation movements but often played key roles and contributed unique perspectives.

Certainly, between 1870 and 1940, women proved critical in the emerging crusade to save the American West. From birders and botanists to nature illustrators and writers, women collected data, encouraged others to study nature, shaped perceptions of the environment, and supported environmental principles, programs, and projects.

Such women appeared to possess less anxiety about nature than is customarily assumed—or perhaps had none at all. Numerous "all-American girls" seem to have fought "domesticity" on every front, or perhaps they just ignored it as irrelevant to their own lives. If, indeed, the American woman had a "proper sphere," she embraced nature and the outdoors as part of that world. Could it be that the reactionary thought of the post–World War II era dulled American sensitivities to the realities of earlier generations of women?

Rather than avoiding the western "wilderness," American women "conquered" it in their own way—by feminizing it. Especially through written and visual images, women put the West into an accessible, nonthreatening format. These women created a docile West that could, and should, be gentled. They also feminized western vistas, making them more desirable and accessible to the public in general and to women in particular.

Before and after 1940, women also argued eloquently for such concepts as living with nature rather than controlling it and considering native peoples and historic structures as part of western landscapes. Although it is impossible to argue that all men view the environment in an exploitative manner whereas all women perceive it in a nurturing way, women have made unique gender-related contributions to the environmental ethic in the United States. Because women and men interpreted nature in such disparate ways, gender differences demand more scholarly analysis and interpretation than they have received.

Specific areas need attention from researchers. Among them are the fact that long before the term achieved usage, women of all backgrounds proved themselves as "environmentalists." Scholars must analyze in depth Indian and Hispanic women's relationships with, perceptions of, and actions toward nature. Contemporary female conservationists of color are more than willing to point the way and assist in this endeavor.

The romantic view of the American environment also needs rethinking, especially in terms of gender, class, and religion. The romantics were elite thinkers who influenced American thought but did not control it. Other types of people developed their own ideas regarding the environment—and acted on these ideas.

Furthermore, women's involvement indicates that enthusiasm for environmental reform came "up" from the American people rather than "down" from its leaders. Sheer numbers of women refute the idea that environmentalism was a top-down, politician-inspired, legislated movement in the United States. Women played a crucial role in building the national awareness that allowed such leaders as John Muir, Theodore Roosevelt, and Gifford Pinchot to put their ideas into place. Despite Pinchot's claims regarding his thoughtful ride on his horse Jim, when the "conservation" idea flashed into his mind, the history of the conservation movement needs to expand its boundaries. It was not a legislative coup; it came from concerned people all over the nation.

Women also constituted a major force in the conservation movement in terms of numerical mass. From thousands of signatures on petitions to millions of club women, American women pushed ever-cautious leaders forward into an unknown and unexplored realm of action. Had it not been for the emergence of the idea of women as conservators or the exceptional women's club movement, would environmentalism have ever gotten off the ground? If the movement had not offered outlets for feminist sentiments, would environmentalism have attracted the numbers so necessary to its implementation?

The intersections between women's clubs, feminism, and the American conservation movement offer a rich and seemingly unlimited area of scholarly exploration. We need to know more, for example, about how environmental action became a vote for Mom and country.

Women not only helped forge the conservation movement but also had significant impact on environmentally related industries. Women stimulated such local and national "wilderness" businesses as horse rentals, dude ranches, books related to the environment, nature photography, and advertising copywriting for such giants as the Great Northern Railroad, corporations that granted women little recognition, power, or prestige in return for enhancing profits.

Lastly, women revolutionized their own lives in the process. Whether feminist in philosophy or not, women learned how to network, use political processes to their advantage, infiltrate men's organizations and male-dominated professions, and develop such sophisticated philosophies as ecofeminism. Women's history and environmental history are thus inextricably intertwined.

Clearly, inclusion of women's achievements revises and corrects the history of American environmentalism. In the preceding pages, examples are numerous, yet there are thousands—perhaps millions—more women who were involved in saving the American West. Adding women also reshapes environmental history as an endeavor, for the inclusion of women raises such other issues as gender relations, the impact of race and social class, and power balances between groups. "Feminist analysis" is more than a shibboleth; it creates insights that allow an issue to be reconstructed and reconceptualized.

Rethinking environmental history's conventional interpretations would allow us to rethink environmentalism itself. Even in the face of attention-grabbing social problems, contemporary Americans still have to confront their relationship with nature. Without the earth as a livable and hospitable home, the existence of social problems will not matter.

Giving a holistic interpretation to environmental history could put the United States on the track to a more effective conservation plan, both regionally and nationally. Part of such an approach promises to bring the past and present of women and nature to the foreground. Appreciation of these women's perceptions may well suggest alternatives for the future.

NOTE ON SOURCES

The primary resources for the topic of American women in the conservation movement are vast and varied. The challenge is to locate and extract them from libraries and archives that are only beginning to catalog such topics as "conservation" and "environment" and that often overlook most women's sources when they do so. Most librarians and archivists, however, are excited by the topic and are more than willing to help.

Even with such assistance, a researcher has to sort through mounds of possibilities and be extra alert to small items in newspapers, magazines, organization minutes, and speeches. Western women's diaries, letters, and reminiscences are also worth pursuing, for they reveal women's attitudes and activities in relation to landscapes, use of resources, and conservation policies.

Collections that contain pertinent American women's materials used in this study are the Historical Society of Arizona, Tucson; Special Collections, University of Arizona, Tucson; Arizona State Museum, University of Arizona, Tucson; Autry Museum of Western Heritage and Braun Library of the Southwest Museum, both in Los Angeles; Huntington Library, San Marino, California; Special Collections, University of California Library, Berkeley; Colorado State Historical Society, Denver; Denver Public Library, especially the Conservation Collection; Special Collections, and Archives, Norlin Library, University of Colorado at Boulder; Iowa State Historical Society, Iowa City and Des Moines; Kansas State Historical Society, Topeka; Minnesota Historical Society, St. Paul; Montana State Historical Society, especially the Montana American Mothers Bicentennial Project, 1975–76, Helena; Special Collections, Montana State University Library, Bozeman; Nebraska State Historical Society, Lincoln; Special Collections, Getchell Library, University of Nevada, Reno; Nevada Historical Society, Reno; Women's Archives, Dickinson Library, University of Nevada, Las Vegas; Center for Southwest Research, University of New Mexico Library, Albuquerque; State Records Center and Archives, Santa Fe, New Mexico; State Historical Society of North Dakota, Bismarck; Special Collections, University of Oregon Library, Eugene; Lane County Museum, Eugene, Oregon; Oregon Historical Society, Portland; South Dakota State Historical Resource Center, Pierre; Institute of Oral History, University of Texas at El Paso; Special Collections, University of Texas at El Paso; J. Evetts Haley Collection, Nita Stewart Haley Memorial Library, Midland, Texas; Utah State Historical Society and Special Collections, University of Utah Libraries, both in Salt Lake City; Wyoming State Archives, Cheyenne; American Heritage Center, University of Wyoming Library, Laramie; Manuscripts and University Archives, University of Washington Libraries, Seattle; Washington State Library, Olympia.

Not to be overlooked are regional, state, and local historical journals and books, often by obscure publishers, that contain published versions of women's original writings. Two examples are Florence S. Shipek, transcriber, *The Autobiography of Delfina Guero: A Diegueño Indian* (Los Angeles: Dawson's Book Shop, 1968); and Gilbert L. Wilson, transcriber, *Buffalo Bird Woman's Garden* (St. Paul: Minnesota Historical Society Press, 1987).

In addition, women's nature writings can be found in such anthologies as Karen Knowles, ed., *Celebrating the Land: Women's Nature Writings, 1850–1991* (Flagstaff AZ: Northland, 1992); and Marcia Myers Bonta, *American Women Afield: Writings by Pioneering Women Naturalists* (College Station: Texas A&M University Press, 1995). Helpful commentaries appear in John Elder, ed., *American Nature Writers*, 2 vols. (New York: Charles Scribner's Sons, 1996).

Individual women who participated in some aspect of the conservation movement can be identified in a wide variety of reference and guide books: Edward T. James, ed., *Notable American Women, 1607–1950* (Cambridge MA: Belknap Press, 1971); Jennifer James-Wilson, *Washington Women: A Centennial Celebration* (Olympia WA: State Superintendent of Public Instruction, 1992); Phil Kovinick, *The Woman Artist in the American West, 1860–1960* (Fullerton CA: Muckenthaler Cultural Center, 1976); Peggy A. Woleke Kelley, *Women of*

Nebraska Hall of Fame (Omaha: Nebraska International Women's Year Coalition, 1976); Barbara Sicherman and Carol Hurd Green, eds., *Notable American Women: The Modern Period* (Cambridge MA: Belknap Press, 1981); Nell Brown Propst, *Those Strenuous Dames of the Colorado Prairie* (Boulder CO: Pruett, 1982); Barbara Bennett Peterson, ed., *Notable Women of Hawaii* (Honolulu: Univ. of Hawaii Press, 1984); Rosalie Crowe and Diane Tod, *Arizona Women's Hall of Fame* (Phoenix: Arizona Historical Society, 1985); Barbara A. Babcock and Nancy J. Parezo, *Daughters of the Desert: Women Anthropologists and the Native American Southwest, 1880–1980* (Albuquerque: Univ. of New Mexico Press, 1988); Angela Howard Zophy, ed., *Handbook of American Women's History* (New York: Garland, 1990); Betty Penson-Ward, *Idaho Women in History* (Boise ID: Legendary, 1991); Peter E. Palmquist, *A Directory of Women in California Photography, 1900–1920* (Eureka CA: Eureka Printing, 1991); Darlene Clark Hine, ed., *Black Women in America* (Brooklyn NY: Carlson, 1993); Nancy J. Parezo, ed., *Hidden Scholars: Women Anthropologists and the Native American Southwest* (Albuquerque: Univ. of New Mexico Press, 1993); and Patricia Trenton, ed., *Independent Spirits: Women Painters of the American West, 1890–1945* (Los Angeles: Autry Museum of Western Heritage, 1995).

There are also autobiographies and biographies that cover the lives and work of women conservationists, such as Carol Green Wilson, *Alice Eastwood's Wonderland: The Adventures of a Botanist* (San Francisco: California Academy of Sciences, 1955); Helen Winter Stauffer, *Mari Sandoz* (Lincoln: Univ. of Nebraska Press, 1982); Maxine Benson, *Martha Maxwell: Rocky Mountain Naturalist* (Lincoln: Univ. of Nebraska Press, 1986); Lewis L. Gould, *Lady Bird and the Environment* (Lawrence: Univ. Press of Kansas, 1988); Harriet Kofalk, *No Woman Tenderfoot: Florence Merriam Bailey, Pioneer Naturalist* (College Station: Texas A&M Univ. Press, 1989); James J. Yoch, *Landscaping the American Dream: The Gardens and Film Sets of Florence Yoch, 1890–1972* (New York: Harry N. Abrams, 1989); Peggy Pond Church, *Wind's Trail: The Early Life of Mary Austin* (Santa Fe: Museum of New Mexico Press, 1990); Virginia L. Grattan, *Mary Colter: Builder upon the Red Earth* (Grand Canyon AZ: Grand Canyon Natural History Association, 1992); and Necah Stewart Furman, *Caroline Lockhart: Her Life and Legacy* (Seattle: Univ. of Washington Press, 1994).

The number of scholars who write about American women and landscapes is growing. Helpful works include Annette Kolodny, *The Lay of the Land: Metaphor as Experience and History in American Life and Letters* (Chapel Hill: Univ. of North Carolina Press, 1975); Kolodny, *The Land before Her: Fantasy and Experience of the American Frontiers, 1630–1860* (Chapel Hill: Univ. of North Carolina Press, 1984); Sandra Lin Marburg, "Women and Environment: Subsistence Paradigms, 1850–1950," *Environmental Review* 8 (spring 1984): 7–22; Carolyn Merchant, *The Death of Nature: Women, Ecology, and the Scientific Revolution* (New York: Harper & Row, 1980); Merchant, "Women of the Progressive Conservation Movement: 1900–1916," *Environmental Review* 8 (spring 1984): 57–85; Merchant, *Radical Ecology: The Search for a Livable World* (New York: Routledge, 1992); Janice Monk, "Approaches to the Study of Women and Landscape," *Environmental Review* 8 (spring 1984): 23–33; Vera Norwood, "Heroines of Nature: Four Women Respond to the American Landscape," *Environmental Review* 8 (spring 1984): 34–56; Norwood, "Women's Place: Continuity and Changes in Response to Western Landscapes," in *Western Women: Their Land, Their Lives,* ed. Lillian Schlissel, Vicki L. Ruiz, and Janice Monk (Albuquerque: Univ. of New Mexico Press, 1988); Norwood, *Made from This Earth: American Women and Nature* (Chapel Hill: Univ. of North Carolina Press, 1993); and Joni Seager, *Earth Follies: Coming to Feminist Terms with the Global Environmental Crisis* (New York: Routledge, 1993).

Dissertations on aspects of women and environmentalism are also increasing in number. Some of the best include Ellen Huening Mokowski, "Scenic Parks and Landscape Values," University of Illinois, 1987; Madelyn Clare Troxclair, "An Examination of the Wilderness Theme in Twentieth Century American Literature: Revising Myths and Projections Regarding Nature and Women," University of Washington, 1990; Kathleen Davies, "The Goddess in the Landscape: A Tradition of Twentieth Century American Women's Pastoral," Indiana University, 1991; and Gregg Webster Wentzell, "Wildness and the American Mind: The Social Construction of Nature in Environmental Romanticism from Thoreau to Dillard," Miami University, Oxford, Ohio, 1993.

On specific women and conservation topics, the most recent works are Marcia Myers Bonta, *Women in the Field: America's Pioneering Women Naturalists* (College Station: Texas A&M Press, 1991); and

Polly Welts Kaufman, "Challenging Tradition: Pioneer Women Naturalists in the National Park Service," *Forest and Conservation History* 34 (January 1990): 4–16, and *National Parks and the Woman's Voice: A History* (Albuquerque: Univ. of New Mexico Press, 1996).

Research on American peoples of color and environmentalism is growing slowly, and few studies focus on women. Especially useful are George L. Cornell, "Native American Contributions to the Formation of the Modern Conservation Ethic," Ph.D. diss., Michigan State University, 1982, and "The Influence of Native Americans on Modern Conservationists," *Environmental Review* 9 (1985): 104–17; Richard White, "American Indians and the Environment, *Environmental Review* 9 (1985): 101–3; Tey Diana Rebolledo, "Tradition and Mythology," in *The Desert Is No Lady: Southwestern Landscapes in Women's Writing and Art,* ed. Vera Norwood and Janice Monk (New Haven: Yale Univ. Press, 1987); Laura Pulido, "Latino Environmental Struggles in the Southwest," Ph.D. diss., University of California at Los Angeles, 1991; and David Rich Lewis, *Neither Wolf Nor Dog: American Indians, Environment, and Agrarian Change* (New York: Oxford Univ. Press, 1994).

Miscellaneous sources are also enlightening. For instance, collections of tourist brochures and other travel literature from the American West can be found at the Autry Museum of Western Heritage and the Braun Library, Southwest Museum, both in Los Angeles. Some women's guidebooks to the outdoors are S. Anna Gordon, *Camping in Colorado* (New York: Author's Publishing, 1879); and Grace Gallatin Thompson Seton, *A Woman Tenderfoot* (New York: Doubleday, Page, 1905). More recent works include Judith Niemi, *The Basic Essentials of Women in the Outdoors* (Merrillville IN: ICS Books, 1990); Judith Niemi and Barbara Wieser, eds., *Rivers Running Free: Canoeing Stories by Adventurous Women* (Seattle: Seal Press, 1992); and Anne LaBastille, *Women and Wilderness* (San Francisco: Sierra Club Books, 1980). Several women's travel books are Carrie Adell Strahorn, *Fifteen Thousand Miles by Stage* (New York: Putnam, 1911); Septima M. Collis, *A Woman's Trip to Alaska* (New York: Cassell, 1890); and, more recently, Debbie S. Miller, *Midnight Wilderness: Journeys in Alaska's Arctic National Wildlife Refuge* (San Francisco: Sierra Club Books, 1990).

The European background to American women's involvement in environmentalism was primarily researched at the Bodleian Library,

University Museum, and Ashmolean Museum, both in Oxford, England; and the Marianne North Gallery in the Royal Botanic Gardens at Kew, England. Especially useful published studies are Dorothy Middleton, *Victorian Lady Travellers* (New York: E. P. Dutton, 1965); Leo Hamalian, ed., *Ladies on the Loose: Women Travellers of the 18th and 19th Centuries* (South Yarmouth MA: John Curley, 1981); Val Williams, *Women Photographers: The Other Observers, 1900 to the Present* (London: Virago Press, 1986); Meriel Buxton, *Ladies of the Chase* (London: Sportsman's Press, 1987); Dea Birkett, *Spinsters Abroad: Victorian Lady Explorers* (Oxford: Basil Blackwell, 1989); Marion Tinling, ed., *Women into the Unknown: A Sourcebook on Women Explorers and Travelers* (New York: Greenwood Press, 1989); Tinling, *With Women's Eyes: Visitors to the New World* (Hamden CT: Archon Books, 1993); Marina Benjamin, ed., *Science and Sensibility: Gender and Scientific Enquiry, 1780–1945* (Oxford: Blackwell, 1991); Marni L. Stanley, "The Imperial Mission: Women Travellers and the Propaganda of Empire," D.Phil. thesis, St. Hilda's College, 1990; Sara Mills, *Discourses of Differences: An Analysis of Women's Travel Writing and Colonialism* (London: Routledge, 1991); Patricia Phillips, *The Scientific Lady: A Social History of Women's Scientific Interests, 1520–1918* (London: Weidenfield & Nicolson, 1992); Elizabeth A. Bohls, *Women Travel Writers and the Language of Aesthetics, 1716–1818* (Cambridge: Cambridge Univ. Press, 1995); Deborah Kellaway, *The Virago Book of Women Gardeners* (London: Virago Press, 1995); and Society for the History of Natural History, *Women and Natural History* (Oxford: Bodleian Library, 1996).

For additional details on primary collections and on published sources, please see the endnotes, which include full references and give additional citations. In addition, the chapter organization of endnotes identifies specific women as botanists, writers, club women, and so forth.

Above all, be prepared to travel, to ask numerous questions, and to consider unlikely sources, which sometimes turn out to be rewarding.

NOTES

Introduction

1. Terry Tempest Williams, *Refuge: An Unnatural History of Family and Place* (New York: Random House, 1991).

2. *Newsweek*, 3 November 1997, 19.

1 · "Wimmin Is Everywhere"

1. Quoted in Dorothy K. Gray, *Women of the West* (Millbrae CA: Les Femmes, 1976), 143.

2. Among those who argue that Indians were sound environmentalists are J. Baird Callicott, "Traditional American Indian and Traditional Western European Attitudes towards Nature: An Overview," in *Environmental Philosophy: A Collection of Readings,* ed. Robert Elliot and Aron Gare (University Park: Pennsylvania State Univ. Press, 1983), 231–59; J. Donald Hughes, *American Indian Ecology* (El Paso: Texas Western Press, 1983); Jeanne Kay, "Native Americans in the Fur Trade and Wildlife Depletion," *Environmental Review* 9 (summer 1985): 118–30; and Marjane Ambler, *Breaking the Iron Bonds: Indian Control of Energy Development* (Lawrence: Univ. Press of Kansas, 1990). See also Kent C. Ryden, *Mapping the Invisible Landscape: Folklore, Writing, and the Sense of Place* (Iowa City: Univ. of Iowa Press, 1993), 242–87. For nature as a theme in Indian history, see J. Donald Hughes, "Ecology and Development as Narrative Themes of World History," *Environmental History Review* 19 (spring 1995): 1–16.

Other analysts point out that Indians depleted certain resources, and that they respond, like whites, to technology and economic incentives. See, for instance, John Baden, Richard Stroup, and Walter Thurman, "Myths, Admonitions and Rationality: The American Indian as a Resource Manager," *Economic Inquiry* 19 (January 1981): 132–43; and J. Baird Callicott, "American Indian Land Wisdom? Sorting Out the Issue," *Journal of Forest History* 33 (January 1989): 35–42.

3. As told to Florence S. Shipek, *The Autobiography of Delfina Guero: A Diegueño Indian* (Los Angeles: Dawson's Book Shop, 1968). For the importance of women as resource managers in subsistence societies, consult Dounia Loudiyi and Alison Meares, *Women in Conservation: Tools for Analysis and a Framework for Action* (Ashland OH: Book-Masters, 1993). See also Vera Norwood, "Women's Place: Continuity and Change in Response to Western Landscapes," in *Western Women: Their Land, Their Lives,* ed. Lillian Schlissel, Vicki L. Ruiz, and Janice Monk (Albuquerque: Univ. of New Mexico Press, 1988), 159–62.

4. As told to Gilbert L. Wilson, comp., *Buffalo Bird Woman's Garden* (St. Paul: Minnesota Historical Society Press, 1987): 10–14, 119–20.

5. "An Indian Woman Deplores the Soreness of the Land, Recorded in 1925," in *Major Problems in American Environmental History,* ed. Carolyn Merchant (Boston: D. C. Heath, 1993), 261–62.

6. The ways in which Hispanics arranged the landscape are described in Robert H. Lister and Florence C. Lister, *Those Who Came Before* (Albuquerque: Univ. of New Mexico Press, 1993), 45–55. An example of seeking riches is found in Cynthia Russ Ramsay, "Domínquez and Escalante in the Southwest," in *Into the Wilderness,* ed. Lowell Georgia (Washington DC: National Geographic Society, 1978), 8–33. Hispanic ideas of nature are analyzed in Laura Pulido, "Latino Environmental Struggles in the Southwest" (Ph.D. diss., University of California at Los Angeles, 1991), 11–14.

7. For Hispanics' reliance on nature for healing, see Michael Moore, *Los Remedios: Traditional Herbal Remedies of the Southwest* (Santa Fe: Red Crane Books, 1990). Women writers' ideas of nature are discussed in Tey Diana Rebolledo, "Tradition and Mythology," in *The Desert Is No Lady: Southwestern Landscapes in Women's Writing and Art,* ed. Vera Norwood and Janice Monk (New Haven: Yale Univ. Press, 1987), 96–97. See also Norwood, "Women's Place," 160–61.

8. Marianne L. Stoller, "Peregrinas with Many Visions: Hispanic Women Artists of New Mexico, Southern Colorado, and Texas," in Norwood and Monks, *Desert Is No Lady,* 125–35.

9. John R. Stilgoe, *Common Landscape of America, 1580 to 1845* (New Haven: Yale Univ. Press, 1982), ix–x, 7–12, 34–43. That some Hispanic policies remained after white conquest is shown in Michael C. Meyer, "The Living Legacy of Hispanic Groundwater Law in the Contemporary Southwest," *Journal of the Southwest* 31 (autumn 1989): 287–99.

10. David Rich Lewis, *Neither Wolf nor Dog: American Indians, Environment, and Agrarian Change* (New York: Univ. of Oxford Press, 1994), 3–21.

11. For examples, see Friedrich Heer, *The Intellectual History of Europe* (Cleveland: World, 1953); and Franklin L. Baumer, *Modern European Thought: Continuity and Change in Ideas, 1600–1950* (New York: Macmillan, 1977).

12. Yasuhide Kawashime and Ruth Tone, "Environmental Policy in Early America: A Survey of Colonial Statutes," *Journal of Forest History* 27 (October 1983): 168–79; and James A. Jolly, "The Colonists' Attitudes toward the Land," *Journal of the Lancaster County Historical Society* 2 (1995): 2–12.

13. Nelson Van Valen, "James Fenimore Cooper and the Conservation Schism," *New York History* 62 (July 1981): 289–306; and Lee Clark Mitchell, *Witnesses to a Vanishing America: The Nineteenth-Century Response* (Princeton NJ: Princeton Univ. Press, 1981), xiii–xvi, 23–64, 189–212.

14. That conservation ideas began during the Civil War era is argued in Hans Huth, *Nature and the American: Three Centuries of Changing Attitudes* (Lincoln: Univ. of Nebraska Press, 1957), 192–212; James B. Trefethen, *An American Crusade for Wildlife* (New York: Winchester Press, 1975), 69–79; and Donald J. Pisani, "Forest and Conservation, 1865–1890," *Journal of American History* 72 (September 1985): 340–59.

For a description of the Great Plains as a desert, see Richard N. Ellis, ed., "General Pope's Report on the West, 1866," *Kansas Historical Quarterly* 35 (winter 1969): 345–72. For the Great Plains as a garden, see Leo E. Oliva, "Our Frontier Heritage and the Environment," *American West* 9 (January 1972): 44–47, 61–63; and Frederick Turner, *Beyond Geography: The Western Spirit against the Wilderness* (New York: Viking Press, 1980), 259–69.

The variety of attitudes toward land is demonstrated in Gilbert C.

Fite, "'The Only Thing Worth Working For': Land and Its Meaning for Pioneer Dakotans," *South Dakota History* 15 (winter 1985), 2–25; and Robert Bunting, "The Enviromnment and Settler Society in Western Oregon," *Pacific Historical Review* 64 (August 1995): 413–32.

15. George L. Cornell, "Native American Contributions to the Formation of the Modern Conservation Ethic" (Ph.D. diss., Michigan State University, 1982); Cornell, "The Influence of Native Americans on Modern Conservationists," *Environmental Review* 9 (1985): 104–17; and Richard White, "American Indians and the Environment, *Environmental Review* 9 (1985): 101–3.

16. Brooke Hindle, "Jane Colden," in *Notable American Women, 1607–1950,* ed. Edward T. James (Cambridge MA: Belknap Press, 1971), 1:357–78.

17. Phillis Wheatly, "An Hymn to the Morning," in Merchant, *Major Problems,* 171–72.

18. Quoted in Carolyn Merchant, *Ecological Revolutions: Nature, Gender, and Science in New England* (Chapel Hill: Univ. of North Carolina Press, 1989), 252. See also Carolyn Merchant, "The Theoretical Structure of Ecological Revolutions," *Environmental Review* 11 (winter 1987): 265–74.

19. Regina A. Brown, "Geology," in James, *Notable American Women,* 2:229.

20. Annie Houlhac Coffin, "Maria Martin," in James, *Notable American Women,* 2:505–6; and Marcia Myers Bonta, *Women in the Field: America's Pioneering Women Naturalists* (College Station: Texas A&M Univ. Press, 1991), 9–17.

21. Merchant, *Ecological Revolutions,* 250–54.

22. Lazella Schwarten, "Kate Furbish," in James, *Notable American Women,* 2:686–87.

23. Brown, "Geology," in James, *Notable American Women,* 2:230.

24. The idea of the wilderness as fun is explored in Ellen Huening Mokowski, "Scenic Parks and Landscape Values" (Ph.D. diss., University of Illinois, 1987).

25. The quotation is from Alan Axelrod and Charles Phillips, eds., *Environmentalists: A Biographical Dictionary from the 17th Century to*

the Present (Oxford, England: Facts on File, 1993), xi. Some examples of books that slight women are Roderick Nash, ed., *The American Environment: Readings in the History of Conservation*, 2d ed. (New York: Alfred A. Knopf, 1976); and Douglas H. Strong, *Dreamers and Defenders: American Conservationists*, 2d ed. (Lincoln: Univ. of Nebraska Press, 1988); both these books at least include Rachel Carson in their second editions. Similar in their neglect of women are William Schwarz, ed., *Voices for the Wilderness* (New York: Ballantine Books, 1969); and Frank Graham Jr., *Man's Dominion: The Story of Conservation in America* (Philadelphia: J. B. Lippincott, 1971). More recent works that overlook women are Donald Worster, *Nature's Economy: A History of Ecological Ideas*, 3d ed. (Cambridge: Cambridge Univ. Press, 1994); and Max Oeslshlaeger, *The Idea of Wilderness: From Prehistory to the Age of Ecology* (New Haven: Yale Univ. Press, 1991).

26. Gifford Pinchot, *Breaking New Ground* (Washington DC: Island Press, 1947), 323, 326. For Pinchot's development as an environmentalist, see Char Miller, "The Greening of Gifford Pinchot," *Environmental History Review* 16 (fall 1992): 1–20. Also useful is Elmo R. Richardson, "Conservation as a Political Issue: The Western Progressives' Dilemma, 1909–1912," *Pacific Northwest Quarterly* 49 (1958): 49–54.

27. Neal Stevens Burdick, "The Evolution of Environmental Consciousness in Nineteenth-Century America: An Interdisciplinary Study" (Ph.D. diss., Case Western Reserve University, 1981), 4; Michael Payne Branch, "The Enlightened Naturalist: Ecological Romanticism in American Literature" (Ph.D. diss., University of Virginia, 1993); and Daniel G. Payne, "In Sympathy with Nature: American Nature Writings and Environmental Politics, 1620–1920" (Ph.D. diss., State University of New York at Buffalo, 1993).

28. Vera Norwood, *Made from This Earth: American Women and Nature* (Chapel Hill: Univ. of North Carolina Press, 1993) 11–12.

29. Almira Hart Lincoln Phelps, *Familiar Lectures on Botany: Practical, Elementary, and Physiological* (Hartford CT: H. & F. J. Huntington, 1829), 9–15, 128–30, 200–219. See also Frederick Rudolph, "Almira Hart Lincoln Phelps," in James, *Notable American Women*, 2:58–60.

30. Robert Clarke, *Ellen Swallow: The Woman Who Founded Ecology* (New York: Follett, 1973): 113–19; and Janet Wilson James, "Ellen Henrietta Swallow Richards," in James, *Notable American Women*,

3:143–46. See also "The First Woman Graduate of M.I.T.: Ellen H. Richards, Chemist, 1873," in Madeleine B. Stern, *We the Women: Career Firsts of Nineteenth-Century America* (Lincoln: Univ. of Nebraska Press, 1962), 118–44; and H. Patricia Hynes, "Ellen Swallow, Lois Gibbs and Rachel Carson: Catalysts of the American Environmental Movement," *Women's Studies International Forum* 8 (1985): 291–98.

31. Sandra Lin Marburg, "Women and Environment: Subsistence Paradigms, 1850–1950," *Environmental Review* 8 (spring 1984): 7–22.

32. Hamlin Garland, *The Moccasin Ranch: A Story of Dakota* (New York: Harper & Brothers, 1909), 71, 78. Also useful is Robert Thacker, "'Twisting toward Insanity': Landscape and Female Intrapment in Plains Fiction," *North Dakota Quarterly* 52 (summer 1984): 181–94.

33. Quoted in Glenda Riley, *The Female Frontier: A Comparative View of Women on the Prairie and Plains* (Lawrence: Univ. Press of Kansas, 1988), 96. For a similar argument, see Peg Wherry, "At Home on the Range: Reactions of Pioneer Women to the Kansas Plains Landscape," *Kansas Quarterly* 18 (autumn 1986): 71–78; and Julie Roy Jeffrey, "'There Is Some Splendid Scenery': Women's Responses to the Great Plains Landscape," *Great Plains Quarterly* 8 (spring 1988): 69–78.

34. *Thirteenth Census of the United States Taken in the Year 1910,* vol. 4, *Population and Social Statistics* (Washington DC: Government Printing Office, 1872): 462, 486. See also Anne B. Webb, "Forgotten Persephones: Women Farmers on the Frontiers," *Minnesota History* 50 (winter 1986): 134–48.

35. For examples, see Irene Day Feulner, "Elizabeth Jane Russell Day: Biographical Sketch," 1967, Utah State Historical Society, Salt Lake City; and Mary Kidder Rak, Papers, undated, Special Collections, University of Arizona, Tucson. Ranchwomen's work is described in Mary S. Melcher, "Tending Children, Chickens, and Cattle: Southern Arizona Ranch and Farm Women, 1910–1940" (Ph.D. diss., Arizona State University, 1994). That women were among the early farmers in California is demonstrated in Steven Stoll, "The Fruits of Natural Advantage: Horticulture and the Industrial Countryside in California" (Ph.D. diss., Yale University, 1994).

36. Sheryl Patterson-Black, "Women Homesteaders on the Great

Plains Frontiers," *Frontiers* 1 (spring 1976): 67–88; Lonnie E. Underhill and Daniel F. Littlefield Jr., "Women Homeseekers in Oklahoma Territory, 1889–1901," *Pacific Historian* 17 (fall 1973): 36–47; Paula M. Bauman, "Single Women Homesteaders in Wyoming, 1880–1930," *Annals of Wyoming* 58 (spring 1986): 40–53; and Katherine Harris, *Long Vistas: Women and Families on Colorado Homesteads* (Niwot: Univ. Press of Colorado, 1993). Examples of women homesteaders of color are found in Nell Brown Propst, *Those Strenuous Dames of the Colorado Prairie* (Boulder CO: Pruett, 1982), 19–23.

37. "Early Days in Kansas," *South Kansas Tribune*, 16 July 1930; and LaVerne R. Johnson, "Myrtle Rigby: A Lady Homesteader," 1983, Utah State Historical Society, Salt Lake City.

Stories of women homesteaders are numerous. See Jeanne L. Wuillemin, A Homesteader's Letter, undated, South Dakota State Historical Resource Center, Pierre; Myrtle Yeoman Holm, "Homestead Days," 24 June 1905, South Dakota State Historical Research Center, Pierre; Bess Cobb, Letter to "Dear Helen," 31 July 1907, State Historical Society of North Dakota, Bismarck; Susan Strawbridge, Papers, 1913–28, Iowa State Historical Society, Des Moines; Harriet Joor, "Two Women Homesteaders," *Craftsman* 27 (January 1915): 436–40; Laura Frances Colston, "Two Girls on a Ranch," *Wide World Magazine*, 16 January 1916, 210–19, and 16 February 1916, 346–52; Edith Eudora Kohl, *Land of the Burnt Thigh* (New York: Funk & Wagnalls, 1938); Mary Culbertson, "Experiences in Wyoming," 1939, Wyoming State Archives, Cheyenne; Ada Blayney Clarke, "Pothook Pioneer: A Reminiscence," *Nebraska History* 39 (March 1958): 41–56; Paul Corey, "Bachelor Bess: My Sister," *South Dakota Historical Collections* 37 (1974): 1–101; Fern Spencer Dumbrill, "A Woman's Memories of Homesteading," in *Wyoming Homestead Heritage*, ed. Charles F. Spencer, 175–99 (Hicksville NY: Exposition Press, 1975); Lynette Wert, "The Lady Stakes a Claim," *Persimmon Hill* 6 (spring 1976): 18–23; Enid Bern, ed., "They Had a Wonderful Time: The Homesteading Letters of Anna and Ethel Erickson," *North Dakota History* 45 (fall 1978): 4–31; and Henry Kilian Goetz, "Kate's Quarter Section: A Woman in the Cherokee Strip," *Chronicles of Oklahoma* 61 (fall 1983): 246–67.

38. Stories of ranchwomen can be found in Olive Letitia Brown, "Reminiscences," undated, Arizona Historical Society, Tucson; [no author],

"Only Two Women in Panhandle," undated, and [no author], "Mrs. E. R. Bradley," 17 January 1927, both in J. Evetts Haley Collection, Nita Stewart Haley Memorial Library, Midland TX; "Carrie Roberts," Biography, Montana American Mothers Bicentennial Project, 1975–76, Montana State Historical Society, Helena; Propst, *Those Strenuous Dames of the Colorado Prairie*; Denice Wheeler, "The Feminine Frontier: Wyoming Women . . . 1850–1900," 1987, Utah State Historical Society, Salt Lake City; and Elizabeth Maret, *Women of the Range: Women's Roles in the Texas Beef Cattle Industry* (College Station: Texas A&M Univ. Press, 1993).

39. María de Jesús Domínquez, "Inventory of Separate Property of Married Woman," 6 November 1862, Huntington Library, San Marino CA.

40. Susan McSween Barber, Papers, undated, Center for Southwest Research, University of New Mexico Library, Albuquerque. For a similar tale, see Emma Altman, "Story of Her Life," in "The Family Story," sec. 4, University of Texas at El Paso.

41. Con Marshall, "Wife Builds Vast Wyoming Cattle Spread While Spouse Works Mines," late 1960s, J. Evetts Haley Collection, Nita Stewart Haley Memorial Library, Midland TX.

42. Carl V. Larson, "The Women of the Mormon Battalion," 1989, Utah State Historical Society, Salt Lake City.

43. Mrs. E. J. Guerin, *Mountain Charley; or, The Adventures of Mrs. E. J. Guerin, Who Was Thirteen Years in Male Attire* (Norman: Univ. of Oklahoma Press, 1968); and "Gold Hill Women," *Gold Hill News*, 28 October 1865, 3:2. For other adventure stories, see Annie D. Tallent, *The First White Woman in the Black Hills* (Mitchell SD: Educator Supply, 1923), 128–29. See also Tallent, *The Black Hills; or, The Last Hunting Ground of the Dakotahs* (Sioux Falls SD: Brevet Press, 1974).

44. Kate Dare Whittlesey Resley, Diary, 1899, Special Collections, University of Texas at El Paso.

45. For information on Nellie Cashman, see Harriet Rochlin, "The Amazing Adventures of a Good Woman," *Journal of the West* 12 (April 1973): 281–95. Poetry is quoted from Della M. Baker, Memoir, 1938, Special Collections, University of Oregon Library, Eugene. Also en-

lightening are Georgia White, Diary, 21 February 1898 to 29 September 1898, Georgia White Collection, Yukon Archives, Whitehorse, Yukon Territory, Canada; and Inga Sjoneth Kolloen, "Crossing the Chilcoot Pass," 9 March to 25 June 1898, Manuscripts, University of Washington Libraries, Seattle. See also James H. Duckeer, "Gold Rushers North: A Census Study of the Yukon and Alaskan Gold Rushes, 1896–1900," *Pacific Northwest Quarterly* 85, no. 3 (July 1994): 82–92.

46. Josephine C. Scott, "A Thousand Miles of Desert and Mountains: A Prospecting Trip across Nevada and over the Sierras, March 14–September 9, 1914," Special Collections, Getchell Library, University of Nevada, Reno.

47. [No author], "Mrs. Luella Moyer: Campbell County Pioneer," 1936, Wyoming State Archives, Cheyenne.

48. Pearl Baker, *Robber's Roost Recollections* (Logan: Utah State Univ. Press, 1976), 151–53.

49. Florence Hughes, Interview Transcript, 30 September 1979, American Heritage Center, University of Wyoming Library, Laramie.

50. Scholars have spent a good deal of time defining such concepts as nature, environment, ecology, landscape, and wilderness, and have analyzed such factors as the influence of Christianity on environmental values, but few scholars have examined how these concepts differ in meaning to women and men. See, for instance, Michael Frome, *Battle for the Wilderness* (New York: Praeger, 1974), 11–16; Morgan Sherwood, "The End of American Wilderness," *Environmental Review* 9 (1983): 197–208; Dennis Roth, "The National Forests and the Campaign for Wilderness Legislation," *Journal of National Agricultural Laboratory Associates* 8 (1983): 161–86; Max Oelschlaeger, *The Idea of Wilderness: From Prehistory to the Age of Ecology* (New Haven: Yale Univ. Press, 1991); and Susan Power Bratton, *Christianity, Wilderness, and Wildlife: The Original Desert Solitaire* (Scranton: Univ. of Scranton Press, 1993). Women's view of nature is analyzed in Annette Kolodny, *The Lay of the Land: Metaphor as Experience and History in American Life and Letters* (Chapel Hill: Univ. of North Carolina Press, 1975); and Kolodny, *The Land before Her: Fantasy and Experience of the American Frontiers, 1630–1860* (Chapel Hill: Univ. of North Carolina Press, 1984).

51. Ramsay, "Domínquez and Esclante in the Southwest," 10.

52. Jeanne Smith Carr, Papers, 1842–1903, Huntington Library, San Marino CA.

53. Carr, Papers; and Ronald H. Limbaugh, "John Muir's Life and Legacy," in *John Muir: Life and Work*, ed. Sally M. Miller (Albuquerque: Univ. of New Mexico Press, 1993), 3–5.

54. John Muir, Papers, 1902–55, Letters to Katharine Putnam Hooker, 2 August 1911, 29 August 1911, and 19 September 1911; Letters to Florence Merriam Bailey, 8 March 1907 and 27 March 1913, Huntington Library, San Marino CA.

55. Quoted in Peggy A. Voleke Kelley, *Women of Nebraska Hall of Fame* (Omaha: Nebraska International Women's Year Coalition, 1976), 50. See also Julius Sterling Morton, Papers, 1814–1960, Nebraska State Historical Society, Lincoln; and "Arbor Lodge Gained Much from Caroline Norton," *Lincoln Sun, Journal and Star*, 12 April 1974.

56. Frances B. Cogan, *All-American Girl: The Ideal of Real Womanhood in Mid-Nineteenth-Century America* (Athens: Univ. of Georgia Press, 1989).

57. Bonta, *Women in the Field*, 18–29, 42–48. A useful discussion of married and single women scientists is found in Nancy G. Slack, "Nineteenth-Century American Women Botanists: Wives, Widows, and Work," in *Uneasy Careers and Intimate Lives: Women in Science, 1789–1979*, ed. Pnina G. Abir-Am and Dorinda Outram (New Brunswick NJ: Rutgers Univ. Press, 1987), 77–103.

58. William Campbell Steere, "Elizabeth Gertrude Knight Britton," in James, *Notable American Women*, 3:243–44; and Milton B. Trautman, "Margaret Morse Nice," in *Notable American Women: The Modern Period*, ed. Barbara Sicherman and Carol Hurd Green (Cambridge MA: Belknap Press, 1980), 506–7.

59. Jim O'Brien, "Environmentalism as a Mass Movement: Historical Notes," *Radical America* 17 (1983): 7–11.

60. Polly Welts Kaufman, *National Parks and the Woman's Voice: A History* (Albuquerque: Univ. of New Mexico Press, 1996), 30–32.

61. O'Brien, "Environmentalism as a Mass Movement," 11, suggests that men's conservation organizations limited themselves by class and race. Women's groups formed a similar structure.

62. For problems of Indian women, see, for instance, Robert S. McPherson, "From Dezba to 'John': The Changing Role of Navajo Women in Southeastern Utah," *American Indian Culture and Research Journal* 18 (1994): 187–209.

63. Maria de Los Angeles G. Pompa, Interview Transcript, 22 April 1983; and Margaret Candelaria, Interview Transcript, 5 August 1976; both at the Institute of Oral History, University of Texas at El Paso.

64. Juanita [no last name given], Interview Transcript, 1976; and Belén B. Robles, Interview Transcript, 26–27 April 1976; both at the Institute of Oral History, University of Texas at El Paso.

65. Juanita Gastello, Interview Transcript, 18 November 1977; and Herminia M. Chávez, Interview Transcript, 19 November 1977; both at the Institute of Oral History, University of Texas at El Paso.

66. "Eulalia Elias," in Rosalie Crowe and Diane Tod, *Arizona Women's Hall of Fame* (Phoenix: Arizona Historical Society, 1985), 31–32.

67. Bonta, *Women in the Field,* 103–14; and Marcia Myers Bonta, ed., *American Women Afield: Writings by Pioneering Women Naturalists* (College Station: Texas A&M Univ. Press, 1995), 142.

68. Norwood, *Made from This Earth,* 12; Eric Jay Dolin, "Black Americans' Attitudes toward Wildlife," *Journal of Environmental Education* 20 (fall 1988): 19; and Sondra Yvonne Millner, "Free Grace in the Wilderness: An Aesthetic Analysis of Land and Space in African American Culture: In the Narratives of Henry Bibb, Harriet Jacobs and Josiah Benson" (Ph.D. diss., Temple University, 1994), 2–3, 21, 37–38, 101–2, 107–10.

69. Era Bell Thompson, *American Daughter* (St. Paul: Minnesota Historical Society Press, 1986).

70. Quoted in Norwood, *Made from This Earth,* 207.

71. Drusilla Nixon, Interview Transcript, 11 December 1975; and Frances Hills, Interview Transcript, 12 October 1985; both at the Institute of Oral History, University of Texas at El Paso.

72. Nathan Hare, "Black Ecology," in Merchant, *Major Problems,* 479–82; and Evelyn C. White, "Black Women and the Wilderness," in *The Stories That Shape Us: Contemporary Women Write about the*

West, ed. Theresa Jordan and James Hepworth (New York: W. W. Norton, 1995), 376–83.

73. Leigh-Wai Doo, "Florence Wai Kyiu Young," 112–14, and Miya Soga, "Sei Tanizawa Soga," 352–55; both in *Notable Women of Hawaii,* ed. Barbara Bennett Peterson (Honolulu: Univ. of Hawaii Press, 1984).

74. Pulido, "Latino Environmental Struggles," 18–19, 22–27.

75. For example, during the 1870s, Maria E. Fernald, the wife and mother of entomologists, began her own work—cataloguing small moths in Maine. Marilyn Bailey Ogilvie, "Marital Collaboration: An Approach to Science," in Abir-Am and Outram, *Uneasy Careers,* 104–25; and Bonta, *Women in the Field,* 150.

2 · The European Legacy

1. Although learned women existed in many cultures, adventurous outdoors women did not. See, for example, Patricia H. Labalme, ed., *Beyond Their Sex: Learned Women of the European Past* (New York: New York Univ. Press, 1984).

2. Norwood, *Made from This Earth,* 11–12.

3. Norwood, *Made from This Earth,* 5.

4. Dorinda Outram, "Before Objectivity: Wives, Patronage, and Cultural Reproduction in Early Nineteenth-Century French Science," in Abir-Am and Outram, *Uneasy Careers,* 19–30.

5. Benjamin Wilkes, *English Moths and Butterflies* (London, 1773).

6. John Lightfoot, *Catalogue of the Portland Museum* (London: Kearsley, 1786), which can be found in the Hope Library, University Museum, Oxford University, Oxford, England.

7. Thomas Edward Bowdich and Sarah Bowdich, *An Introduction to the Ornithology of Cuvier* (Paris: Treuttel & Wurtz, 1821), *Excursions in Madeira and Porto-Santo* (London, 1825), and *Taxidermy* (London: Longman, 1820).

8. Ann B. Shteir, "Botany in the Breakfast Room: Women and Early Nineteenth-Century British Plant Study," in Abir-Am and Outram, *Uneasy Careers,* 31–44; and Mary Ward, *The Microscope,* 3d ed. (London: Groombridge, 1869), 5. Also useful are D. E. Allen, "The Women Members of the Botanical Society of London, 1836–1856," *British Jour-*

nal for the History of Science 13 (1980): 250–54; Graeme Gooday, "'Nature' in the Laboratory: Domestication and Discipline with the Microscope in Victorian Life," British Journal for the History of Science 24 (1991): 307–41; and Ludmilla Jordanova, "Gender and the Historiography of Science," British Journal for the History of Science 26 (1993): 469–83.

9. Mary Anning, Letter to William Buckland, June 1832; and Pencil Drawing of Squaloraja Found at Lyme Regis, December 1829; both are located in the Buckland Archive, University Museum, Oxford University, Oxford, England. A coprolite collected by Mary Anning is in the Geological Collections, University Museum, Oxford. See also Hugh Torrens, "Mary Anning (1799–1847) of Lyme: The Greatest Fossilist the World Ever Knew," British Journal for the History of Science 28 (1995): 257–84. An overview of women's struggles in science is found in Patricia Phillips, The Scientific Lady: A Social History of Women's Scientific Interests, 1520–1918 (London: Weidenfield & Nicolson, 1992).

10. Elizabeth Philpot, Letter to Mrs. Buckland, 9 December 1833, Buckland Archives, University Museum, Oxford University, Oxford, England; and Fossil Ink Sac, Geological Collections, University Museum, Oxford.

11. Eleanor Ormerod, Royal Agricultural Society posters of the Turnip-Fly or Flea-Beetle and the Daddy-Long-Legs, ca. 1882; Notes for Observations of Injurious Insects, 1879–81; "Report of Observations of Injurious Insects, 1882–1900"; Letter to Professor J. O. Westwood, 20 April 1888; "Ox Hide with Perforation from Ox-Warble Flies," 1888; and "Important to Farmers and Fraziers: Warbles in Hides," 1888; all are located in the Hope Library, University Museum, Oxford University, Oxford, England; and Ormerod, Guide to the Methods of Insect Life (London: Simpkin, Marshall, 1884). See also Virginia Woolf, "Miss Ormerod," Dial 77 (1924): 466–74; and J. F. McDiarmid Clark, "Eleanor Ormerod (1828–1902) as an Economic Entomologist: Pioneer of Purity Even More Than of Paris Green," British Journal for the History of Science 25 (1993): 431–52.

12. Miriam Rothschild, Fleas, Flukes and Cuckoos (London: Collins, 1952); Rothschild, A Colour Atlas of Insect Tissues via the Flea (London: Wolfe, 1986); Rothschild, Dear Lord Rothschild: Birds, Butterflies

and History (Philadelphia: ISI Press, 1983); Rothschild, *Butterfly Cooing like a Dove* (London: Doubleday, 1991); and [no author], *An Illustrated Catalogue of the Rothschild Collection of Fleas in the British Museum*, vol. 1 (London, 1953)

13. Mrs. Alfred Gatty, *Parables from Nature* (London: Bell & Daldy, 1857), viii, 140–41. For a discussion of the male view of sexuality in nature, see Londa Schiebinger, "The Private Life of Plants: Sexual Politics in Carl Linnaeus and Erasmus Darwin," in *Science and Sensibility: Gender and Scientific Enquiry, 1780–1945*, ed. Marina Benjamin (Oxford, England: Blackwell, 1991), 121–43.

14. Marvin Perry, *An Intellectual History of Modern Europe* (Boston: Houghton Mifflin, 1992), 281–86.

15. Phelps, *Familiar Lectures on Botany.*

16. Priscilla Wakefield, *An Introduction to Botany* (London: E. Newberry, 1796), 1; and Wakefield, *Instinct Displayed, in a Collection of Well-Authenticated Facts, Exemplifying the Extraordinary Sagacity of Various Species of the Animal Creation* (London: Darton, Harvey, & Darton, 1814), x–xi, 177–78, 289.

17. Christina Rossetti, *Sing-Song: A Nursery Rhyme Book* (London: George Routledge, 1872). During the early twentieth century, noted sex educator and paleontologist Marie Stopes, who also believed in reaching children, published *Study of Plant Life for Young People* (London: A. Moring, 1906).

18. "Maria Sibylla Merian," in Natalie Zemon Davis, *Women on the Margins: Three Seventeenth-Century Lives* (Cambridge MA: Harvard Univ. Press, 1995), 140–202; and Maria Sibylla Merian, *Flowers, Butterflies, and Insects* (New York: Dover, 1991).

19. Merian's first work, *Der Raupen wunderbare Verwandelung und sonderbare Blumennahrun*, 2 vols. (Nuremberg and Frankfurt, 1679–83), can be found in the Ashmoleian Museum, Oxford, England. Her master work, *Dissertatio de generatione el metamorphosibus insectorum Surinamensium*, 2d ed. (1719), is in the University Library in Oxford, England.

20. Marianne North Gallery, Royal Botanic Garden, Kew, England.

21. Quoted in Marianne North, *A Vision of Eden: The Life and Work of*

Marianne North (London: Royal Botanic Gardens, Kew, 1980), 84.

22. Quoted in North, *Vision of Eden*, 88, 192, 193, 196.

23. Val Williams, *Women Photographers: The Other Observers, 1900 to the Present* (London: Virago Press, 1986), 11–12, 14–15, 18–20.

24. Williams, *Women Photographers*, 22–24.

25. Deborah Kellaway, ed., *The Virago Book of Women Gardeners* (London: Virago Press, 1995), ix–xvi.

26. Jane Loudon, *Ornamental Flowers* (London: Studio Editions, 1991), 5–6.

27. Loudon, *Ornamental Flowers*, 12; and Jane Loudon, *Ladies Magazine of Gardening*, vol. 1 (London: William Smith, 1842).

28. Kellaway, *Virago Book of Women Gardeners*, ix–x.

29. Betty Massingham, *Miss Jekyll: Portrait of a Great Gardener* (London: Country Life, 1966), 162–75; and Joan Edwards, *Gertrude Jekyll: Before the Boots, the Gardens, and the Portrait* (London: Museum of Garden History, 1993), 4–5, 9, 20, 24–25.

30. Quoted in Kellaway, *Virago Book of Women Gardeners*, xiii.

31. Kellaway, *Virago Book of Women Gardeners*, xvi–xvii, 127.

32. See, for example, Alice Morse Earle, *Old Time Gardens* (New York: Macmillan, 1901); and Helena Rutherfurd Ely, *A Woman's Hardy Garden* (New York: Macmillan, 1903; reprint, 1990).

33. Stella Nicholas, comp., *Education, Friendship, and Fun: A History of the National Association of Women's Clubs* (n.p.: National Association of Women's Clubs, 1994), 3–5.

34. Society for the History of Natural History, *Women and Natural History* (Oxford, England: Bodleian Library, 1996), 14–15.

35. The International Association for the Total Suppression of Vivisection, *The Woman and the Age* (London: E. W. Allen, 1881), 5, 15, 18. For more information, see Mary Elston, "Women and Anti-Vivisection in Victorian England, 1870–1900," in *Vivisection in Historical Perspective*, ed. Nicolas A. Rupke (London: Croom Helm, 1987), 259–94.

36. Society for the History of Natural History, *Women and Natural History*, 5–7.

37. Quoted in Society for the History of Natural History, *Women and Natural History*, 27.

38. Society for the History of Natural History, *Women and Natural History*, 17.

39. Lynn McDonald, *The Women Founders of the Social Sciences* (Ottawa, Ontario: Carleton Univ. Press, 1994), 108–9, 205, 220–21, 245–46.

40. Melissa Leach and Cathy Green, *Gender and Environmental History: Moving beyond the Narratives of the Past in Contemporary Women-Environment Policy Debates* (Brighton, England: Institute of Developmental Studies, 1995), 1.

41. Francis Gribble, *The Early Mountaineers* (London: T. Fisher Unwin, 1899), 240.

42. Quoted in Gribble, *Early Mountaineers*, 241.

43. Quoted in Gribble, *Early Mountaineers*, 241.

44. Gribble, *Early Mountaineers*, 241–49.

45. Mrs. Cole, *A Lady's Tour round Monte Rosa* (London: Longman, Brown, Green, Longmans & Roberts, 1859), 1.

46. Bill Birkett and Bill Peascod, *Women Climbing: Two Hundred Years of Achievement* (London: A & C Black, 1989), 18–22.

47. Birkett and Peascod, *Women Climbing*, 31–35; and Shirley Angell, *Pinnacle Club: A History of Women Climbing* (Glasgow: Pinnacle Club, 1988), 1–4.

48. Meriel Buxton, *Ladies of the Chase* (London: Sportsman's Press, 1987), 14–35.

49. Buxton, *Ladies of the Chase*, 43–67.

50. Lady Greville, ed., *Ladies in the Field: Sketches of Sport* (London: Ward & Downy, 1894), iii–iv.

51. Lady Greville, *Ladies in the Field*, 3–4.

52. Lady Greville, *Ladies in the Field*, 147, 272, 285.

53. Lady Greville, *Ladies in the Field*, 235–36, 243.

54. *Sportswoman* 1 (1908), unpaged.

55. Buxton, *Ladies of the Chase,* 102, 133, 145–56, 172.

56. Dorothy Middleton, *Victorian Lady Travellers* (New York: E. P. Dutton, 1965), 3–4, 7, 9.

57. I. G. Simmons, *Environmental History: A Concise Introduction* (Oxford, England: Blackwell, 1993), 175.

58. Theresa S. Dougal, "Spreading Their Wings: The Travel Narrative as an Alternative Genre for Late Eighteenth-Century Women Writers" (Ph.D. diss., University of Chicago, 1994), 1–60, 107–39.

59. A Lady Pioneer, *The Indian Alps and How We Crossed Them* (New York: Dodd, Mead, 1876), vii–viii.

60. Middleton, *Victorian Lady Travellers,* 3–15; and Leo Hamalian, ed., *Ladies on the Loose: Women Travellers of the 18th and 19th Centuries* (South Yarmouth MA: John Curley, 1981), xii–xvi.

61. Margaret Fountaine, *Love among the Butterflies* (London: Collins, 1980); and Fountaine, *Butterflies and Late Loves* (London: Collins, 1986). See also a series of *Danaida chrysippus* collected by Margaret Fountaine, ca. 1925, Hope Collection, University Museum, Oxford University, Oxford, England.

62. Mary Kingsley, "Journey into the Jungle," in Hamalian, *Ladies on the Loose,* 533, 547; and Middleton, *Victorian Lady Travellers,* 149–76.

63. Elizabeth A. Bohls, *Women Travel Writers and the Language of Aesthetics, 1716–1818* (Cambridge: Cambridge Univ. Press, 1995), 89–107; Wollstonecraft is quoted on 145. Also helpful is Katharine S. H. Turner, "Women Travel Writers of the Eighteenth Century," (M.Phil. thesis, Oxford University, 1990).

64. Bohls, *Women Travel Writers,* 82–89.

65. Quoted in Marni L. Stanley, "The Imperial Mission: Women Travellers and the Propaganda of Empire" (D.Phil. thesis, St. Hilda's College, Oxford University, 1990), 167.

66. Quoted in "Maria Theresa Longworth Visits Celebrated Sites," in *With Women's Eyes: Visitors to the New World,* ed. Marion Tinling (Hamden CT: Archon Books, 1993), 103.

67. Sara Mills, *Discourses of Differences: An Analysis of Women's Travel Writing and Colonialism* (London: Routledge, 1991), 27–29,

83–94. The quotations are from "Ida Pfeiffer, 1853," 84, and "Lady Duffus Hardy, 1880," 145, 149, in Tinling, *With Women's Eyes*, 84.

68. Isabella L. Bird, *A Lady's Life in the Rocky Mountains* (London: John Murray, 1879). Also consult Pat Barr, *A Curious Life for a Lady: The Story of Isabella Bird* (New York: Doubleday, 1970); and Anne Gatti, *Isabella Bird Bishop* (London: Hamish Hamilton, 1988). Bird's Hawaiian journey is described in Isabella Bird, *Six Months in Hawaii* (London: John Murray, 1875).

69. "Isabella Bird Describes Nature in the Rockies, 1873," in Merchant, *Major Problems*, 385–86; Vera L. Norwood, "Heroines of Nature: Four Women Respond to the American Landscape," *Environmental Review* 8 (spring 1984): 37–40; and Norwood, *Made from This Earth*, 8.

70. Rose Pender, *A Lady's Experiences in the Wild West in 1883* (London: George Tucker, 1888), v–vii, 1–28.

71. Pender, *Lady's Experiences*, 33–36.

72. Pender, *Lady's Experiences*, 17, 78.

73. Quoted in "Constance Gordon Cumming, 1878," in Tinling, *Through Women's Eyes*, 138, 140.

74. Middleton, *Victorian Lady Travellers*, 1–18. For additional examples of women travelers, see W. H. Davenport Adams, *Celebrated Women Travellers of the Nineteenth Century* (London: W. Swan Sonnenschein, 1883); and Dea Birkett, *Spinsters Abroad: Victorian Lady Explorers* (Oxford, England: Basil Blackwell, 1989).

3 · Botanizers, Birders, and Other Naturalists

1. Joseph Ewan, "Alice Eastwood," in Sicherman and Green, *Notable American Women*, 216.

2. Bonta, *Women in the Field*, 93–99.

3. Ewan, "Alice Eastwood," in Sicherman and Green, *Notable American Women*, 217; and Bonta, *Women in the Field*, 100–101.

4. Quoted in Carol Green Wilson, *Alice Eastwood's Wonderland: The Adventures of a Botanist* (San Francisco: California Academy of Sciences, 1955), 87.

5. Duane Isely, *One Hundred and One Botanists* (Ames: Iowa State Univ. Press, 1994). Earlier works that slight women are Alexander B. Adams, *Eternal Quest: The Story of the Great Naturalists* (New York: G. P. Putnam's Sons, 1969); and John K. Terres, ed., *Discovery: Great Moments in the Lives of Outstanding Naturalists* (Philadelphia: J. B. Lippincott, 1961). Not one woman appears in Elsa Guerdrum Allen, "The History of American Ornithology before Audubon," *Transactions of the American Philosophical Society* 43 (1951): 387–583.

6. Bonta, *Women in the Field*, 71.

7. Janice Emily Bowers, *A Sense of Place: The Life and Work of Forrest Shreve* (Tucson: Univ. of Arizona Press, 1988), 21–23, 30, 66–67, 82, 95, 148. Also helpful on Shreve and the issue of forgotten women scientists are George E. Webb, "Leading Women Scientists in the American Southwest: A Demographic Portrait, 1900–1950," *New Mexico Historical Review* 68 (January 1993): 41–61; and George E. Webb, "A Woman's Place Is in the Lab: Arizona's Women Research Scientists, 1910–1950," *Journal of Arizona History* 34 (spring 1993): 45–64.

8. Lilla Irvin Leach Collection, 1972, Special Collections, University of Oregon Library, Eugene.

9. Leach Collection.

10. Leach Collection.

11. Paul Brooks, *Speaking for Nature: How Literary Naturalists from Henry Thoreau to Rachel Carson Have Shaped America* (Boston: Houghton Mifflin, 1980), 165.

12. Florence Merriam Bailey, Obituary, 1948, Center for Southwest Research, University of New Mexico Library, Albuquerque; and Paul H. Oehser, "Florence Merriam Bailey," in James, *Notable American Women*, 2:82–83.

13. "Florence Merriam Bailey on the Early Audubon Women, 1900," in Merchant, *Major Problems*, 389.

14. Harriet Kofalk, *No Woman Tenderfoot: Florence Merriam Bailey, Pioneer Naturalist* (College Station: Texas A&M Univ. Press, 1989), 90, 143–45. For a survey of the "feather" controversy, see Robin W. Doughty, *Feather Fashions and Bird Preservation* (Berkeley: Univ. of California Press, 1975); and Harry Kersey Jr., *Pelts, Plumes, and Hides:*

White Traders among the Seminole Indians, 1870–1930 (Gainesville: Univ. Press of Florida, 1975).

15. Kofalk, *No Woman Tenderfoot*, 162–67, 181; and Bailey, Obituary.

16. Dorothy Dimsdale, "Good Things Survive," *Western Tanager* 57 (July/August 1991): 1.

17. Dimsdale, "Good Things Survive," 1–2. For a discussion of animal rights, see Lisa Mighetto, *Wild Animals and American Environmental Ethics* (Tucson: Univ. of Arizona Press, 1991), especially 14–16.

18. Dimsdale, "Good Things Survive," 2–4.

19. Dora Jane Isenberg Cole, "Mary Dorothea Rice Isenberg," in Peterson, *Notable Women of Hawaii*, 161–64.

20. Bonta, *Women in the Field*, 49–50.

21. Rianna M. Williams, "Annie Montague Alexander: Explorer, Naturalist, Philanthropist," *Hawaiian Journal of History* 28 (1994): 113–18.

22. Bonta, *Women in the Field*, 54–55.

23. Williams, "Annie Montague Alexander," 119, 125.

24. Jennie McCowen, "Women in Iowa," *Annals of Iowa* 3 (October 1884): 105.

25. Laura A. Linton, Biographical Data File, 1955–56, Minnesota Historical Society, St. Paul; and Jean C. Dahlberg, "Laura A. Linton and Lintonite," *Minnesota History* 38 (March 1962): 21–23.

26. Bonta, *Women in the Field*, 153.

27. Bonta, *Women in the Field*, 51–52, 55.

28. Quoted in Bonta, *Women in the Field*, 74–75.

29. Clara Field McCarthy, "Clara's Episodes: A Reflection of Early Wyoming, 1909–1911," 1964, Wyoming State Archives, Cheyenne; and "Luvenia Conway Roberts," in *Texas Tears and Texas Sunshine: Voices of Frontier Women*, ed. Jo Ellen Powell Exley (College Station: Texas A&M Univ. Press, 1985), 197–98.

30. Wilson, *Alice Eastwood's Wonderland*, 50, 55–56.

31. Wilson, *Alice Eastwood's Wonderland*, 65; and Bonta, *Women in the Field*, 115.

32. Edith Van Allen Murphey, Papers, 1939–53, Special Collections, Getchell Library, University of Nevada, Reno.

33. Pictured in Dimsdale, "Good Things Survive," 3, 5.

34. See, for example, the clothing mishaps of Eliza R. Lythgoe, "Pioneer Blood," 1936, Wyoming State Archives, Cheyenne; and Mary Olivette Taylor Bunton in Exley, *Texas Tears and Texas Sunshine*, 231–33.

35. Leach Collection, Special Collections, University of Oregon, Eugene.

36. Bonta, *Women in the Field*, 117; and Bonta, *American Women Afield*, 159–60.

37. Nell Stevenson, Diary, 1907, Colorado Historical Society, Denver.

38. "Pioneer Boulder Woman, Martha Maxwell, Brought Fame to Colorado," *Boulder Camera*, 21 August 1958; and photograph section in Maxine Benson, *Martha Maxwell: Rocky Mountain Naturalist* (Lincoln: Univ. of Nebraska Press, 1986), unpaged.

39. Quoted in Mary Dartt, *On the Plains and among the Peaks; or, How Mrs. Maxwell Made Her Natural History Collection* (Philadelphia: Claxton, Remsen & Haffelfinger, 1879), 119.

40. "Pioneer Boulder Woman," *Boulder Camera*, 21 August 1958.

41. Quoted in Williams, "Annie Montague Alexander," 117.

42. Mary Hetty Bonar, Diary, 1885, State Historical Society of North Dakota, Bismarck.

43. Carrie Sweetser, Diary, 1897–1935, Special Collections, University of Oregon Library, Eugene.

44. Sally Gregory Kohlstedt, "Nature Study," in *Handbook of American Women's History*, ed. Angela Howard Zophy (New York: Garland, 1990), 423–34.

45. Hunter Dupree and Marian L. Gade, "Mary Katharine Layne Curran Brandegee," in James, *Notable American Women*, 1:228–29.

46. Bonta, *Women in the Field*, 61–69.

47. Bonta, *Women in the Field*, 182–83, 209–10; and Marianne Gosztonyi Ainley, "Field Work and Family: North American Women Orni-

thologists, 1900–1950," in Abir-Am and Outram, *Uneasy Careers*, 63–67.

48. Bonta, *Women in the Field*, 51–52.

49. Edith Clements, Papers, 1911–49, Nebraska State Historical Society, Lincoln. Also revealing in its sophistication is an early monograph, Edith Schwartz Clements, *The Relation of Leaf Structure to Physical Factors*, 1905, reprinted from *Transactions of the American Microscopical Society*, Special Collections, University of Nebraska Library, Lincoln.

50. Quoted in Glenda Riley, *Inventing the American Woman* (Wheeling IL: Harlan Davidson, 1995), 1:155.

51. Charlotte Haywood, "Lydia White Shattuck," in James, *Notable American Women*, 3:273–74; and Riley, *Inventing the American Woman*, 2:203.

52. Katharine Brandegee, Letters, 1900–1902, in Harvey Monroe Hall, Papers, 1896–1932, Bancroft Library, University of California, Berkeley.

53. Riley, *Inventing the American Women*, 2:257–59.

54. "Ruth Harris Thomas," in Bonta, *American Women Afield*, 233–34.

55. Wilson, *Alice Eastwood's Wonderland*, 38.

56. Quoted in Bonta, *Women in the Field*, 102.

4 · Writers and Poets

1. Daniel G. Payne, "In Sympathy with Nature: American Nature Writing and Environmental Politics, 1620–1920" (Ph.D. diss., State University of New York at Buffalo, 1993).

2. For a review of Austin's life, see Peggy Pond Church, *Wind's Trail: The Early Life of Mary Austin* (Santa Fe: Museum of New Mexico Press, 1990).

3. Norwood, "Heroines of Nature, 42–43.

4. Helen MacKnight Doyle, *Mary Austin: Woman of Genius* (New York: Gotham House, 1939), xiii.

5. Mary Austin, Clipping File, undated, Center for Southwest Re-

search, University of New Mexico Library, Albuquerque; and Jo W. Lyday, *Mary Austin: The Southwest Works* (Austin: Steck-Vaughn, 1968), 7.

6. Albert Brantley Harwell Jr., "Writing the Wilderness: A Study of Henry Thoreau, John Muir, and Mary Austin" (Ph.D. diss., University of Tennessee, 1992), 182–87.

7. Peter Wild, *Pioneer Conservationists of Western America* (Missoula MT: Mountain Press, 1979), 83, 85, 87.

8. Melody Graulich, ed., *Western Trails: A Collection of Short Stories by Mary Austin* (Reno: Univ. of Nevada Press, 1987), 3–4.

9. Branch, "Enlightened Naturalist"; Gregg Webster Wentzell, "Wildness and the American Mind: The Social Construction of Nature in Environmental Romanticism from Thoreau to Dillard" (Ph.D. diss., Miami University, Oxford OH, 1993); and Michael P. Branch, "Early Romantic Natural History Literature," in *American Nature Writers,* ed. John Elder (New York: Charles Scribner's Sons, 1996), 2:1059–77.

10. Kathleen Davies, "The Goddess in the Landscape: A Tradition of Twentieth Century American Women's Pastoral" (Ph.D. diss., Indiana University, 1991), 1–39.

11. Norwood, *Made from This Earth,* 25–41.

12. Jeanne Kay and Craig J. Brown, "Mormon Beliefs about Land and Natural Resources, 1847–1877," *Journal of Historical Geography* 11 (July 1985): 253–67; Dan L. Flores, "Agriculture, Mountain Ecology, and the Land Ethic: Phases of the Environmental History of Utah," in *Working the Range: Essays on the History of Western Land Management and the Environment,* ed. John R. Wunder (Westport CT: Greenwood Press, 1985), 157–86; and Thomas G. Alexander, "Stewardship and Enterprise: The LDS Church and the Wasatch Oasis Environment, 1847–1930," *Western Historical Quarterly* 25 (autumn 1994): 341–66.

13. Charlotte L. Forten [later Charlotte Forten Grimké], *The Journal of Charlotte L. Forten: A Free Negro in the Slave Era* (New York: Collier Books, 1961), 46–47.

14. Karen Knowles, ed., *Celebrating the Land: Women's Nature Writings, 1850–1991* (Flagstaff AZ: Northland, 1992), 3–5; Lou Rodenberger, "Trends in Western Women's Writing," in Western Literature Association, *A Literary History of the American West* (Fort Worth: Texas

Christian Univ. Press, 1987), 1178; and Madelyn Clare Troxclair, "An Examination of the Wilderness Theme in Twentieth Century American Literature: Revising Myths and Projections Regarding Nature and Women" (Ph.D. diss., University of Washington, 1990). Also helpful on this point are the articles found in "Women and Environmental History," special issue, *Environmental Review* 8 (spring 1984).

15. That women led the way in realistic writing is argued in Jeraldine Parker, "'Uneasy Survivors': Five Women Writers, 1896–1923" (Ph.D. diss., University of Utah, 1973).

16. Quoted in Mark I. West, ed., *Westward to a High Mountain: The Colorado Writings of Helen Hunt Jackson* (Denver: Colorado Historical Society, 1994), 61.

17. Helen Hunt Jackson, *Bits of Travel at Home* (Boston: Roberts Brothers, 1879), 311.

18. Davies, "Goddess in the Landscape."

19. Vicki Pierarski, *Westward the Women: An Anthology of Western Stories by Women* (Garden City NY: Doubleday, 1984), 6.

20. Pierarski, *Westward the Women,* 4. Meanwhile, Mary Hallock Foote, an eastern artist who came west with her husband during the 1870s, wrote vivid descriptions of Colorado, Idaho, and California. In Foote's case, she was the brave heroine, for she traveled and observed firsthand. In particular, she penned revealing accounts of the mining frontier, including an 1883 description of a mine into which she personally descended. Pierarski, *Westward the Women,* 5. See also Mary Hallock Foote, *A Victorian Gentlewoman in the Far West* (San Marino CA: Huntington Library, 1972); and Melody Graulich, "Mary Hallock Foote, 1847–1938," *Legacy* 3 (1986): 43–52.

21. Troxclair, "Examination of the Wilderness Theme," 237–39. Also useful is Phachee Yuvajita, "The Changing Images of Women in Western American Literature as Illustrated in the Works of Willa Cather, Hamlin Garland, and Mari Sandoz" (Ph.D. diss., University of Oregon, 1985).

22. David Robertson, "Bioregionalism in Nature Writing," in Elder, *American Nature Writers,* 2:1018.

23. Agnes C. Laut, *The Freebooters of the Wilderness* (New York: Moffat, Yard, 1913), 420, 426–34.

24. Edith E. Kohl, Obituary, undated, Denver Public Library.

25. Barbara Rippey, "Mari Sandoz: Novelist as Historian" (Ph.D. diss., University of Nebraska, 1989); Rippey, "Mari Sandoz' Historical Perspective: Linking Past and Present," *Platte Valley Review* 17 (winter 1989): 60–68; Rosemary Whitaker, "Violence in *Old Jules* and *Slogum House*," *Western American Literature* 16 (November 1981): 217–24; Katherine A. Mason, "Greed and the Erosion of the Pioneer Ethic: Selected Novels of Mari Sandoz," *Platte Valley Review* 17 (winter 1989): 92–101; and Sandoz, Obituary, "Western Historian Dies in New York," 1950, Denver Public Library. The best biographical treatment of Sandoz is Helen Winter Stauffer, *Mari Sandoz* (Lincoln: Univ. of Nebraska Press, 1982).

26. Helen W. Stauffer, "Mari Sandoz," in Western Literature Association, *A Literary History of the American West*, 767, 771. Additional helpful essays are Betsy Downey, "'She Does Not Write like a Historian': Mari Sandoz and the Old and New Western History," *Great Plains Quarterly* 16 (winter 1996): 9–28; and Lisa R. Lindell, "Recasting Epic Tradition: The Dispossessed as Hero in Sandoz's *Crazy Horse* and *Cheyenne Autumn*," *Great Plains Quarterly* 16 (winter 1996): 43–53.

27. Claire Mattern, "Mari Sandoz: Her Use of Allegory in Slogum House" (Ph.D. diss., University of Nebraska-Lincoln, 1981); and Glenda Riley, "Mari Sandoz's *Slogum House*: Woman as Greed," *Great Plains Quarterly* 16 (winter 1996): 29–41. See also Mari Sandoz, *The Buffalo Hunters* (New York: Hastings House, 1954); and Sandoz, *The Beaver Men* (New York: Hastings House, 1964).

28. Mari Sandoz, *Slogum House* (Boston: Little, Brown, 1937), 394.

29. Katherine Bagg Hastings, Biographical File, undated, Arizona Historical Society, Tucson.

30. Opal Whiteley, Papers, 1911–22, Special Collections, University of Oregon Library, Eugene.

31. Whiteley, Papers.

32. Whiteley, Papers.

33. Benjamin Hoff, *The Singing Creek Where the Willows Grow* (New York: Penguin Books, 1986), 194, 292. Another look at child nature writers is found in Penelope Franklin, ed., *Private Pages: Diaries of*

American Women, 1830s–1970s (New York: Ballantine Books, 1986), 3–62.

34. Florence Merriam Bailey, *My Summer in a Mormon Village* (Boston: Houghton, Mifflin, 1894), 1, 171.

35. Bailey also revised her earlier study of birds in Glacier National Park. See Florence Merriam Bailey, "The Birds," in *Wild Animals of Glacier National Park* (Washington DC: Government Printing Office, 1918). See also Florence Merriam Bailey, *Birds of New Mexico* (Washington DC: Judd & Detweiler, 1928).

36. Necah Stewart Furman, *Caroline Lockhart: Her Life and Legacy* (Seattle: Univ. of Washington Press, 1994), xix, 144–46. Similarly, during the 1930s, Colorado ranchwoman Florence G. Means spoke and wrote opposing the wholesale cutting of Christmas trees. Means also advocated shelter-belts of trees to counteract Colorado's dust storms. Florence G. Means, "Reflections of a Rancher's Wife," 1972, Special Collections, Norlin Library, University of Colorado at Boulder.

37. Piekarski, *Westward the Women*, 8.

38. Piekarski, *Westward the Women*, 44, 51, 72, 79–80.

39. Mary Roberts Rinehart, *Through Glacier Park: Seeing America First* (Boston: Houghton Mifflin, 1916), 5–7.

40. Rinehart, *Through Glacier Park*, 7, 14, 20, 24.

41. Mary Roberts Rinehart, *The Out Trail* (New York: George H. Doran, 1923), 1, 17.

42. Grant Overton, *American Nights Entertainment* (New York: D. Appleton, 1923), 43–44.

43. Quoted in Christopher Merrill, "The Forms of American Nature Poetry," in Elder, *American Nature Writers*, 2:1079–97.

44. Ella Higginson, *When the Birds Go North Again* (New York: Macmillan, 1898), 3. Also see Ella Higginson, *The Voice of April-Land and Other Poems* (New York: Macmillan, 1903), 5–6; and Higginson, *Alaska: The Great Country* (New York: Macmillan, 1909).

45. Lilian White Spencer, "Mesa Verde—A.D. 1000," *Forum* 71 (March 1924): 289; and Margaret W. Ross, Biographical File, undated, Arizona Historical Society, Tucson.

46. Fannie Elizabeth Still, Biographical File, undated, Arizona Historical Society, Tucson; Lillian A. Shuey, *Among the Redwoods* (San Francisco: Whitaker & Bay, 1901); and Rena S. Matthews, Papers, 1884–1962, Arizona Historical Society, Tucson.

47. Phoebe M. Bogan, "The Desert Uncompromising," in "Poems of Desert Moods," undated, in Bogan, Papers, 1909–26, Arizona Historical Society, Tucson.

48. Bogan, "Desert Uncompromising."

49. Olephia "Leafy" King, "Dust and Desire" and "Good Morning Nevada," undated, in King, Papers, 1920–77, Special Collections, Getchell Library, University of Nevada, Reno.

50. King, "Coyote's Tale," in King, Papers.

51. Karen S. Langlois, "Mary Austin and Lincoln Steffens," *Huntington Library Quarterly* 49 (1986): 357; and Marjorie Pryse, ed., *Stories from the Country of Lost Borders* (New Brunswick NJ: Rutgers Univ. Press, 1987), xiv.

52. Mary Austin, *Earth Horizon: An Autobiography* (Albuquerque: Univ. of New Mexico Press, 1991), 78, 228.

53. Austin, *Earth Horizon*, 157, 376.

54. Austin, *Earth Horizon*, 386–87.

55. Austin, *Earth Horizon*, 391–92.

56. Wild, *Pioneer Conservationists of Western America*; Benay Blend, "Mary Austin and the Western Conservation Movement: 1900–1927," *Journal of the Southwest* 30 (spring 1988): 12–34; Esther Lanigan Stineman, *Mary Austin: Songs of a Maverick* (New Haven: Yale Univ. Press, 1989); Edwin R. Bingham, "American Wests through Autobiography and Memoir," *Pacific Historical Review* 56 (February 1987): 7–13; and Morley Baer, *Room and Time Enough: The Land of Mary Austin* (Flagstaff AZ: Northland Press, 1979), 1.

57. Harwell, "Writing the Wilderness"; John P. O'Grady, *Pilgrims to the Wild: Everett Ruess, Henry David Thoreau, John Muir, Clarence King, Mary Austin* (Salt Lake City: Univ. of Utah Press, 1993); and Ann H. Zwinger, ed., *Writing the Western Landscape: Mary Austin and John Muir* (Boston: Beacon Press, 1994).

5 · Visual Image-Makers

1. Florence Yoch, "Fitting the Land for Human Use," *California Arts and Architecture*, July 1930, 19, 20, 72.

2. "Women Achieve Fame as Landscape Artists," *Pasadena Post*, 29 May 1932.

3. James J. Yoch, *Landscaping the Dream: The Gardens and Film Sets of Florence Yoch, 1890–1972* (New York: Harry N. Abrams, 1989), 3.

4. Phil Kovinick, *The Woman Artist in the American West, 1860–1960* (Fullerton CA: Muckenthaler Cultural Center, 1976), 1; and Virginia Scharff, "Women Envision the West, 1890–1945," in *Independent Spirits: Women Painters of the American West, 1890–1945*, ed. Patricia Trenton (Los Angeles: Autry Museum of Western Heritage, 1995), 1–8. For women working in traditional forms, see Vera L. Norwood, "'Thank You for My Bones': Connections between Contemporary Women Artists and the Traditional Arts of Their Foremothers," *New Mexico Historical Review* 58 (January 1983): 57–78; and Rita Gonzalez-Mahoney, "Interviews," in "Women Artists and Writers of the Southwest," special issue, *New America: A Journal of American and Southwest Culture* 3 (1982): 106–13.

5. Kovinick, *Woman Artist*, 13. Meanwhile, Helen Henderson Chain of Denver painted Colorado landscapes and other points of interest. Like Brodt, Chain also liked majestic scenes, yet she often interjected humor into her work. At the same time, Mary Hallock Foote illustrated her writing about the West with original drawings, some of the best of which were in her series "Pictures of the Far West" in the magazine *Century*, 1888 and 1889. Kovinick, *Woman Artist*, 15, 23.

6. Alice Stewart Hill, Papers, undated, Denver Public Library.

7. Annegret Ogden, "Love and Marriage: Five California Couples," *Californians*, July/August 1987, 13.

8. Kovinick, *Woman Artist*, 22, 25, 41, 47.

9. Elsa Jemne, Diary, ca. 1920s, Montana Historical Society, Helena; and Kirby Lambert, "The Lure of the Parks," *Montana: The Magazine of Western History* 46 (spring 1996): 47.

10. Kovinick, *Woman Artist*, 50; Kirby Lambert, "Lure of the Parks," 43; and Nancy Acord, "Women of the WPA Art Projects: California

Murals, 1933–1943," in *Yesterday and Tomorrow: California Women Artists*, ed. Sylvia Moore (New York: Midmarch Arts Press, 1989), 1–36. WPA programs also helped women photographers. See Marta Weigle, ed., *New Mexicans in Cameo and Camera: New Deal Documentation of Twentieth-Century Lives* (Albuquerque: Univ. of New Mexico Press, 1985).

11. Susan Landauer, "Searching for Selfhood: Women Artists of Northern California," and Patricia Trenton, "'Islands on the Land': Women Traditionalists of Southern California," both in Trenton, *Independent Spirits*, 9–76.

12. Kovinick, *Woman Artist*, 14, 17.

13. Ilene Susan Fort, "The Adventuresome, the Eccentrics, and the Dreamers: Women Modernists of Southern California," in Trenton, *Independent Spirits*, 75–106.

14. "Mary Russell Ferrell Colton," in Crowe and Tod, *Arizona Women's Hall of Fame*; and Kovinick, *Woman Artist*, 17. For other areas in the West, see Vicki Halper, "Northwestern Exposure"; Sarah J. Moore, "No Woman's Land: Arizona Adventurers"; Sandra D'Emilio and Sharyn Udall, "Inner Voices, Outward Forms: Women Painters in New Mexico"; Susan Landauer with Becky Duval Reese, "Lone Star Spirits"; Erika Doss, "'I *Must* Paint': Women Artists of the Rocky Mountain Region"; Joni L. Kinsey, "Cultivating the Grasslands: Women Painters in the Great Plains"; all are found in Trenton, *Independent Spirits*, 107–273.

15. Georgia O'Keeffe, Papers, 1920s–70s, Center for Southwest Research, University of New Mexico Library, Albuquerque.

16. O'Keeffe, quoted in *Albuquerque Journal*, 26 April 1975.

17. Quoted in Georgia O'Keeffe, *Catalogue*, "Georgia O'Keeffe, Exhibition of Oils and Pastels," 22 January–17 March 1939, Amon Carter Museum of Western Art, Fort Worth TX, unpaged.

18. Peter E. Palmquist, "Pioneer Women Photographers in Nineteenth-Century California," *California History* 71 (spring 1992): 122; and Eliza W. Withington, "How a Woman Makes Landscape Photographs," *Philadelphia Photographer* 13 (1876): 357–79. A useful overview is Martha A. Sandweiss, ed., *Photography in Nineteenth-Century America* (New York: Abrams, 1991).

19. *San Francisco Examiner,* 14 March 1895.

20. Peter E. Palmquist, "Photographers in Petticoats," *Journal of the West* 21 (April 1982): 60–64. An example of a woman's treatise is found in Maude E. Chase, "The Orthochromatic Plate in Landscape Photography," *California Camera Club,* 564 (1912): 46–47.

21. Palmquist, "Pioneer Women Photographers," 124; and Tracey Baker, "Nineteenth-Century Minnesota Women Photographers," 15–23, and Kathleen L. Miller, "The Cabinet Card Photograph: Relic of a Gilded Age," 29–41, both in *Photography in the West,* ed. Peter E. Palmquist (Manhattan KS: Sunflower Univ. Press, 1989).

22. Catharine Weed Barnes, "Why Ladies Should Be Admitted to Membership in Photographic Societies," *American Amateur Photographer* 1 (December 1889): 223–24.

23. Dorothy Miller, "The Artists in Kern River Canyon," *Sunset Magazine* 12, no. 2 (December 1903): 129–34.

24. Adamson Family, "Diary of a Trip," 1916, Nebraska State Historical Society, Lincoln.

25. [No author], "The Artistic Vision of Myrta Wright Stevens," *Montana: The Magazine of Western History* 24 (summer 1975): 36–47; Donna M. Lucey, "Evelyn J. Cameron: Pioneer Photographer and Diarist," *Montana: The Magazine of Western History* 41 (summer 1991): 42–55; Lucey, *Photographing Montana, 1894–1928: The Life and Work of Evelyn Cameron* (New York: Alfred A. Knopf, 1990); and Utah Women's History Association, *A Woman's View: The Photography of Elfie Huntington, 1868–1949* (Salt Lake City: Utah Arts Council, 1988). Photographs by Stevens and Cameron can be found at the Montana Historical Society in Helena.

26. Ira W. Martin, "Women in Photography," *Pictorial Photography in America* 5 (1929): unpaged. A similar argument appeared earlier in Miss M. E. Sperry, "Women and Photography," *Pacific Coast Photographer* 3 (October 1894): 153–54.

27. Quoted in Anne Brigman, "The Glory of the Open," *Camera Craft* 33 (April 1926): 155, 158; and Brigman, "Just a Word," *Camera Craft* 15 (March 1908): 87–88. See also Emily J. Hamilton, "Some Symbolic Nature Studies from the Camera of Annie W. Brigman," *Craftsman* 12 (September 1907): 660–64.

28. Brigman, "Glory of the Open," 156–59, 161–62. A sizable number of Brigman photographs are housed at the Oakland Museum in Oakland CA.

29. Laura M. Adams, "The Picture Possibilities of Photography," *Overland Monthly* 36 (September 1900): 241–45. A few years later, Helen Davie also attacked the question of photography as art. Davie maintained that "photography is generally recognized as an art, one in which the individuality of the worker may be as forcibly expressed as in sculpture or in painting." Yet she stated that the sciences were also in debt to photography. Helen Davie, "Women in Photography," *Camera Craft* 13 (August 1904): 130–38.

30. Flora Lewis Marble, "Geographical and Landscape Photography," *Photographic Times* 43 (September 1911): 337.

31. Sidney Allan, "A Poet of Sunshine and Mist—A Recorder of Atmosphere: Maude Wilson," *Photo Era* 27 (December 1911): 283–85.

32. Beatrice B. Bell, "Fog-Photography," in *Camera Fiends and Kodak Girls II: 50 Selections by and about Women in Photography, 1840–1930*, ed. Peter E. Palmquist (New York: Midmarch Arts Press, 1989), 175–77.

33. Michael Henry, "Alice Hare: Views of California Beauty," in *A Directory of Women in California Photography, 1900–1920*, ed. Peter E. Palmquist (Eureka CA: Eureka Printing, 1991), 159–62.

34. George F. Frick, "Martha Daniel Logan," in *Notable American Women*, 2:419–20.

35. Jane Loudon, *Gardening for Ladies and Companion to the Flower Garden* (New York: Wiley & Halstead, 1849), 16–17; and Harriet Beecher Stowe and Catharine E. Beecher, *American Woman's Home; or, Principles of Domestic Science* (New York: J. B. Ford, 1869), frontispiece, 384–86.

36. Norwood, *Made from This Earth*, 104.

37. Norwood, *Made from This Earth*, 125–27.

38. Norwood, *Made from This Earth*, 129–30.

39. McKenny is described in Mrs. George H. Funk, "Reminiscences of an Early School Teacher in Washington," 1956, Washington State Library, Olympia; and Frances Carol Locher, ed., *Contemporary Authors*

(Detroit: Gale Research, 1978), 422. Two of McKenny's well-known earlier books were *Birds in the Garden and How to Attract Them* (New York: Grosset & Dunlap, 1939) and *A Book of Wild Flowers* (New York: Macmillan, 1939).

40. Polly Welts Kaufman, *National Parks and the Woman's Voice: A History* (Albuquerque: Univ. of New Mexico Press, 1996), 36–40.

41. Diana Balmori, Diane Kostial McGuire, and Eleanor M. McPeck, *Beatrix Farrand's American Landscapes: Her Gardens and Campuses* (New York: Sagapress, 1985), 6–7.

42. Balmori, McGuire, and McPeck, *Beatrix Farrand's American Landscapes*, 22, 24–25, 201–2.

43. Norwood, *Made from This Earth*, 115.

44. Annie G. Rockefellow, Biographical File, undated, Arizona Historical Society, Tucson.

45. "Mary Colter," in Crowe and Tod, *Arizona Women's Hall of Fame*, 48–49; and Virginia L. Grattan, *Mary Colter: Builder upon the Red Earth* (Grand Canyon AZ: Grand Canyon Natural History Association, 1992), 1–19.

46. "Mary Colter," in Crowe and Tod, *Arizona Women's Hall of Fame*, 49; and Grattan, *Mary Colter*, 20–40. See also Claire Sheperd-Laniers, "Trading on Tradition: Mary Jane Colter and the Romantic Appeal of Harvey House Architecture," *Journal of the Southwest* 38 (summer 1996): 163–95.

47. "Mary Colter," in Crowe and Tod, *Arizona Women's Hall of Fame*, 48–50; and Grattan, *Mary Colter*, 25–31.

48. Grattan, *Mary Colter*, 20–22.

49. Grattan, *Mary Colter*, ix, 25, 32.

50. Yoch, "Fitting the Land," 20.

51. Yoch, *Landscaping the American Dream*, 9–10.

52. Senga Mortimer, "Pioneers in Gardening," *Traditional Home* (September 1995), 36.

53. Quoted in "Helena Modjeska, 1876–93," in *Through Women's Eyes*, 137. See also Helena Modjeska, *Memories and Impressions: An*

Autobiography (New York: Macmillan, 1910); and Theodore Payne, *Life on the Modjeska Ranch in the Gay Nineties* (Los Angeles: Kruckeberg Press, 1962).

6 · Club Women and Other Activists

1. See, for example, Sandra Haarsager, *Organized Womanhood: Cultural Politics in the Pacific Northwest, 1840–1920* (Norman: Univ. of Oklahoma Press, 1997).

2. Phebe Kerrick Warner, "Mary Ann Goodnight," undated, J. Evetts Haley Collection, Nita Stewart Haley Memorial Library, Midland TX.

3. Warner, "Mary Ann Goodnight."

4. *Temple (Texas) Telegram*, 27 July 1931; and *Brady (Texas) Standard*, 4 August 1931.

5. Riley, *Inventing the American Woman*, 2:181–83.

6. Benson's Women's Club, "Arizona Litany," undated, "A Collect for Club Women," undated, and "An Arizona Creed," ca. 1922–43, Arizona Federation of Women's Clubs, Papers, undated, Arizona Historical Society, Tucson; and "Why Save a Forest? Dedication Address of Federation Forest," 1949, General Federation of Women's Clubs, Records, 1896–1923, and Manuscripts, University of Washington Libraries, Seattle.

7. Mrs. Ernest E. Knudsen, "History of Utah Federation of Women's Clubs, 1893 to 1952," Utah State Historical Society, Salt Lake City; and Roberta Bernard, "Preservation of Beauty Spots," *Women's Forum* 2 (summer 1929): 17.

8. Quoted in Jennie McCowen, "Women in Iowa," *Annals of Iowa* 3 (October 1884): 104.

9. Ebell Club, Papers, 1904–10; Highland Park Ebell Club, Papers, 1907–8; and Charles Lummis, Letter to "Dear Mrs. Hunt," 22 April 1905, Mary H. Hunt, Letters, 1905; all in Braun Library, Southwest Museum, Los Angeles.

10. Sam Davis, *The History of Nevada* (Reno: Elins, 1913), 773; U-Wah-Un Study Club, Papers, 1919–60s, Women's Archives, Dickinson Library, University of Nevada, Las Vegas; and Goldfield NV Women's Club Constitution and By-Laws, 1928, and Goldfield Women's Club

Meeting Minutes, 1906–13, Women's Archives, Dickinson Library, University of Nevada, Las Vegas.

11. Mildred Forgeon Rich, *Memories* (n.p., 1971), 22. For other Idaho examples, see Betty Penson-Ward, *Idaho Women in History* (Boise ID: Legendary, 1991).

12. Aurora Club, Papers, 1913–38, Special Collections, University of Utah Libraries, Salt Lake City.

13. Frances B. Cameron and Barbara B. Lyons, "Ethel Frances Smith Baldwin," in Peterson, *Notable Women of Hawaii*, 19–22.

14. For a general overview, see Alfred Runte, *National Parks: The American Experience* (Lincoln: Univ. of Nebraska Press, 1979); Runte, *Yosemite: The Embattled Wilderness* (Lincoln: Univ. of Nebraska Press, 1990); Douglas H. Strong, "Preservation Efforts at Lake Tahoe, 1880 to 1980," *Journal of Forest History* 25 (April 1981): 78–97; Robert M. Utley, "America's National Parks," *American History Illustrated* 17 (March 1982): 12–20; William C. Everhart, *The National Park Service* (Boulder CO: Westview Press, 1983); Richard C. Davis, ed., *Encyclopedia of American Forest and Conservation History* (New York: Macmillan, 1983); David A. Clary, *Timber and the Forest Service* (Lawrence: Univ. Press of Kansas, 1986); William K. Wyant, *Westward in Eden: The Public Lands and the Conservation Movement* (Berkeley: Univ. of California Press, 1982); and Robert W. Righter, *Crucible for Conservation: The Creation of Grand Teton National Park* (Boulder: Colorado Associated Univ. Press, 1982).

One study that includes a few women is Hal Rothman, *America's National Monuments: The Politics of Preservation* (Lawrence: Univ. Press of Kansas, 1989). Hal Rothman, *"I'll Never Fight Fire with My Bare Hands Again": Recollections of the First Forest Rangers of the Inland Northwest* (Lawrence: Univ. Press of Kansas, 1994), all about men, gives a very different picture than Polly Welts Kaufman, *National Parks and the Woman's Voice: A History* (Albuquerque: Univ. of New Mexico Press, 1996). A woman-oriented view of Canadian parks, similar to Kaufman's perspective, is found in PearlAnn Reichwein, "Beauty, Health, and Moral Uplift: Guardians of the Rockies," *Beaver* (Winnipeg, Manitoba) 74 (August/September 1994): 4–13.

15. Kaufman, *National Parks and Woman's Voice*, 28–30.

16. Rosalie Edge, Papers, 1929–55, Conservation Collection, Denver Public Library.

17. Edge, Papers, 1929–55.

18. Kaufman, *National Parks and Woman's Voice*, 36–40.

19. *Woman Citizen*, November 1912, 13, Nevada Historical Society, Reno; and Nevada Federation of Women's Clubs, Correspondence and Papers, 1913–72, Nevada Historical Society, Reno.

20. Utah Federation of Women's Clubs, Official Year Book, 1918–20, Utah State Historical Society, Salt Lake City.

21. U.S. Department of Agriculture, Forest Service, "Forestry and Conservation Programs for Utah Women's Clubs," ca. late 1930s, Utah State Historical Society, Salt Lake City.

22. Forest Service, "Forestry and Conservation Programs."

23. Mrs. Ernest E. Knudsen, "History of Utah Federation of Women's Clubs, 1893 to 1952," compiled 1952, Manuscripts, Utah State Historical Society, Salt Lake City.

24. Arizona Federation of Women's Clubs Papers, "An Arizona Creed," ca. 1922–43, Arizona Historical Society, Tucson; and special issue on Alaska, *Woman's Forum* 2 (summer 1929).

25. Riley, *Inventing the American Woman*, 2:182.

26. Carolyn Merchant, "Women of the Progressive Conservation Movement: 1900–1916," *Environmental Review* 8 (spring 1984): 62–63.

27. Quoted in Merchant, *Major Problems*, 353–55. For the growth of the animal rights movement in the United States, see Thomas R. Dunlap, *Saving America's Wildlife* (Princeton NJ: Princeton Univ. Press, 1988).

28. National Federation of Women's Clubs, *General Federation Bulletin* 10 (April 1912): 14–16.

29. Richard C. Berner, *Seattle, 1900–1920* (Seattle: Charles Press, 1991), 99.

30. Federation of Women's Clubs, Records, 1896–1923, Manuscripts, University of Washington Libraries, Seattle.

31. Federation of Women's Clubs, Records.

32. National Association of Colored Women, *National Notes* 28, no. 8 (May 1926): 6, 8.

33. National Association of Colored Women, *National Notes,* 23.

34. Dorothy Salem, "National Association of Colored Women," in *Black Women in America,* ed. Darlene Clark Hine (Brooklyn: Carlson, 1993), 842–51; and National Association of Colored Women, "Strength of the Federation of Colored Women's Clubs, Inc., Nationally and Locally," undated, Denver Public Library. A similar example from a different part of the West is found in St. Paul's Pilgrim Baptist Church, Ladies Aid Society Records, 1910–22, Minnesota Historical Society, St. Paul.

35. Salem, "National Association of Colored Women"; and National Association of Colored Women, "Strength of the Federation of Colored Women's Clubs."

36. See, for example, Ted C. Hinckley, "Glimpses of Societal Change among Nineteenth-Century Tlingit Women," *Journal of the West* 32 (July 1993): 12–24.

37. The Little Flower Club, ca. 1920s, Arizona Historical Society, Tucson.

38. Administration of Mrs. Amy P. S. Stacy, undated, Washington Federation of Women's Clubs, Records, 1896–1923, Manuscripts, University of Washington Libraries, Seattle.

39. Florence Humphrey Church, Nevada Federation of Women's Clubs, Correspondence, etc., 1913–72, Nevada Historical Society, Reno.

40. Lucy Browne Johnson, Papers, 1846–1937, Kansas State Historical Society, Topeka.

41. [No author], *Nebraska Women through the Years, 1867–1994* (Lincoln NE: Johnson, 1967), 55.

42. Susan R. Schrepfer, *The Fight to Save the Redwoods: A History of Environmental Reform, 1917–1978* (Madison: Univ. of Wisconsin Press, 1983); and Lillian Power, "Cherilla Lillian Storrs Lowrey," in Peterson, *Notable Women of Hawaii,* 245–48.

43. John Gilbert Chittenden Babcock, "The Role of Public Discourse in the Soil Conservation Movement, 1865–1935" (Ph.D. diss., University of Michigan, 1985).

44. Eleanor Ferrall, "With Pen in Hand: Josephine Clifford McCrackin Opens the Battle to Save the Redwoods," Women in Forestry 5 (1983): 15–16.

45. Peggy A. Voleke Kelley, Women of Nebraska Hall of Fame (Omaha: Nebraska International Women's Year Coalition, 1976), 70–82.

46. Rodman Wilson Paul, "Harriet Williams Russell Strong," in James, Notable American Women, 3:405–6.

47. Quoted in Gloria Ricci Lothrop, "Women Pioneers and the California Landscape," Californians 4 (May-June 1986): 16–23.

48. Polly Welts Kaufman, "Challenging Tradition: Pioneer Women Naturalists in the National Park Service," Forest and Conservation History 34 (January 1990): 5.

49. Denver Post, 19 September 1920, 10. See also Denver Times, 18 July 1919, 15.

50. Kaufman, "Challenging Tradition," 7–9.

51. Kaufman, "Challenging Tradition," 5, 12.

52. Rebecca Ann Conard, "The Conservation of Local Autonomy: California's Land Policies, 1900–1966" (Ph.D. diss., University of California–Santa Barbara, 1984).

53. Sharlot Madbrith Hall, Papers, undated, and Biographical File, undated, Arizona Historical Society, Tucson.

54. E. Shan Correa, "Emma Kaili Metcalf Beckley Nakuina," in Peterson, Notable Women of Hawaii, 279–81; and [no author], New Mexico Blue Book, 1923, State Records Center and Archives, Santa Fe.

55. "Frances Lillian Willard Munds," in Crowe and Tod, Arizona Women's Hall of Fame, 56–58.

56. Delila M. Abbott, "Women Legislators of Utah, 1896–1976," 1976, Utah State Historical Society, Salt Lake City.

57. Nan Wood Honeyman, Political Correspondence, 1932–50, Special Collections, University of Oregon, Eugene.

58. Isabelle F. Story, *The National Parks and Emergency Conservation* (Washington DC: Government Printing Office, 1933).

59. *Temple (Texas) Telegram,* 28 July 1931; *Fort Worth Star Telegram,* 2 August 1931; and *Dallas Morning News,* 2 August 1931.

60. *Quanah (Texas) Tribune Chief,* 4 August 1931.

61. *San Antonio Express,* 9 February 1934; and Stephen Chalmus Head, *A History of Conservation in Texas, 1860–1963* (Lubbock: Texas Tech University, 1982).

7 · Climbers and Other Athletes

1. Elinor E[ppich] Kingery, Papers, 1959, Colorado Historical Society, Denver.

2. Kingery, Papers.

3. Found in Leonard Daughenbaugh, "On Top of Her World: Anna Mills' Ascent of Mt. Whitney," *California History* 64 (winter 1985): 42.

4. Julia Archibald Holmes, "A Journey to Pike's Peak," *Sibyl* (Middletown NY) 3 (15 March 1859): 1. For a description of atmospheric currents and other conditions on Pikes Peak, see James H. Smith, "A Winter on Pike's Peak," *Youth's Companion,* 10 March 1887, 105–6.

5. Holmes, "Journey to Pike's Peak," 3.

6. Quoted from Julia Archibald Holmes, "A Lady on the Summit of Pike's Peak," *(Lawrence) Kansas Herald,* 20 November 1858. See also Gail King, "She Climbed Pikes Peak in Bloomers," *Empire Magazine,* 2 April 1978, 26, 28; "From the Rocky Mountains," *Lawrence (Kansas) Republican,* 7 October 1858, 2; Julia Archibald Holmes, *A Bloomer Girl on Pike's Peak, 1858* (Denver: Denver Public Library, 1949); and Julia Archibald Holmes, Papers, undated, Denver Public Library.

7. Margaret Solomon, "A Study of Feminism as a Motif in 'A Journey to Pike's Peak and New Mexico' by Julia Archibald Homes," in *Women and Western American Literature,* ed. Helen Winter Stauffer and Susan J. Rosowski (Troy NY: Whitston, 1982), 28–39.

8. Paul Schullery, ed., *Island in the Sky: Pioneering Accounts of Mount Rainier, 1833–1894* (Seattle: Mountaineers, 1987), 125–40.

9. Schullery, *Island in the Sky.*

10. Schullery, *Island in the Sky.*

11. *Virginia (Nevada Territory) Evening Bulletin,* 7 August 1863; *Boulder County (Colorado) News,* 26 August 1871; and *Greeley (Colorado) Sun,* 14 August 1873.

12. Daughenbaugh, "On Top of Her World," 47–48; and *Boulder County (Colorado) News,* 10 September 1873.

13. Annegret Ogden, "We All Climbed Whitney in Skirts," *Californians* 6 (January/February 1988): 10–11, 59.

14. Janet Robertson, *The Magnificent Mountain Women: Adventures in the Colorado Rockies* (Lincoln: Univ. of Nebraska Press, 1990), 20–21.

15. Robertson, *Magnificent Mountain Women,* 22–23. For more on fascinating guide and naturalist Enos Mills, see Enos Mills, *The Story of Estes Park and a Guide Book* (Denver: Outdoor Life, 1905); Enos A. Mills, *The Adventures of a Nature Guide* (New York: Doubleday, Page, 1920); and Hildegarde Hawthorne and Esther Burnell Mills, *Enos Mills of the Rockies* (Boston: Houghton Mifflin, 1935).

16. "First Woman to Climb Mt. Ruby," *Humboldt (Nevada) Star,* 27 August 1913, sec. 3, 4; and Sherry L. Smith, "A Woman's Life in the Teton Country: Geraldine L. Lucas," *Montana: The Magazine of Western History* 44 (summer 1994): 18–33.

17. David Mazel, ed., *Mountaineering Women: Stories by Early Climbers* (College Station: Texas A&M Univ. Press, 1994), 9; and Esther Merriam, *Harper's Bazar* 44 (November 1910): 634. From 1917 to the late 1920s, Rocky Mountain National Park guide Elizabeth Burnell was one of the first women naturalists to lead nature walks for women and men. Burnell also supervised nature study for the Los Angeles schools during the winter months and coauthored the *Field Book of Birds of Southwest United States.*

18. Robertson, *Magnificent Mountain Women,* 28–29.

19. Quoted in Bertha Snow Adams, "Would a Girl Guide Keep You Climbing?" *Illustrated World* 38 (December 1922): 549, 632; and Herman Howard Matteson, "How Much of a Coward Are You?" *Sunset Magazine* 48 (June 1922): 39.

20. Richard C. Berner, *Seattle, 1900–1920: From Boomtown, Urban Turbulence, to Restoration* (Seattle: Charles Press, 1991), 99.

21. For more information on the Sierra Club, see Anne Farrar Hyde, "Temples and Playgrounds: The Sierra Club in the Wilderness, 1901–1922," *California History* 66 (September 1987): 208–20; Michael P. Cohen, *The History of the Sierra Club, 1891–1970* (San Francisco: Sierra Club Books, 1988); Tom Turner, *Sierra Club: 100 Years of Protecting Nature* (New York: Harry N. Abrams, 1991); Roderick W. Nash, "The Sierra Club's Centennial in Historical Perspective: Introduction to the Special Issue," *California History* 71 (summer 1992): 155–59; and Sierra Club Records, 1896–1991, and Sierra Club Members Papers, 1892–1990 (which include a few women), Bancroft Library, University of California, Berkeley.

22. Robert Martin Price, Papers, 1890–99, Special Collections, Getchell Library, University of Nevada, Reno.

23. Price, Papers.

24. Jennie Ellsworth Price, "A Woman's Trip through the Tuolumne Cañon," *Sierra Club Bulletin* 2 (1897–99): 174–84.

25. Price, "Woman's Trip," 184.

26. Mountaineers Climbing Committee, Records, 1906–92, Manuscripts, University of Washington Libraries, Seattle.

27. Mountaineers Climbing Committee, Records.

28. Mountaineers Climbing Committee, Records.

29. Berner, *Seattle*, 98.

30. Anna W. Newman, "My Summer with the Mountaineers," Records, 1906–92, Manuscripts, University of Washington Libraries, Seattle.

31. Newman, "My Summer with the Mountaineers."

32. *Mountaineer*, 1924, 8–9, Special Collections, University of Washington Libraries, Seattle.

33. *Mountaineer*, 1924, 10–11.

34. Minutes of the Board of Trustees, Mountaineers, Records, 1906–91, Manuscripts, University of Washington Libraries, Seattle; and Berner, *Seattle*, 99.

35. Lucretia Vaile, "Auditing the Club Scrapbooks with Personal Observations and Reminiscences from Many Sources," *Trail and Timberline* 42 (April 1962): 4–5.

36. Lucretia Vaile, "Colorado Mountain Club—1912," *Trail and Timberline* 42 (April 1962): 47–48.

37. Agnes S. Hall, "Trip from Palmer Lake to Pike's Peak and Back with a Pack Horse," undated, Denver Public Library.

38. Pearl V. Turner, "August 10, 1914," Papers, Special Collections, Norlin Library, University of Colorado at Boulder.

39. Turner, "August 10, 1914."

40. Turner, "August 10, 1914."

41. "8th Annual Outing of the Colorado Mountain Club," Directory of Participants—1919, Pearl V. Turner, Papers, 1914–24, Special Collections, Norlin Library, University of Colorado at Boulder.

42. Quoted in "Dedicated to Giant Forest," High Sierra Horseback Trip, August 1992, in Turner, Papers.

43. Turner, Notes in photograph album, 1922 and 1924, in Turner, Papers.

44. Laura Makepeace, "Fort Collins, 1922–1962," *Trail and Timberline* 42 (April 1962): 64–65.

45. Riley, *Inventing the American Woman*, 2:185.

46. Glenda Riley, *The Life and Legacy of Annie Oakley* (Norman: Univ. of Oklahoma Press, 1994), 112–44. Also helpful is Shirl Kaspar, *Annie Oakley* (Norman: Univ. of Oklahoma Press, 1992). West of the Mississippi River, many women followed Annie Oakley's lead by making names for themselves in the rodeo arena. Bertha Kaepernik Blancett and Lucille Mulhall of Oklahoma achieved acclaim as top riders and frequent rodeo award winners. Both followed Oakley's model by wearing skirts when competing and often by riding sidesaddle. Even Texan Tad Lucas, champion trick rider during the 1920s to 1940s, retained the essence of Annie Oakley's femininity.

47. Grace Gallatin Thompson Seton, *A Woman Tenderfoot* (New York: Doubleday, Page, 1905), unpaged.

48. Riley, *Inventing the American Woman*, 2:185.

49. See, for example, Bulah Liles Patterson, Interview Transcript, 27 October 1983, Institute of Oral History, University of Texas at El Paso.

50. Virginia Culin Roberts, "Horseback to Mount Baldy: A Ranchwoman's Holiday, 1913," *Journal of Arizona History* 21 (spring 1980): 25–42.

51. Eaton's Ranch, Brochure, 1922, and Wranglin' Notes of the Wolves Club, 1924; both are located at the Autry Museum of Western Heritage, Los Angeles.

52. Valley Ranch, Brochures, 1924, 1929, Autry Museum of Western Heritage, Los Angeles.

53. Kathleen Mitchell Newton, Diary, ca. 1900, in Papers, 1927, Lane County Museum, Eugene, Oregon; Ida Brewington Pittman, Collection, 1945–77, Women's Archives, Dickinson Library, University of Nevada, Las Vegas; and Mrs. S. E. Webster, Scrapbook, 1923–25, Nebraska State Historical Society, Lincoln.

54. Borghild Marie Bergstedt Paulsen, "Mor Remisces," 1970, Special Collections, University of Utah Libraries, Salt Lake City.

55. Robertson, *Magnificent Mountain Women*, 36–44.

56. Quoted in Judith Niemi, *The Basic Essentials of Women in the Outdoors* (Merrillville IN: ICS Books, 1990), 1.

57. "She's a big game guide, Mrs. Fannie Steele has packed and hunted," *Post Empire*, special hunting issue, 4 October 1959, 10.

58. Judith Pryor, "The Girl Scouts of America," in Zophy, *Handbook of American Women's History*, 233.

59. Pryor, "Girl Scouts of America."

60. Sarah Addington, "The First Girl Scout," *Good Housekeeping*, February 1927; and Fern G. Brown, *Daisy and the Girl Scouts: The Story of Juliette Gordon Low* (Morton Grove IL: Albert Whitman, 1996), 66.

61. Myra G. Gutin, *The President's Partner: The First Lady in the Twentieth Century* (New York: Greenwood Press, 1989), 44–47; and Lou Henry Hoover, Letters to Mary Austin, 1911–27, Huntington Library, San Marino CA.

62. Foxboro Ranches, Brochure, undated, Arizona Historical Society, Tucson.

63. Camp Chonokis, Brochure, in Camp Chonokis, Records, 1879–1982, Special Collections, Getchell Library, University of Nevada, Reno.

64. Camp Chonokis, Brochure.

65. Camp Chonokis, Brochure.

66. Camp Chonokis, Brochure.

67. Camp Chonokis, Brochure.

68. Robertson, *Magnificent Mountain Women*, 55–56.

69. Kingery, Papers.

70. Kingery, Papers; and C. W. Buchholtz, "Paradise Founded: The Beginnings of Rocky Mountain National Park," *Colorado Heritage* 1 (1984): 2–17.

8 · *Travelers and Tourists*

1. Lloyd E. Hudman, "Tourism and the American West," *Journal of the West* 33 (July 1994): 67–76.

2. Margaret Long, "Our Summering of 1890," Yellowstone Journal, 1890, Archives, Norlin Library, University of Colorado at Boulder.

3. Long, "Our Summering of 1890."

4. Long, "Our Summering of 1890."

5. Margaret Long, "Biographical Sketch of Margaret Long," undated, Archives, Norlin Library, University of Colorado at Boulder.

6. Margaret Long, Travel Diary, 29 May–6 November 1919, Archives, Norlin Library, University of Colorado at Boulder.

7. Margaret Long, Notes, "Writings on the Desert," undated, and Notes, "Research concerning Death Valley," undated, Archives, Norlin Library, University of Colorado at Boulder.

8. An overview of Long and her writings can be found in Walt Wheelock, *Gentlewomen Adventurers in Death Valley* (Death Valley CA: Annual Death Valley 49ers Encampment, 1986).

9. *(Denver) Rocky Mountain News*, 2 February 1930.

10. *Los Angeles Times*, 26 January 1930.

11. Margaret Long, Research Notes, undated, Archives, Norlin Library, University of Colorado at Boulder.

12. Russel B. Nye, "Ann Newport Royall," in James, *Notable American Women, 1607–1950*, 2:204–5; and Marion Tinling, ed., *Women into the Unknown: A Sourcebook on Women Explorers and Travelers* (New York: Greenwood Press, 1989), 241. Novelist Harriet Beecher Stowe also journeyed abroad and wrote of her experiences. See Leo Hamalian, ed., *Ladies on the Loose: Women Travellers of the 18th and 19th Centuries* (South Yarmouth MA: John Curley, 1981), 62, 70.

13. S. Anna Gordon, *Camping in Colorado* (New York: Author's Pub., 1879).

14. Mary Alice Keating, "Two Girls in a Buggy: The Story of a Three-Hundred-Mile Drive through California Valleys," *Sunset Magazine* 11 (August 1903): 319–29. A dissenting view is found in Carrie Adell Strahorn, *Fifteen Thousand Miles by Stage* (New York: G. P. Putnam's Sons, 1911), which gained an enduring reputation as a classic narrative of riding stagecoaches during the 1870s and 1880s. Strahorn recorded unmitigated details about poor lodgings, food, and travel conditions.

15. Barbara Jane Dickey, "Women Travelers in Nineteenth Century Colorado: 'And Though Rather a Rough Trip, Is Quite Practical for Ladies'" (M.A. thesis, University of Utah, 1980), 18–46.

16. Anne F. Hyde, "Cultural Filters: The Significance of Perception in the History of the American West," *Western Historical Quarterly* 24 (August 1993): 351–74.

17. Serena J. Washburn, Autobiography, 1836–1904, Special Collections, Montana State University Library, Bozeman.

18. Septima M. Collis, *A Woman's Trip to Alaska* (New York: Cassell, 1890), i, 194. A similar account is found in Mrs. James Edwin Morris, *A Pacific Coast Vacation* (New York: Abbey Press, 1901).

19. Ella Carroll, "Pleasant Memories," undated, Archives, Norlin Library, University of Colorado at Boulder.

20. Minneapolis Tourist Club, Records, 1891–1965, Minnesota Historical Society, St. Paul.

21. Letter, "Dear Miss Moynihan," 27 January 1926, from the All-Year Club of Southern California, copy in author's possession.

22. Mrs. May Humphreys Stacy, Papers, undated, Arizona Historical Society, Tucson; and Sandra L. Myres, ed., "An Arizona Camping Trip: May Banks Stacey's [sic] Account of an Outing to Mount Graham in 1879," *Arizona and the West* 23 (spring 1981): 53–64.

23. Stacy, Papers; and Myres, "An Arizona Camping Trip," 53–64.

24. Marian Redington Abbott, "Marian Redington Abbott on Her Turn-of-the-Century Camping Trip," *Oregon Historical Society* 88 (summer 1987): 196–203. Another account of a woman who had a "wonderful" time camping is found in Della M. Todd's Daily Journal, 5 July 1911 to 5 July 1912, American Heritage Center, University of Wyoming Library, Laramie.

25. Nellie Martin Wade, "Through Interior Alaska on Horseback and the Scenic Coast Route," 1907, Oregon Historical Society, Portland, Oregon.

26. Brigitta Maria Ingemanson, "Under Cover: The Paradox of Victorian Women's Travel Costume," in *Women and the Journey: The Female Travel Experience*, ed. Bonnie Frederick and Susan H. McLeod (Pullman: Washington State Univ. Press, 1993), 5–19.

27. Olin D. Wheeler, *Wonderland 1901* (St. Paul MN: Northern Pacific Railroad, 1901), 20–26, 104.

28. Julia Elsing Collection, "Diary of an Auto Trip," 1919, Arizona Historical Society, Tucson; and Menno Duerksen, "The Lincoln Highway: West of Cheyenne the Going Gets Rough," *Cars and Parts*, October 1979, 14.

29. Evalyn A. Bentley, Papers, undated, Arizona Historical Society, Tucson. An earlier trip is described in Bentley, "Presimeda Pass," *Associated Arizona Producer*, 1 February 1929, unpaged.

30. An account of one catarrh sufferer appears in Maria P. Heppin, Letter to "Mrs. G. H. Scribner," 17 June 1882, Nevada Historical Society, Reno. For Denver and the Southwest, see Susan Jane Edwards, "Nature as Healer: Denver, Colorado's Social and Built Landscapes of Health, 1880–1930" (Ph.D. diss., University of Colorado at Boulder, 1994).

31. "The Colorado Sanitarium," 1896, Boulder, Colorado, brochure in author's possession.

32. "Colorado Sanitarium."

33. Colorado Promotion and Publicity Committee, "Colorado: Its Hotels and Resorts," 1904, 5, 18, brochure in author's possession.

34. Maud F. Bucholz, Diary, 1902–5, Arizona Historical Society, Tucson; and Norah Hammersly Laing, "Dreamy Draw," *Wide World Magazine* (London), 1924, 411–16.

35. Pearl Rosemary Poole Peterson, Journal and Papers, 1894–1944, Minneapolis Historical Society, St. Paul.

36. Chicago and North Western Railway, "The Enchanted Summer-Land," undated, 34, 45, brochure in author's possession.

37. James S. Brust and Lee H. Whittlesey, "'Roughing It up the Yellowstone to Wonderland': The Nelson Miles/Colgate Hoyt Party in Yellowstone National Park, September 1878," *Montana: The Magazine of Western History* 46 (spring 1986): 56–64.

38. Roland G. Kaiser, "Edna Fay Kaiser," Montana American Mothers Bicentennial Project, 1975–76, Montana State Historical Society, Helena; and Mary B. Richards, *Camping Out in the Yellowstone* (Salem MA: Newcomb & Grass, 1910), 3–10, 62. The latter includes Yellowstone letters originally written in 1882.

39. Kirby Lambert, "The Lure of the Parks," *Montana: The Magazine of American History* 46 (spring 1996): 42–55. Regarding the growing sentiment to see America first, see Marguerite S. Shafer, "'See America First': Re-Envisioning Nation and Region through Western Tourism," *Pacific Historical Review* 65 (November 1996): 559–81.

40. Nell Buchan, "Pioneer Memories," 1975, Wyoming State Archives, Cheyenne. For a similar account, see Jessie P. Mudgett in the same collection.

41. C. Van Tassell, *Truthful Lies of Yellowstone Park* (St. Paul MN: Pioneer, 1923), 11.

42. *The Compete Campers Manual; or, How to Camp Out and What to Do* (n.p., 1903), 34, 37; and Denver and Rio Grande System, *Camping in the Rocky Mountains: A Cheap and Delightful Way to Spend Your Summer* (Denver: n.p., 1907), 10, 27, 31, 47; copies in author's possession.

43. Captain John Hance, Papers, undated, Arizona Historical Society, Tucson.

44. Carrie E. LeConte, *Yo Semite, 1878: Adventures of N and C* (San Francisco: Book Club of California, 1964), 99. See also Carrie Ober, "Log Book of 1901 Cruise of the N.P.," 1901, Special Collections, University of Washington Libraries, Seattle. Also helpful in understanding Yosemite are Stanford E. Demars, *The Tourist in Yosemite, 1855–1985* (Salt Lake City: Univ. of Utah Press, 1991); and Kate Nearpass Ogden, "Yosemite Valley as Image and Symbol: Paintings and Photographs from 1855 to 1880" (Ph.D. diss., Columbia University, 1992).

45. Dorothy M. Johnson, "Carefree Youth: Dudes in Glacier," *Montana: The Magazine of Western History* 24 (summer 1975): 59.

46. Estes Park Chamber of Commerce, *Estes Park, Colorado: Rocky Mountain National Park* (n.p., ca. 1935); and Yosemite National Park Company, *Yosemite: All-Year-Round National Park, California: YTS Tours* (n.p., 1922); both in author's possession.

47. Chicago and North Western Railway, "Enchanted Summer-Land," 1–5.

48. Southern Pacific Railroad, *California for the Tourist: The Charm of the Land of Sunshine by Summit, Sea and Shore* (San Francisco: Southern Pacific, 1910), 45, 84, 89, copy in author's possession.

49. Union Pacific Railroad, *Western Wonderlands* (Omaha: n.p., 1931), 3, 21.

50. A. C. Harvey, *Harvey and Co.'s Popular California Excursions* (n.p., 1887), copy in author's possession.

51. Harveycars, *Motor Drives out from the Alvarado, Albuquerque* (Chicago: W. J. Black, 1927); Harveycars, *Roads to Yesterday* (Chicago: W. J. Black, 1927); and Harveycars, *Harveycar Motor Cruises off the Beaten Path in the Great Southwest* (Chicago: W. J. Black, 1929); originals at Braun Library, Southwest Museum, Los Angeles. For more on the Harvey company, see Marta Weigle and Barbara Babcock, eds., *The Great Southwest of the Fred Harvey Company and the Santa Fe Railroad* (Tucson: Univ. of Arizona Press, 1996).

52. "Amy Cornwall Neal," in Crowe and Tod, *Arizona Women's Hall of Fame*, 74–75. For more information on the Harvey Girls, see Tom Vinegar, ed., *Harvey Girls' Recipes: From the Pages of the Santa Fe*

Magazine, 1910–1913 (Albuquerque: Vinegar Tom Press, 1972); Lesley Poling-Kempes, *The Harvey Girls: Women Who Opened the West* (New York: Marlowe, 1989); Poling-Kempes, *Far From Home: West by Rail with the Harvey Girls* (Lubbock: Texas Tech Univ. Press, 1994); and Juddi Morris, *The Harvey Girls: The Women Who Civilized the West* (New York: Walker, 1994).

53. Arizona Wonder Circuit Tours, Prospectus, 1924, Arizona Historical Society, Tucson.

54. Cave of the Winds Scenic Attraction Company, *The Wonderful Cave of the Winds, Manitou, Colorado* (Colorado Springs: n.p., ca. 1920s), copy in author's possession; and *National Forest Dude Ranch Vacation*, ca. 1925, Autry Museum of Western Heritage, Los Angeles.

55. "From 'Bunk' to 'Bunkie,'" Photograph Album, ca. 1925, Diamond G Ranch, 1930s, and Bar BC Ranch, Brochure, Victor ID, early 1920s; both at Autry Museum of Western Heritage, Los Angeles.

56. Frost and Richards Ranch, Brochure, 1913, Autry Museum of Western Heritage, Los Angeles.

57. Bar BC Ranch, Brochure.

58. Remuda Guest Ranch, Brochure, ca. 1925; Diamond G. Ranch of the Rockies, 1925; Guest Ranches of Southern Arizona, Brochure, 1928; and Dude Ranches Out West, Brochure, 1931; all at Autry Museum of Western Heritage, Los Angeles.

59. Four Bear Ranch, Brochure, early 1930s; Pierson Dude Ranch, Brochure, 1930s; and Santa Fe Dude Ranch Country, Brochure, 1937; all at Autry Museum of Western Heritage, Los Angeles.

60. LX-Bar Ranch, Brochure, 1931, Autry Museum of Western Heritage, Los Angeles.

61. "Ranch Life in the Buffalo Bill Country [Wyoming]," Brochure, 1928, Autry Museum of Western Heritage, Los Angeles.

62. I. H. Larcom, *Welcome to My West: I. H. Larcom, Dude Rancher, Conservationist, Collector* (Cody WY: Buffalo Bill Historical Center, 1982).

63. Wheelock, *Gentlewomen Adventurers in Death Valley*, 5, 7.

64. Wheelock, *Gentlewomen Adventurers in Death Valley*, 3, 5, 11.

9 · Beyond the Land

1. Karen Knowles, ed., *Celebrating the Land: Women's Nature Writings, 1850–1991* (Flagstaff AZ: Northland, 1992), 126.

2. Glenda Riley, *Women and Indians on the Frontier, 1825–1915* (Albuquerque: Univ. of New Mexico Press, 1984), 205–8; and Frederick Turner, "The Terror of Wilderness," *American Heritage* 28 (February 1977): 58–65.

3. Quoted in Flora Warren Seymour, "Our Indian Problem," *Forum* 71 (March 1924): 274. For the rhetoric of Indian reform, consult Brigitte Georgi-Findlay, *The Frontiers of Women's Writing: Women's Narratives and the Rhetoric of Westward Expansion* (Tucson: Univ. of Arizona Press, 1996), 240–51.

4. Frank Linderman, *Pretty-Shield: Medicine Woman of the Crows* (Lincoln: Univ. of Nebraska Press, 1972).

5. Mary Crow Dog, "Civilize Them with a Stick," in Jordan and Hepworth, *Stories That Shape Us*, 91.

6. Cheryl Walker, *Indian Nation: Native American Literature and Nineteenth-Century Nationalism* (Durham NC: Duke Univ. Press, 1997), 185.

7. Mary Austin, "The Folly of the Officials," *Forum* 71 (March 1924): 287.

8. Richmond L. Clow, ed., "Autobiography of Mary C. Collins, Missionary to the Western Sioux," *South Dakota Historical Collections* 41 (1982): 3–64; Mary G. Burdette, ed., *Young Women among Blanket Indians: The Heroine of Saddle Mountain* (Chicago: R. R. Donnelley & Sons, 1897); and The Missionary Committee, "Women's National Indian Association," Report, 17 November 1885, Braun Library, Southwest Museum, Los Angeles. Also helpful is Ruth Ann Alexander, "Women in South Dakota Missions," *Anglican and Episcopal History* 63 (September 1994): 334–62.

9. Quoted in "From Our Matrons," *Ramona Days* (Santa Fe: Ramona Industrial School of the University of New Mexico, 1887), 19; and *Reports of Superintendents and Others in Charge of Indians, Arizona* (Washington DC: Government Printing Office, 1909), 12.

10. Ruth Ann Alexander, "Finding Oneself through a Cause: Elaine

Goodale Eastman and Indian Reform in the 1880s," *South Dakota History* 22 (winter 1992): 1–37.

11. Elizabeth Baker Bohan, "Rancho Guajome: The Real Home of Ramona," *Rural Californian*, November 1894, 1–8; and Ella H. Enderlein, "Carlos and Ramona," *Sunset Magazine* 11 (May 1903): 44–47.

12. "Gold Hill Women," Pamphlet File, 1981, Archives, Norlin Library, University of Colorado at Boulder. Nevada women also owned and managed tourist camps at Goldfield. See Goldfield nv, Advertising Card for Goldfield Auto Camp, undated, Women's Archives, Dickinson Library, University of Nevada, Las Vegas.

13. California Petroleum Corporation, Easy Fold Maps of California Highways, undated, and New Mexico State Tourist Bureau, Recreational Map of New Mexico: Land of Enchantment, 1941; both maps in author's possession. A helpful discussion is found in Hal K. Rothman, "Selling the Meaning of Place: Entrepreneurship, Tourism, and Community Transformation in the Twentieth-Century American West," *Pacific Historical Review* 65 (November 1996): 525–57.

14. A useful biographical treatment is Evelyn I. Banning, *Helen Hunt Jackson* (New York: Vanguard, 1973). For analysis of Jackson, see Valerie Sherer Mathes, "Helen Hunt Jackson and the Ponca Controversy," *Montana: The Magazine of Western History* 39 (winter 1989): 42–53; Mathes, "The California Mission Indian Commission of 1891: The Legacy of Helen Hunt Jackson," *California History* 72 (winter 1993–94): 338–59; and Mathes, *Helen Hunt Jackson and Her Indian Reform Legacy* (Austin: Univ. of Texas Press, 1990).

15. Pierarski, *Westward the Women*, 5.

16. Katharine Luomala, "Martha Warren Beckwith," in Peterson, *Notable Women of Hawaii*, 26–30.

17. Mary Austin, "The Folly of the Officials," *Forum* 71 (March 1924): 288.

18. Mary Austin, Clipping File, undated, Center for Southwest Research, University of New Mexico Library, Albuquerque.

19. Mary Austin, Letter to "Dear Charles," 28 December 1918, in *Literary America, 1903–1934: The Mary Austin Letters*, ed. T. M. Pearce (Westport ct: Greenwood Press, 1979), 26; and James Ruppert, "Mary

Austin's Landscape Line in Native American Literature," *Southwest Review* 68 (autumn 1983): 376–90.

20. Austin, Clipping File.

21. Ann Nolan Clark, Clipping File, undated, Center for Southwest Research, University of New Mexico Library, Albuquerque.

22. Clark, Clipping File.

23. Zitkala-Ša, *American Indian Stories* (Lincoln: Univ. of Nebraska Press, 1985); Anna Moore Shaw, *A Pima Past* (Tucson: Univ. of Arizona Press, 1974); and K. Tasianina Lomawaima, *They Called It Prairie Light: The Story of Chilocco Indian School* (Lincoln: Univ. of Nebraska Press, 1994).

24. Norwood and Monk, *Desert Is No Lady*, 226. See also Joan M. Jensen, *One Foot on the Rockies: Women and Creativity in the Modern American West* (Albuquerque: Univ. of New Mexico Press, 1995), 37–58.

25. Kovinick, *Woman Artist*, 32.

26. Mrs. E. H. Kemp, "Photographing in Hopi Land," *Camera Craft* 6 (December 1905): 247–55.

27. Kate Cory, *The Hopi Photographs: Kate Cory, 1905–1912* (La Cañada CA: Chaco Press, 1986), 2.

28. Mildred Ring, "Kodaking the Indians," *Camera Craft* 24 (February 1924): 71–76, and quoted in Margaretta K. Mitchell, *Recollections: Ten Women of Photography* (New York: Viking Press, 1979), 121. See also Bobbi Rahder, "Gendered Stylistic Differences between Photographers of Native Americans at the Turn of the Century," *Journal of the West* 35 (January 1996): 86–95.

29. N. A. Wog, "Artist with the Camera," *Camera Craft* 24 (May 1917): 189–92.

30. Kovinick, *Woman Artist*, 36.

31. James C. Faris, "Laura Gilpin and the 'Endearing' Navajo," *History of Photography* 21 (spring 1997): 60–66; and "Laura Gilpin, Retrospective, 1910–1974," Center for Southwest Research, University of New Mexico Library, Albuquerque. The university also has a taped interview with Laura Gilpin, 1975. The bulk of her photographs are at the

Amon Carter Museum of Western Art, Fort Worth TX. To understand the work of Laura Gilpin, one must consult Martha A. Sandweiss, *Laura Gilpin: An Eduring Grace* (Fort Worth TX: Amon Carter Museum, 1986).

32. Kovinik, *Woman Artist*, 22, 25, 41.

33. Virginia L. Grattan, *Mary Colter: Builder upon the Red Earth* (Grand Canyon AZ: Grand Canyon Natural History Association, 1992), 42.

34. Grattan, *Mary Colter*, 84.

35. Grattan, *Mary Colter*, 75, 80, 84.

36. Austin, "Folly of the Officials," 286.

37. Mrs. Ernest E. Knudsen, "History of Utah Federation of Women's Clubs, 1893 to 1952," compiled 1952, Utah State Historical Society, Salt Lake City.

38. "Maie Bartlett Heard," in Crowe and Tod, *Arizona Women's Hall of Fame*, 62–63; and Eula Parker Murphy, "Maie Bartlett Heard," undated, Arizona Historical Society, Tucson.

39. History and Landmarks Section of California Federation of Women's Clubs, "Historic Facts and Fancies," undated, Braun Library, Southwest Museum, Los Angeles.

40. Grace Meeker, Miscellaneous Papers, undated, Kansas State Historical Society, Topeka; and Beng Poh Yoskikawa, "Elizabeth Carter Bogardus," in Peterson, *Notable Women of Hawaii*, 47–48.

41. Alice Baltzell Addenbrooke, Papers, 1934–57, Nevada Historical Society, Reno; and Clipping, "Jennie's Babies Remembered," 1952, in Agnes Wright Spring Collection, Special Collections, Norlin Library, University of Colorado at Boulder. For an overview of historical preservation, see Hal Rothman, *Preserving Different Pasts: The American National Monuments* (Urbana: Univ. of Illinois Press, 1989).

42. Nancy Ostreich Lurie, "Matilda Coxe Evans Stevenson," in James, *Notable American Women*, 2:373–74; Nancy J. Parezo, "Matilda Coxe Stevenson: Pioneer Ethnologist," in *Hidden Scholars: Women Anthropologists and the Native American Southwest*, ed. Nancy J. Parezo (Albuquerque: Univ. of New Mexico Press, 1993), 38–62; and Matilda Coxe Stevenson, *Thirtieth Annual Report of the Bureau of American*

Ethnology to the Secretary of the Smithsonian Institution, 1908–1909 (Washington DC: Government Printing Office, 1915).

43. Quoted in the *Buffalo (New York) Courier*, 31 August 1896. See also Alice Cunningham Fletcher, *Twenty-Seventh Annual Report of the Bureau of American Ethnology* (Washington DC: Government Printing Office, 1911).

44. "Louisa Wetherill," in Crowe and Tod, *Arizona Women's Hall of Fame*, 23–25; and Kathryn Gabriel, ed., *Marietta Wetherill: Reflections of Life with the Navajos in Chaco Canyon* (Boulder CO: Johnson Books, 1992).

45. Edith Van Allen Murphey, Papers, 1939–53, Special Collections, Getchell Library, University of Nevada, Reno.

46. Ruth Laughlin, Biography, undated, Center for Southwest Research, University of New Mexico Library, Albuquerque; Clara Lee Fraps Tanner, Papers, undated, Arizona Historical Society, Tucson; and Museum of New Mexico and Museum of American Archaeology at Santa Fe, Announcement Number One, February 1910, Braun Library, Southwest Museum, Los Angeles. See also Linda S. Cordell, "Women Archaeologists in the Southwest," in Parezo, *Hidden Scholars*, 202–20.

47. Elsie Clews Parson, Women of New Mexico Collection, undated, Center for Southwest Research, University of New Mexico Library, Albuquerque; Barbara A. Babcock, ed., *Pueblo Mothers and Children: Essays by Elsie Clews Parsons, 1915–1924* (Santa Fe NM: Ancient City Press, 1991); Louis A. Hieb, "Elsie Clews Parsons in the Southwest," in Parezo, *Hidden Scholars*, 63–75; and Pat Paton, "Ruth Underhill Remembered: A Backward Glance into the Life of a Noted Anthropologist," *Colorado Heritage* 1 (1985): 14–21. Also revealing are U.S. Soil Conservation Service, Collection, 1936, Center for Southwest Research, University of New Mexico Library, Albuquerque; and Constance Darrow Knowles, "A History of Lumbering in the Truckee Basin from 1856 to 1936," WPA Project Report for the Forest Survey Division, California Forest and Range Experiment Station, 26 October 1942, Nevada Historical Society, Reno.

48. Sophie Alberle, Biography and Clippings, undated, and Florence Hawley Ellis, Clippings, undated, both at the Center for Southwest Research, University of New Mexico Library, Albuquerque; Louise Lamphere, "Gladys Reichard among the Navajo," in Parezo, *Hidden*

Scholars, 157–88; Natalie F. S. Woodbury and Millicent C. McIntosh, *Gladys A. Reichard, 1893–1955* (New York: Barnard College, 1955); and Robert S. McPherson, "From Dezba to 'John': The Changing Role of Navajo Women in Southeastern Utah," *American Indian Culture and Research Journal* 18 (1994): 187–209.

49. For other women, see Barbara A. Babcock, "The Leading Edge: Women Anthropologists in the Native American Southwest, 1880–1945," *El Palacio* 92 (1986): 41–49; and Barbara A. Babcock and Nancy J. Parezo, *Daughters of the Desert: Women Anthropologists and the Native American Southwest, 1880–1980* (Albuquerque: Univ. of New Mexico Press, 1988).

50. The attack on tourists is reported in Rex C. Myers, ed., *Lizzie: The Letters of Elizabeth Chester Fish, 1864–1893* (Missoula MT: Mountain Press, 1989), 48–49.

51. Dorothy M. Johnson, "Carefree Youth with Dudes in Glacier," *Montana: The Magazine of Western History* 24 (summer 1975): 48–49.

52. Harveycars, "Indian Detour," Brochure, undated, Braun Library, Southwest Museum, Los Angeles.

53. "Nampeyo," in Crowe and Tod, *Arizona's Women's Hall of Fame,* 85–86.

54. Annie B. Schencks, "Journal: Camping Tour in Rocky Mountains," August 1871, Colorado Historical Society, Denver.

55. Carroll, "Pleasant Memories."

56. New Mexico State Tourist Bureau, Recreational Map, 1941.

57. Grace M. Sparkes, Papers, 1911–60, Arizona Historical Society, Tucson; and "Grace M. Sparkes," in Crowe and Tod, *Arizona Women's Hall of Fame,* 21–22.

58. Sparkes, Papers; and Jennifer DeWitt, "'When They Are Gone. . .': The Smoki People of Prescott and the Preservation of Indian Culture," *Journal of Arizona History* 37 (winter 1996): 319–36.

59. Sparkes, Papers.

10 · Since 1940

1. Examples of recent works that generally overlook women are John K. Terres, ed., *Discovery: Great Moments in the Lives of Outstanding*

Naturalists (Philadelphia: J. B. Lippincott, 1961); Alexander B. Adams, *Eternal Quest: The Story of the Great Naturalists* (New York: G. P. Putnam's Sons, 1969); Robin W. Doughty, *Wildlife and Man in Texas: Environmental Change and Conservation* (College Station: Texas A&M Univ. Press, 1983); and David Pepper, *The Roots of Modern Environmentalism* (London: Croom Helm, 1984). Notable volumes that include women are Richard H. Stroud, ed., *National Leaders of American Conservation* (Washington DC: Smithsonian Institution Press, 1985); and Derrick Jensen, *Listening to the Land: Conversations about Nature, Culture, and Eros* (San Francisco: Sierra Club Books, 1995).

2. For example, see George H. Stankey and Richard Schreyer, "Attitudes toward Wilderness and Factors Affecting Visitor Behavior: A State-of-Knowledge Review," in *Proceedings—National Wilderness Research Conference: Issues, State-of-Knowledge, Future Directions,* comp. Robert C. Lucas (Ogden UT: Intermountain Research Station, 1985); and Rachel Kaplan and Stephen Kaplan, *The Experience of Nature* (New York: Cambridge Univ. Press, 1989).

3. Steven Davis, "Pluralism and Ecological Values: The Case of the Siskiyou National Forest, 1983–1992" (Ph.D. diss., Loyola University, Chicago, 1994).

4. Michael K. Heimen, "Race, Waste, and Class: New Perspectives on Environmental Justice," *Antipode* 28 (April 1996): 111–21; Laura Pulido, Steve Sidawi, and Robert O. Vos, "An Archaeology of Environmental Racism in Los Angeles," *Urban Georgraphy* 17 (1 July–15 August 1996): 419–39; and Annie Gilbert Coleman, "The Unbearable Whiteness of Skiing," *Pacific Historical Review* 65 (November 1996): 583–614.

5. Quoted in Jensen, *Listening to the Land,* 222–31.

6. Quoted in Jensen, *Listening to the Land,* 123. For information about other Hispanic activists, consult Laura Pulido, *Environmentalism and Economic Justice: Two Struggles in the Southwest* (Tucson: Univ. of Arizona Press, 1996).

7. Grace Greenwood, *New Life in New Lands* (New York: J. B. Ford, 1873), 384.

8. Christine June Cuomo, "Ecological Feminism as Environmental Ethics" (Ph.D. diss., University of Wisconsin-Madison, 1992).

9. Elizabeth Dodson Gray, *Green Paradise Lost*, 2d ed. (Wellesley MA: Roundtable Press, 1981); Carolyn Merchant, *The Death of Nature: Women, Ecology, and the Scientific Revolution* (San Francisco: Harper & Row, 1980); and Joni Seager, *Earth Follies: Coming to Feminist Terms with the Global Environmental Crisis* (New York: Routledge, 1993). For a much fuller treatment of this complex philosophy, see Carolyn Merchant, ed., *Ecology* (Atlantic Highlands NJ: Humanities Press, 1994).

10. From Hogan's poem "oil," quoted in Lorraine Anderson, ed., *Sisters of the Earth: Women's Prose and Poetry about Nature* (New York: Vintage Books, 1991), 310.

11. Carolyn Merchant, *Radical Ecology: The Search for a Livable World* (New York: Routledge, 1992), 1. Also see Merchant's earlier essays, "Earthcare: Women and the Environment," *Environment* 23 (June 1981): 6–13, and "Gender and Environmental History," *Journal of American History* 76 (March 1990): 1117–21.

12. Quoted in Jensen, *Listening to the Land*, 46, 49.

13. Cecile Jackson, "Women/Nature or Gender/History? A Critique of Ecofeminist 'Development,'" *Journal of Peasant Studies* 20 (1993): 389–418; Karen J. Warren, "Feminism and Ecology: Making Connections," *Environmental Ethics* 9 (spring 1987): 2–20; Warren, "The Power and the Promise of Ecological Feminism," *Environmental Ethics* 12 (summer 1990): 125–46; and Melissa Leach and Cathy Green, *Gender and Environmental History: Moving beyond the Narratives of the Past in Contemporary Women-Environment Policy Debates* (Brighton, England: Institute of Developmental Studies, 1995).

14. Derek Richter, ed., *Women Scientists: The Road to Liberation* (London: Macmillan, 1982).

15. Paul Brooks, *The House of Life: Rachel Carson at Work* (Boston: Houghton Mifflin, 1972); Douglas H. Strong, *Dreamers and Defenders: American Conservationists* (Lincoln: Univ. of Nebraska Press, 1976), 177–95; Ralph H. Lutts, "Chemical Fallout: Rachel Carson's *Silent Spring*, Radioactive Fallout, and the Environmental Movement," *Environmental Review* 9 (fall 1985): 210–25; and Lisa Budwig, "Breaking Nature's Silence: Pennsylvania's Rachel Carson," *Pennsylvania Heritage* 18 (fall 1992) 30–37.

16. Florence Hart Carr, "Helen Blackburn Hoover: Scientist, Naturalist, Writer" (master's thesis, Hamline University, St. Paul, 1993). See also Helen Hoover, *A Place in the Woods* (New York: Alfred A. Knopf, 1969); and Hoover, *The Years of the Forest* (New York: Alfred A. Knopf, 1973). In another case, a U.S. Park Service botanist, Pauline Patraw, pursued conservation activities throughout her career. During the early 1980s, after her retirement, Patraw helped local Girl Scouts develop a nature trail in New Mexico's Hyde State Park. Gail D. Tierny, *Roadside Plants of Northern New Mexico* (Santa Fe NM: Lightning Tree Press, 1983), 5.

17. Karen Harden McCracken, *Connie Hagar: The Life History of a Texas Birdwatcher* (College Station: Texas A&M Univ. Press, 1986), xv–xvi, 17, 276.

18. Tierney, *Roadside Plants*, 5 (for an account of Leonora S. M. Curtin); and Barbara L. Davis, *Birds of the Southwest* (Tucson: Treasure Chest, 1986), 4.

19. Florence Page Jacques, *Snowshoe Country* (Minneapolis: Univ. of Minnesota Press, 1944). In a similar vein is Sally Carrighar, *One Day on Beetle Rock* (New York: Alfred A. Knopf, 1945), and *One Day at Teton Marsh* (New York: Alfred A. Knopf, 1947).

20. A. Clay Schoenfeld, "The Environmental Movement as Reflected in the American Magazine," *Journalism Quarterly* 60 (autumn 1983): 470–75.

21. Schoenfeld, "Environmental Movement," 470–75.

22. Scott Slovic, *Seeking Awareness in American Nature Writing* (Salt Lake City: Univ. of Utah Press, 1992), 3–20. Also helpful is Annette Kolodny, "Letting Go Our Grand Obsessions: Notes toward a New Literary History of the American Frontiers," *American Literature* 64 (March 1992): 1–18; and Susan Rhoades Neel, "A Place of Extremes: Nature, History, and the American West," *Western Historical Quarterly* 25 (winter 1994): 489–505.

23. Several anthologies offer examples of women's writings, including Pierkarski, *Westward the Women*; Robert C. Baron and Elizabeth Darby Junkin, eds., *Of Discovery and Destiny: An Anthology of American Writers and the American Land* (Golden CO: Fulcrum, 1986); Anderson, *Sisters of the Earth*; and Karen Knowles, ed., *Celebrating the*

Land: Women's Nature Writings, 1850–1991 (Flagstaff AZ: Northland, 1992). Interpretive essays are found in Elder, *American Nature Writers,* 2 vols.

For an example of authors who offer definitions and recommendations, see Clifford and Isabel Ahlgren, *Lob Trees in the Wilderness* (Minneapolis: Univ. of Minnesota Press, 1984). For male writers' acceptance of women's presence in the West, see Donald J. Greiner, *Women Enter the Wilderness: Male Bonding and the American Novel of the 1980s* (Columbia: Univ. of South Carolina Press, 1991). Also helpful is Patricia Greiner, "Radical Environmentalism in Recent Literature Concerning the American West," *Rendezvous* 19 (1983): 8–15.

24. Ann Zwinger, *Beyond the Aspen Grove* (New York: Random House, 1970); Zwinger, with Beatrice E. Willard, *Land above the Trees: A Guide to American Alpine Tundra* (New York: Harper & Row, 1972); Zwinger, *Run, River, Run: A Naturalist's Journey Down on the Great Rivers of the West* (New York: Harper & Row, 1975); Zwinger, *Wind in the Rock* (New York: Harper & Row, 1978); and Zwinger, *The Mysterious Lands: A Naturalist Explores the Four Great Deserts of the Southwest* (New York: E. P. Dutton, 1989).

25. From "What Moon Drove Me to This?" quoted in Anderson, *Sisters of the Earth,* 3.

26. Quoted in Anderson, *Sisters of the Earth,* 336–38.

27. For ranchwomen, see, for example, Sue Hubbell, *A Country Year: Living the Questions* (New York: Random House, 1983); Linda M. Hasselstrom, *Going over East: Reflections of a Woman Rancher* (Golden: Fulcrum, 1987); and Hasselstrom, *Windbreak: A Woman Rancher on the Northern Plains* (Berkeley: Barn Owl Books, 1987). For information on African-American writers, a useful work is David Lionel Smith, "African Americans, Writing, and Nature," in Elder, *American Nature Writers,* 2:1003–12.

28. Jeanne Russell Janish, Collection, 1883–1994, Women's Archives, Dickinson Library, University of Nevada, Las Vegas.

29. Stroud, *National Leaders of American Conservation,* 11–12.

30. Lois Crisler, Papers, 1940–73, Manuscripts, University of Washington Libraries, Seattle.

31. Kathy Zimmerer, "Silken Threads and Golden Butterflies: Asian-Americans," in Moore, *Yesterday and Tomorrow*, 179–92.

32. Heather Anderson, "Artists of the California Landscape, 1850–1950," in Moore, *Yesterday and Tomorrow*, 74; and Rita Gonzalez-Mahoney, "Interviews," *New America: A Journal of American and Southwest Culture* 4 (1982): 33.

33. Annette L. Flugger, Papers, undated, Denver Public Library.

34. Nellie T. Bush, Biographical File, 1888–1963, Arizona Historical Society, Tucson. For a look at another club woman and conservationist west of the Mississippi River, see Mary Linn Wernet, "Conservation through Mutual Cooperation: A History of Mrs. Lee Craig Levy's Work with the Louisiana Forestry Commission," *North Louisiana Historical Association* 16 (1985): 23–34.

35. Edith H. Herman, Papers, 1964–81, Minnesota Historical Society, St. Paul.

36. Merritt H. and Lilly E. Starkweather, Papers, 1916–82, Arizona Historical Society, Tucson.

37. Lilly E. Starkweather, "Conservation High-Lights," address presented 11 March 1952, Starkweather, Papers.

38. Malcolm F. and Mildred Hargraves, Papers, 1922–87, Minnesota Historical Society, St. Paul. During the 1970s, Patricia Emerson of Seattle directed a league project to evaluate citizen environmental programs in Washington State. The survey, funded by the U.S. Army Corps of Engineers, culminated in league recommendations for a series of reports and booklets advocating enhanced citizen participation in environmentalism. Edith H. Herman, Papers, 1964–89, Minnesota Historical Society, St. Paul.

39. Lewis L. Gould, *Lady Bird and the Environment* (Lawrence: Univ. Press of Kansas, 1988), 1–2, 7, 222–45.

40. Maurine B. Neuberger, Papers, 1950–67, Special Collections, University of Oregon Library, Eugene; and "Clara Botzum," in Crowe and Tod, *Arizona Women's Hall of Fame*, 17–20.

41. Double K Mountain Ranch, Records, 1958–72, Special Collections, University of Washington Libraries, Seattle. Also in Washington State, Emily Haig spoke and lobbied to keep Mount Rainer National Park

free of trams and such commercialization as billboards. Later, during the 1960s and 1970s, Louise Marshall used her position as editor of the *Signpost*, a newsletter for hikers and backpackers, to advocate keeping Washington State "green." Emily Huddart Haig, Papers, 1958–70; and Louise B. Marshall, Papers, 1965–75, both in Manuscripts, University of Washington Libraries, Seattle.

42. Velma B. Johnston, Papers, undated, Denver Public Library.

43. Johnston, Papers.

44. Polly Welts Kaufman, *National Parks and the Woman's Voice: A History* (Albuquerque: Univ. of New Mexico Press, 1996), 121–47.

45. Kaufman, *National Parks and the Woman's Voice*, 121; and Elaine Pitt Enarson, *Woods-Working Women: Sexual Integration in the U.S. Forest Service* (University: Univ. of Alabama Press, 1984), ix–x, 146–49. Meanwhile, Minnie Stevens became the first woman creel census taker and in 1959 the only woman hatchery supervisor in Arizona. A fishing enthusiast herself, Stevens operated the Sterling Springs fish hatchery for twenty-seven years. "Minnie Stevens," in Crowe and Hall, *Arizona Women's Hall of Fame*, 14–16.

46. Stroud, *National Leaders of American Conservation*, 389; Owings was quoted in Ann LaBastille, *Women and Wilderness* (San Francisco: Sierra Club Books, 1980), 145.

47. Quoted in Arlene Blum, *Annapurna: A Woman's Place* (San Francisco: Sierra Club Books, 1980), 2.

48. Blum, *Annapurna*.

49. Colorado alone can claim a long list of famous women climbers, including Elizabeth (Betsy) Strong Cowles Partridge, Ruth Ewald Gay, Inestine Roberts, and Molly Higgins, to name just a few. Robertson, *Magnificent Mountain Women*, 143–78.

50. Such other states as Wyoming had active women as well. In 1945, two Wyoming women climbed to the Continental Divide to be the first people to transverse Dinwoody Glacier on skis. Marianne Stevenson Magnuson, "Operation Petticoat," *Ski Illlustrated*, March 1947, 21–23, 41–42; and Paulsen, "Mor Remisces."

51. Sara Machetanz, Papers, 1954–61, Special Collections, University

of Oregon, Eugene; and Susan Butcher, interview by author and others, Fairbanks AK, 18 May 1990.

52. See for example, Stella Dysart, Biographical File, undated, Center for Southwest Research, University of New Mexico Library, Albuquerque.

53. Agnes Morehead Holland, *Brush Country Woman* (College Station: Texas A&M Univ. Press, 1988); Agnes Morley Cleaveland, *Satan's Paradise* (Boston: Houghton Mifflin, 1948), 1–2; and Cleaveland, Biographical File, undated, Center for Southwest Research, University of New Mexico Library, Albuquerque.

54. Debbie S. Miller, *Midnight Wilderness: Journeys in Alaska's Arctic National Wildlife Refuge* (San Francisco: Sierra Club Books, 1990), xvi–xvii.

55. Federation of Western Outdoor Clubs, Records, 1931–53, Special Collections, University of Oregon, Eugene. The quotation is found in *Bulletin of the Federation of Western Outdoor Clubs* 12 (July 1945): 7.

56. Polly Dyer, Papers, 1953–93, Manuscripts, University of Washington Libraries, Seattle.

57. Judith Niemi and Barbara Wieser, eds., *Rivers Running Free: Canoeing Stories by Adventurous Women* (Seattle: Seal Press, 1992), 199. Also useful is LaBastille, *Women and Wilderness*. Such trips also appealed to women of color. During the 1970s, Minnesotan Heart Warrior Chosa canoed the Boundary Waters Canoe Area. After a 1974 trip, Chosa offered campouts that included talks on women's medicine from a Native American viewpoint. Niemi and Wieser, *Rivers Running Free*, 233.

58. Niemi and Wieser, *Rivers Running Free*, 264–65.

59. Niemi and Wieser, *Rivers Running Free*, 39, 203. See also Justine Kerfoot, *Woman of the Boundary Waters: Canoeing, Building, Mushing and Surviving* (Grand Marais MN: Women's Times, 1986). Another example is Gertrude Maxwell, who began guiding hunters in Idaho in 1934. In a 1980 interview she said, "Packed hunters commercially for 30 years. Ranched and raised cattle most of my life." Gertrude Maxwell, Interview Transcript, 1980, OH 449, Idaho State Historical Society, Boise.

60. Ann S. Addington, interview by author, Denver, 1 May 1995.

61. Jensen, *Listening to the Land*, 123.

62. Clarissa Brown Winsor, Biographical File, undated, Arizona Historical Society, Tucson; and "Clarissa Brown Winsor," in Crowe and Tod, *Arizona Women's Hall of Fame*, 92–93. Still other women activists continued women's traditional interest in preserving aspects of the West's built environment. Erna Gunther of Washington State directed the Washington State Museum and also served on the advisory board on historic sites to the State Parks and Recreation Commission, where she tried to save Yakima Indian paintings and Squamish sites.

63. For examples of practitioners of various approaches to anthropology, see Babcock and Parezo, *Daughters of the Desert*; and Jeanne Armstrong, "Deserts and Dreams: The Life of Gwyneth Harrington, 1894–1978," *Journal of the Southwest* 30 (winter 1988): 522–34.

64. Margaret M. Wheat, Papers, 1908–88, Special Collections, Getchell Library, University of Nevada, Reno. For other examples, consult Parezo, *Hidden Scholars*.

65. Reva Beck Bosone, Papers, 1978, University of Utah Libraries, Salt Lake City.

66. Anderson, *Sisters of the Earth*, 335.

67. "Winona LaDuke on Indians' Place in the Ecosystem, 1990," in Merchant, *Major Problems*, 543–44.

68. Quoted in Jensen, *Listening to the Land*, 182.

Conclusion

1. Merchant, "Gender and Environmental History," 1117–21; Janice Monk, "Approaches to the Study of Women and Landscape," *Environmental Review* 8 (spring 1984): 23–33; and Vera Norwood, "Western Women and the Environment," *New Mexico Historical Review* 65 (April 1990): 267–75.

INDEX

Abbott, Sarah E., 156
Aberle, Sophie B. D., 167
A-Birding on a Bronco (Bailey), 74
Addenbrooke, Alice Baltzell, 165
African-American women: club
  movement and, 105–6; ecological
  romanticism of, 66; environmen-
  talism of, 19–20. *See also* women
  of color
Alexander, Addie, 117
Alexander, Annie Montague, 48–49,
  50, 52, 55, 58–59
Alice Eastwood Herbarium, 61
Allen, Paula Gunn, 178
All-Year Club of Southern Califor-
  nia, 140
Alpine Club, 185
Alpine Laboratory (Colorado), 59
*The American Book of Flowers and
  Sentiments* (Hale), 22
American Men of Science, 61
American Naturalist (journal), 6
American Ornithologists' Union, 47
The American Rhythm (Austin),
  159
American Society of Landscape Ar-
  chitects, 92
American Trappers Association
  (ATA), 74

American West: characterized as
  haven for women, 68; curative
  powers of the, 143–45; described
  by women nature writers, 67–76,
  176–79; female travelers through,
  40, 135–53; increased tourism of,
  143–52; women artists' imagery
  of, 81–90; women's promotion of
  reclaiming, 108–9
The American Woman's Home
  (Beecher), 91
American women naturalists: amateur vs. professional status of,
  56–58; birders as, 46–48; botanical tradition of, 43–46; club activities by, 97–113; early environmental commitment by, 6–7; as
  environmental threat, 54–56;
  field experience of, 50–54; garden
  landscaping by, 90–93; ignored by
  male scientists, 8–9; outdoor
  clothing adopted by, 51–53; philosophies of, 60–61; professional
  networking by, 58–59; professional prejudice against, 59–60;
  traveling and travel writing by,
  37. *See also* European women
  naturalists; women's environmentalism

263

In the WOMEN IN THE WEST series